"There is no authority evidenced in this but the man himself. If there are others like him, if we are not all somewhat as he is, provided he write truthfully and out of a gifted mind, he has a right to speak and needs no other authority."
—William Carlos Williams (1942, "A Counsel of Madness")

"In my eyes Kenneth Patchen is now and will remain one of the outstanding figures in American letters. He represents all that a poet should represent, whether expressing himself in verse, in prose, in paint, or in action. . . . Patchen stands out like a shining warrior, a herald of peace and truth, endowed with invincible heart and integrity. No one can read him without being affected and influenced in his own life and work. It is not only the youth who are indebted to him but all of us, even unto the last and most fanatically ardent defender of the Word."
—Henry Miller (1957, *Poemscapes*, cover)

"One could say that it contains the animal honesty of Whitman, and the desperate exaltation of Hart Crane, and the simple delight in sense perception of D.H. Lawrence. . . .His work is brave and original, and it is suffused throughout with the compassion of a strong, free spirit."
—William Packard (1968 *New York Times*, Oct. 20)

"Patchen's work is a Bible torn out of America's heart. It is the prophet's urgent warning. It is a righteous refusal to accept the end of man... Patchen is the wounded Cupid of the American Dream."
—David Meltzer (1970, *Contemporary Poets*, 839, 840)

"Kenneth Patchen was a poet; he was that all the time. He is that still. That is what is meant by 'Poet.' The poetry never stops working if it is real."
—Miriam Patchen (1977 *Kenneth Patchen: A Collection* xii)

Kenneth Patchen (1952) photo by Chester Kessler

Bottom Dog Press

Selected Correspondence of Kenneth Patchen

Edited and Introduced by Allen Frost
Foreword by Larry Smith

Bottom Dog Press
Huron, Ohio

ISBN 978-1-933964-54-6 (soft cover)
ISBN 978-1-933964-55-3 (hard cover)
Bottom Dog Press
PO Box 425
Huron, OH 44839
http://smithdocs.net

Credits:
General Editor: Larry Smith
Cover art is by Kenneth Patchen from the envelope sent to Harvey Breit 1959 and courtesy of the Northwest University Library, Charles Deering McCormick Library of Special Collections.
Dustjacket design by Susanna Sharp-Schwacke

Acknowledgments:

We thank Joel Climenhaga, Miriam Patchen, Jonathan Clark and Larry Smith for their collection of letters and the following library archives indicated in the text with these initials:

ECA	University of Wisconsin at Madison, Special Collections, Alexander Meiklejohn Experimental College Archives.
KPA	Kenneth Patchen Archives, University of California at Santa Cruz, Special Collection.
GUG	John Simon Guggenheim Foundation files.
HAR	Harvard University, Special Collections, Houghton Library.
NDA	New Directions Archives, Norfolk, Connecticut and Northwestern University, Special Collections.
PAP	*Poetry* Magazine Papers at University of Chicago, Special Collections, The Joseph Regenstein Library.
UCLA	University of California at Los Angeles, Special Collection.
UPA	University of Pennsylvania, Charles Patterson Van Pelt Library.
NOR	Northwest University Library, Charles Deering McCormick Library of Special Collections.
HUN	Huntington Library, San Marino, CA
IND	Indiana University, Special Collections, Lilly Library.

Isabel Smith-Stein's letters were shared through biographer Larry Smith. Amos Wilder's photo and correspondence courtesy of the Wilder family, originally appeared in *Sagetrieb* 5, No. 3 Winter 1986. Lawrence Ferlinghetti letter came from Jonathan Clark.

Contents

Foreword by Larry Smith

Kenneth Patchen (1911-1972) produced 36 volumes of poetry, fiction, drawings-and-poems, and picture-poems. He also recorded 4 stunning albums of his work including the dynamic synthesis of poetry-jazz with the Allyn Ferguson and Alan Neil quartets. Since his death 9 volumes of his work have appeared, including the recent *Kenneth Patchen: A Centennial Selection* edited by Jonathan Clark. Patchen's fans and supporters have spanned the globe as well as the decades, among the earliest were Amos Wilder, James Laughlin, Henry Miller, E. E. Cummings, Dylan Thomas, and Kenneth Rexroth, whose letters are for the first time gathered together by the excellent editing of Allen Frost. Patchen is revealed here as the beloved rebel poet whose refusal to accept boundaries led to his innovations in poetry and prose, as well as painting and jazz.

This book could not have been done without the early archival work of Joel Climenhaga, one of Patchen's intimate friends during his later years, and a man who produced all of Patchen's plays and helped sponsor Kenneth Patchen literary festivals around the country. We also thank James Laughlin who opened the New Directions correspondence to us a decade ago. Miriam Patchen served a large role in preserving the letters as well as providing a context for them in the help she provided in my biography, *Kenneth Patchen: Rebel Poet in America* (2000). These letters and Miriam's interviews were the chief source for that biography. You now have them before you to construct your own story of Kenneth Patchen's life and work.

In these letters from and to the author you have the man himself, and an open and honest portrait emerges of a young imaginative boy questing for a vision to encompass and go beyond his working-class roots in Ohio. Reading voraciously at the McKinley Memorial Library in nearby Niles, Ohio, he discovered such literary greats as Dante, Blake, Shelly, Keats, and Dostoevsky, and he shared these with the Literary Club at Warren G. Harding High School with classmates future poet Walter Potashnik (Benton) and Isabel Smith-Stein, his first love. His letters to her at her private school in Tennessee provide the book's opening image of this uncertain and somewhat overcompensating youth. Patchen's education at the University of Wisconsin at Madison is revealed in the correspondence between himself and Alexander Meikeljohn of the Experimental College there, even as he moved on to the Commonwealth Labor College. His letters and papers during the rambling years (1930-1933) as a young radical are lost to us, but begin again with his deep friendship with author Amos Wilder from Boston where he worked for a time, and most importantly, where he met his love and life partner Miriam Patchen. His passionate love letters to her at Smith College are unfortunately lost as well, but we know he sent poems and proposals until she agreed to join him in Greenwich Village in 1934.

Alliances were formed in the Village and with such supporters as critic Lewis Mumford. The story of Patchen's relationship as an "American proletarian poet" with Random House and its editor Bennett Cerf resulted in his first book *Before the Brave* (1936) and his first and only Guggenheim Fellowship. Frost has wisely included samplings of Patchen's annual applications for a Guggenheim (35 years) as informative of his career and as a revelation of his willful character and strong belief in his art. Following the Guggenheim year in Arizona, the Patchens moved to Hollywood, California where he sought to write for films but ended by writing for the W.P.A Writer's Project and growing desperate until he received his first letter from young James Laughlin who had just founded New Directions Publishing. This long relationship between one of America's strongest alternative press editors and its most maverick author is a revelation in itself as friendship develops and is tested. Writing from California in September of 1938, Patchen lays out his fundamental beliefs and plans for friend Amos Wilder. In 1939 we have Patchen's letters to editor-friend James Laughlin, a rich mix of support and dispute that would characterize their literary relationship. And not to be missed is that long handwritten letter from his overseas colleague Dylan Thomas.

Back in the Village during the 1940s, we witness the developing alliance with Henry Miller, one of Patchen's most ardent supporters, especially during his struggle to get his anti-war novel *The Journal of Albion Moonlight* published; witness Miller's *Patchen: Man of Anger and Light* (1946). Patchen himself published no less than 7 books in 1946 through New Directions and other alternative presses...Padell, Grey Walls, United, Bern Porter, and Untide. The Patchens' Village friendship with poet E.E. and Marion Cummings proves crucial to their sustaining the strains of financial loss and physical pain throughout life, even as they move west to San Francisco in the 1950s, following the advice of new friend Kenneth Rexroth.

Exposed in these letters are Patchen's weaknesses: his struggles with pain and for any financial security, his relentless demands with publishers, as well as his strengths: his willful devotion to his art, to others, and to creating a 'new world order' through his art. A caution to thouse who might judge him for his frequent requests for funds from others. It should be noted that he gave as well as he received, so that he and Miriam frequently sent funds to other writers and artists in need. Any funds received were used to keep the writing going, and trust that Miriam never lamented the cost of this struggle to create.

Though correspondence during the 50's and 60's often pertains to arrangements for publications and performances of his poetry-jazz, sustaining correspondence between writer friends reveals Patchen's devotion and fundamental humanity. Included are some of the many love notes he wrote to his life partner, Miriam, while on the road. Though bedridden in their Palo Alto home from back injury and botched operations from 1961-1972, Patchen was able to do his picture-poems, and to handwrite letters to his dearest friends. Witness here, Miriam's long and painful letter of 1962 characterizing for friends and supporters their long years of physical and financial struggle. Editor Frost has wisely chosen to include many graphics of Patchen's revealing and beautiful handwriting here as well as many relevant clippings from the times.

Among last letters to James Laughlin, Kenneth recalls Laughlin's 1939 comment, "I hope we'll get along," and responds, "I think we've done pretty well, getting along." He later writes apologetically, "I trust that you will appreciate that there is nothing personal in my 'strong words,'—What I do is so often done under conditions of nagging pain," and recognizes his friend's long devotion to task, "Thirty years without drawing a really free, relaxed breath—and you're surprised that you get tired..." Such was the man and his humanity. You have the letters before you.

—Larry Smith, March 2012
Huron, Ohio

Introduction by Allen Frost

This is the inspiring story of a supreme artist absolutely committed to his dream. Kenneth Patchen's painted books, novels, prophecies and poems are a testament to life and hope. However, this is also a tale of the adversity he faced: monetary, critical neglect, and a physical pain that kept him bedridden for much of his life. Often these letters are almost shouting with it. "The pain is almost a natural part of me now," Patchen wrote Henry Miller. The agony he endured was contained by his own sheer will and creative power, but also by his circle of friends. This book of correspondence makes that clear. He needs those words of encouragement from Henry Miller. And you can tell that a letter from E.E. Cummings turns his whole day around. Through reading these letters, the path of his life can be drawn following his own words, in a philosophy that he established early on, "It's always because we love that we are rebellious."

AN IMAGINARY WORLD (1929-1933)

From Kenneth Patchen's very first letters, onr can sense that this 16 year old boy will become the poet of humor and protest as he writes young Isabel Smith that he is a rebel for not crossing a 't', inventing a new alphabet, creating a fable about snow. But also, you can feel his unhappiness with the way things are. He already has a vision and his search will take him out of the ordinary. By summer he plans to go to Russia. Instead, he is drawn to a labor college in Arkansas, where he leaves school and throws himself at America. Of this missing time, his wife Miriam later wrote, "His rambles through the country during the depression included most of the classic jobs and situations of such a life with one notable difference: everywhere, he left behind him sheafs of manuscript: forgotten, overlooked, lost—but he was always creating." These years are the start of Patchen's travels, also the beginning of what would become a familiar practice: asking for money.

POETRY AND RANDOM HOUSE (1933-1934)

By 1932, Patchen had made New York City his home, though he was still in motion. He submits poems to *Poetry*, a magazine which will be an ally for years to come. Still in contact with his college mentor, Alexander Meiklejohn, in the letter from July 1933, he dreams of California. More importantly, 1933 is the year he courts Miriam in Boston. This period is documented by friend Amos Wilder, "I found him upstairs in a dismal hall bedroom, flat on his back, and with the shades drawn. He was suffering from sinus trouble and headaches. As his wife, Miriam, later explained, he had had a collapse from fumes while employed in a rubber factory and this had led to a chronic nasal and sinus disorder. On a table were the books of such writers as Conrad Aiken, Lauro de Bosis and Hart Crane, and a litter of yellow sheets of his own verse. He talked of his preferred writers, of his vicissitudes on the road, and of possible openings for publication and income." It is 1934 and Kenneth is already on his back in pain, a recurring condition which will never go away. After an unhappy stay in Ohio and a quick marriage, Kenneth and Miriam return to Greenwich Village. The year ends with a letter from Random House accepting his first book for publication, *Before the Brave.*

BEFORE THE WAR AND THE GUGGENHEIM (1935-1937)

After long dreaming of a house in the country, the Patchens move to a cottage in Rhinebeck, New York, in hopes that Kenneth may provide income by writing. However, once again, he finds himself asking friends for money. In the summer of 1935, he requests an application for a Guggenheim grant, citing his interest in writing in the South. When he wins the award in 1936, he and Miriam leave New York for Santa Fe, New Mexico and Phoenix, Arizona. His request for a second Guggenheim is denied, as it will continue to be for the next 35 years, and the Patchens move on to California.

THE HUNTED CITY (1938)

From Los Angeles, a letter is sent to Leon Trotsky, as Patchen tries and fails to start a radical magazine with New York friend Harvey Breit. Writing for Hollywood films also comes to naught. In his first contact with young James Laughlin of New Directions Publishing, Patchen confides that "a long book is stirring within me." Throughout the year, he works on getting published his next poetry collection *First Will and Testament.*

NEW DIRECTIONS (1939)

Three days after James Laughlin's acceptance of Patchen's second book of poetry, Kenneth responds with a note of anger for having been put off, though he signs off with best wishes. This is the template for their long writing and publishing relationship. Kenneth further hints that he needs to escape California for his work. He begins petitioning friends for money to return east. By spring, the couple arrives in Acton, Massachusetts outside of Concord, working on a farm belonging to Miriam's parents, until Laughlin offers him a job working for his young press at his aunt's estate in Norfolk, Connecticut. It doesn't take long for Laughlin to realize his mistake, as the letters between the two men reveal. While they barrage each other and war is unleashed in Europe, Patchen submits a third application for a Guggenheim, revealing his interest in the Children's Crusade, which he sees as a parallel of the times. Tempering all of this frustration, a long handwritten letter arrives from fellow poet Dylan Thomas.

ALBION MOONLIGHT (1940-1941)

The Patchens return to the Village, this time to Bleecker Street, where Kenneth's "long book" becomes *The Journal of Albion Moonlight.* He makes friendships with Henry Miller and E. E. Cummings, who will be his lifelong supporters. Even with Henry Miller's glowing endorsement, James Laughlin falters with publishing *Moonlight*, leaving Patchen to self-publish it by subscription. This does allow him to take a more active role in the printing of his books, a passion he will continue. Money worries lead Patchen to pawn his typewriter. The end of the year finds him "helpless in bed" apologizing to poet Wallace Stevens for not paying back his loan.

ONE WHO KNOWS (1942-1943)

The Dark Kingdom is published. A chance to live on a houseboat off Long Island is soon scuttled by Patchen's bad back. More desperate letters to Wallace Stevens and to Henry Moe of the Guggenheim follow, coupled with a "steady unrelenting pain in my spine." Work continues on *Cloth of the Tempest*, a collection which also includes his illustrations. His books will more and more feature his artwork, of which he tells Laughlin, "I can get wonderful strange effects."

ON THE SIDE OF THE ANGELS (1944-1945)

A letter arrives from Jasper Wood, a fan from his native Ohio, giving Kenneth a chance to mentor in the art of publishing, first with a literary magazine, then with a book of his own. His all-encompassing advice is illuminating and heartfelt: "Unless the things were done beautifully there's no use in doing them at all."

SLEEPERS AWAKE (1946)
With the end of the world war, Patchen voices support for Ezra Pound, crafting an anti-war manifesto and a defense of life and poetry. Writing to Henry Miller, Patchen identifies his debilitating back trouble as arthritis, and declares his desire to write books along the order of canvases, more evidence of his interest in visual art. He begins work on *Panels for the Walls of Heaven* for Jasper Wood and continues creating his own limited editions. Despite a back operation, Patchen reveals his long working day at the printshop overseeing his new book and then at home writing until dawn. He openly shares all of his publishing frustrations with Miller and Wood.

ON THE RESTRICTED SHELF (1947)
In the winter of 1947, the Patchens move to Old Lyme, Connecticut where Kenneth immediately finds himself in controversy. What began as a simple gift of his *Selected Poems* book to the library backfires as his book is removed from the open shelves. In outrage, Patchen fires off letters to his allies for their written support. In this year's application for a Guggenheim, he proposes going to England to write.

I CHALLENGE THE RIGHT (1948-1949)
"It might feel good not to be in America," Patchen writes Henry Miller, but his back prevents him from such travel. Instead, in contact with Kenneth Rexroth he hopes to move to California by winter. Patchen clearly enjoys Rexroth's company and you can feel their friendship growing. The two share their fury after James Laughlin refutes his own quote appearing in *Partisan Review* which read, "Kenneth Patchen is the most compelling force in American poetry since Whitman." After several angry letters, Patchen and Laughlin make amends and produce Kenneth's next work *Red Wine and Yellow Hair*. However, Patchen soon finds himself in conflict again when *The New York Times* refuses to print an ad for this book. His plan to picket them is stopped at the last minute by his unwilling back.

A VOICE OF FIRE (1950-1951)
In the cold winter of 1950, Patchen writes to Rexroth that he and Miriam are seriously planning a move to California. Support from heiress Doris Duke and a writers' fund which included such figures as T.S. Eliot and Marianne Moore, provide money for another back operation. In the last letter of the year, Patchen tells Rexroth they're on the way to San Francisco in a month.

SAN FRANCISCO (1952-1955)

The Patchens arrive in San Francisco and stay with friends Holly Beye and David Ruff, then move to Green Street. Later Kenneth receives treatment at Stanford while Miriam works in a department store. Letters from E. E. Cummings contain warmth, hope and much needed money. Laughlin and Kenneth's letters reveal further the pressures of working together. Patchen becomes known in San Francisco by poetry readings at the Museum of Art and on the radio. Lawrence Ferlinghetti seeks a manuscript from Patchen for his Pocket Poets Series at City Lights. More hospital operations follow, but nothing stops Kenneth from working on his silk screen portfolios and painted books.

ON ANOTHER PLANET (1956)

The Patchen's relocate to Palo Alto near the clinic where Kenneth will undergo further operations. *Poetry* magazine lends its support by alerting readers to Patchen's plight. Recovering from a full body cast to a steel ribbed brace, Kenneth still writes to his friends, hoping Henry Miller can lend support in republishing Kenneth's novels.

THE WOODS ARE SO FULL (1957)

After learning that their temporary home is to be demolished, Kenneth and Miriam purchase their first and final home at 2340 Sierra Court, Palo Alto. Despite his ailments, Kenneth considers a reading tour, seeking advice from *Poetry*'s longtime editor, Henry Rago. Lawrence Ferlinghetti agrees to reprint *Memoirs of a Shy Pornographer.* Writing to Cummings, Kenneth again mentions plans for a reading tour, and describes the growing Beat scene in San Francisco, which brought *Life* magazine to his door,. He makes it clear that he wants no part in any poetry scene. Kenneth is busy with arrangements for a reading tour featuring a jazz band and making a record. He then finds himself defending his title as the creator of Poetry-Jazz, a claim that brings on more controversy on Kenneth Rexroth's radio program.

ONE DAY, WHEN THIS STORY IS TOLD (1958-1960)

Kenneth has to turn down an invitation to read at the Brussels World Fair. With more operations planned, he searches for foundations and grants. In his 23rd plea for a Guggenheim, he bluntly asks how he could be overlooked and who could possibly be more in need of an award? He notes the severity of his back condition: "between 1937 and 1956 an average of six months out of each year found me helpless in bed."

Musician Alan Neil provides a fascinating look at a 1959 recording session with Kenneth that followed that winter's touring. On his return, Kenneth again undergoes surgery for his back, which results in a "mysterious mishap" in the operating room that leaves him bedridden with permanent crippling pain. Letters to Laughlin, Henry Rago and James Boyer May describe the horrible ordeal. Hoping to secure grant funding, he includes a stark note revealing his monthly income and expenses.

BEHIND THE ICE CURTAIN (1961-1966)

The San Francisco Chronicle announces a tribute program to raise money for Kenneth Patchen featuring local poets, musicians and The Actor's Workshop. While Kenneth recovers from his operation, Miriam takes over the letter writing. A book deal with Doubleday falls through, adding to Patchen's perceived "conspiracy of silence." Finally, Miriam's long letter to Judith Wray reveals the real terror and ordeal she has been through caring for Kenneth with no support. Meanwhile, his work on books continues with *Hallelujah Anyway.*

ON THE SIDE OF LIFE (1967-1971)

Letters arrive from England, where Alex Comfort searches for medical help for his friend. In the summer of 1967, Patchen is finally awarded a major grant of $10,000 from the National Endowment for the Arts. The congratulatory letter includes the note that the award was based on "a host of recommendations from fellow writers, editors and publishers throughout the United States." Negotiations with James Laughlin over Patchen's *Collected Poems* continues. These final letters to Laughlin are nostalgic and conciliatory testifying to their long devoted partnership. A letter from The Beatles' Apple Records, shows the contemporary interest in producing his work. Before his death in 1972 Kenneth Patchen had much more in the works, including a *Patchenopedia.* He leaves us, with an eye on the youth: "Things are a-stir whenever and wherever my work gets over or through those walls."

* * *

This correspondence project began with the Patchen's close friend, Joel Climenhaga. This book wouldn't exist without the work he put in and left waiting to be completed. For the past year spent editing these letters, I have felt Kenneth Patchen's presence in my daily life and dreams. Kenneth Patchen is an artist who will not fade away. I thank all of those persons and libraries who have preserved and shared this correspondence here. Finally, I must thank biographer and editor Larry Smith who has devoted most of his life to Kenneth Patchen's life and work. He supplemented and kept safe this box of letters in Ohio, waiting for the right time. Now, 100 years after the birth of Kenneth Patchen, here are his correspondences, a gift for those people who already love Kenneth Patchen and for those who are about to.

—Allen Frost, March 2012
Bellingham, WA

***Note:** Respectfully, we have kept Patchen's original spellings, irregular indents, and syntax.*

Chapter One: An Imaginary World
1929-1933

To Isabel Smith-Stein from Kenneth Patchen

September 24, 1929
Adams Hall
Experimental College

[Handwritten letter]
Dear Isabel:

I received the missive you sent. I have been changed to another college. Have you heard of the experimental college? I took a test in freshman English and presently I was called in to see my advisor and he said he thought it would be a good idea to take two years in the experimental college and then in my Junior year begin majoring in English. I guess I'll do that.

I don't know so much about this school but the attention of the educational world is focused upon it. They are trying to adapt the course to the interests of the individual. There are no regular classes etc. No grades, I believe until the end of your second year. Not sure.

Boys only. We live in a swell dorm with the proffs and are a regular city and gov. unto ourselves. What do you wish to write about? I've had no experience in writing to female girls and I'll tone my letters and take my cue from your letters. I'll discuss anything. At least I think I will.

Why did you ever go down there to school?

Truly yours
Kenneth Patchen

To Isabel Smith-Stein from Kenneth Patchen

October 4, 1929
Meiklejohn College, Madison, WI

It is never quiet here but I'll write anyway. Everything is running along smoothly and I should be happy but I am not. I always thought I'd like to be with boys who were interesting from the stand point that they would be trying to reason things out. The thing that disgusts me is the wordy, senseless views they seem to have on things in general. I suppose I am subject to moods but the way I feel to-night God could claim me and I wouldn't care in the least. I am beginning to feel a note of futility in it all that I can't get away from. I am almost convinced that there is really nothing worth while living. It seems that all man was created for was to see that his body got enough to eat, was clothed etc. All of these things of the body disgust me.

The thing that pains me most is the fact that I seem to sense or have a feeling that I could make my life worth living. All my life I have been lonely. Because of illness I did not start to school until I was eight years old and it was while I was sick that I had things read to me. I lived in an imaginary world and I believe sometimes that I never really left that world. Thus starting to school my interests were not as those around me and I sort of withdrew into myself. Since childhood I have rarely been happy and I am beginning to have a feeling of revolt against going on like this. Because I am sensitive to a high degree poetry has sort of appealed to me. But lately I am considering whether it is not a sort of a romantic idea that has been thrust upon me.

The country is alive with would-be poets and I'd get a big kick out of socking each and everyone of them in the jaw. To have someone say that this one and that one is a genius fairly makes my blood boil. This is an age of machinery and its poetry is sickening. But at once I seem to be defending good poetry and wishing for better and I seem to be trapped. I can think of beautiful word arrangements but I have resolved not to write until something moves me as I've never been moved before.

There is and has been something lacking in my life and I can't place it. I hate sentimental things and modern poetry seems to be nothing else and I'm at a loss. Just what good it does for a man to be born and eventually die I am unable to see.

Perhaps I am talented in painting, or music etc. I do not know I've never been intensely interested. That gives rise to the question of whether it would be better to be a poor painter and happy than to be a good painter and unhappy. Whether it's better to be an unbalanced genius in poetry, for instance, than to be semi-skilled, in say poetry and science.

But say I shut out everything in my life but the pursuit of creative poetry and in the end find that it does not satisfy me then I'd feel that I had ruined my life for a silly whim.

If I thought that life was some super-being's idea of a practical joke I know what I would do to-morrow. I'd much rather be a swallow and live for a few glamorous years than to live as I am existing now. There has always lurked a doubt in my mind and it's beginning to trouble me now that I have a little time to think. At the moment life holds nothing for me.

I have written this more to act as an escape-valve to my mind than anything else. I am sure that if I were in your place I'd read about half of it and tear the rest up and throw it away. I do not sympathize with myself because I feel that "I" am sort of a disinterested spectator watching what the being which inhabits my body will do next. I can't describe the feeling but it's there.

I thank you for the long letter you wrote to me and if I don't hear from you again I'll understand. I could stand it where you are at school for about five minutes and I'd be through. I hope that you have success in everything you try to do and will always be happy.

Your Friend
Kenneth Patchen

To Isabel Smith- Stein from Kenneth Patchen
[No Date, 1st page missing]

We are going to put on Eugene O'Neil's play 'Beyond the Horizon' in the University theatre in about three weeks. One of the boys has had experience as a professional actor of the stage in Chicago and everyone predicts a big future for him. He read the 'Strange Interlude' aloud to some of us one afternoon.

What alternative do you have to becoming an industrious, middle-class, contented housewife? Isn't that an ideal prospect? I have a definition for the type of husband that usually is found in such a twosome: he is egotistic, impatient, argumentative, brutally intellectual, malicious, querulous, critical, domineering, irritable, earth-bound, arrogant, disingenuous, unpoetical to ignorance and spiritually course and brutish. He shouts his success from the housetops because he is in the depths of him a rotten failure. They have an impulse to form clubs, secret fraternities, masonries, cliques etc. because they like to appear as personages of importance. These unblessed mediocrities have one and only one way to escape out of the crushing consciousness of insignificance; the way of the head.

Among such a group Utopia is child's folly. We are ashamed to be dreamers. Mention the writers or thinkers in the contemporary world in maturity who possess, or are possessed by, great imagination: Dullness & machinery have brought this about I think. Why be a haunted creator when it is easy to be a prosperous merchant or manufacturer? Why be tortured with poetic longing when the rewards of being an advertiser and publicity agent trafficking in sickly verse are temptations not easily put aside. Why be Wm Shakespeare when you can be Eddie Guest?

I am wondering what I will do when I leave school with a degree in English. What can I do? I might try newspaper work but I don't think I'd like it. I may bum my way around the world and try and pick up some information on conditions and sort of get a background. I have thought that it might be well for me to do that and quit school. I think I would learn about as much by doing that.

When this boy from the slums of New York was telling me about how hard he had to work and how much he has suffered I thought of the girls with whom you are going to school and it's quite a contrast. Are their lives as sheltered as chaperons etc. would lead you to believe. I was very much surprised to find that most of the girls seen on the streets and in automobiles are smoking cigarettes. It's all a matter of course. At least that's the impression I got in seeing them. I'm told they drink in the same matter of fact manner. Do they there?

This is all very rambling and disjointed but must serve for nothing better to say. Are there any girls you know who are interested in poetry or writing in general?

Truly yours
Kenneth Patchen

To Isabel Smith- Stein from Kenneth Patchen

February 5, 1930
Wednesday

Dear Isabel:

It is snowing now and the ground is covered with snow. Yesterday it did not snow but the ground was covered with snow. I cannot understand it. If the ground is covered with snow when it does not snow why must it snow in order to have the ground covered with snow. I could elaborate that theme but it is snowing outside and the ground is covered with snow while yesterday it did not snow and yet the ground was covered with snow, so how am I to understand it?

Do you remember snow? Snow is white. It is like cotton. If I were all — I wonder why I didn't cross both of those ts with one stroke. That is important. It means I am conservative. I pride myself upon being a radical and I cross my ts one by one. Just why ts should be crossed I do not know. Is this more of a t than this? t – l. I am thrilled by my new l. I am ashamed of all the crossed ls I've made. I retract them. But can I retract anything when it is snowing?

you may find it hard to believe—damn it—
Do you understand—damn it—why I said
damn it? But—you may find it hard to
believe that over eighty snowflakes have fallen
this year. Why—when you think of it should an
a be a and a b, b; and a c—c, and a d—d, and
so on. I am not going to be restricted by these
old rules. Haven't I already discovered a new
b. I will use my own letters. [illegible]
If you knew what that means you could
explain to me why it must snow on
the ground today in order to have the ground
covered with snow while the ground was
covered with snow yesterday and it did
not snow. I cannot understand this.
That is all of the snow I think of just
now and I'm disturbed to see it snowing
outside when I can't understand why it
should snow. But I like snow. Perhaps
some day I will make a study of snow.
If it doesn't snow tomorrow at least it
snowed yesterday.

Kenneth

To Isabel Smith-Stein from Kenneth Patchen

March 13, 1930
Experimental College

Dear Isabelle:

I felt like a mud-turtle in a turkish bath going through a series of spirals in a pink seaplane at a Rotary Convention in Mineral Ridge Ohio. He said the sunbeams made him laugh but Marx was right about the Stubborn Spinster being a good theory of disarmament. But then if the cloud had lost the race, Morris would have been delighted to receive any less honor and he said I would like a pudding made from the whites of all the Hungarian babies eyes born after sun set in a roller coaster. He took Mrs. Rollands tongue and made a kite because he felt the rain and loved craw-fishes.

The above is my humble rendition of the theme "writing as one young human to another." Listen little one, if ever the opportunity is afforded me, you will be permitted to practice what you disclaim as regards this drinking matter. Never let theories run flat-tired over your sensibilities.

You understand what I mean when I say Paris. Be less obviously subtle in the time anteceding the present.

Russia! Russia,—Tyranny—Oligarchy, intolerance, oppression etc. I warmly admit the truth of what you say and very loudly exclaim bravo (non pour vous mais pour Russia). That is what the masses have always needed. Trample on them; spit in their faces if they are so stupidly stolid as to demur when something is being done for them. We need less education and more stiff-arming. If a New Order Chariot is being rolled down the avenues of world history, crush the flies that make the International Political Horse prance from its predestined course; lubricate the runaway with human blood if necessary but keep the procession moving.

As for acting: "Give me an intelligent parrot for my thrills." Too subtle? You may quote me, while I am on the subject of artistic endeavor, as having brought this statement into being (God knows the thought as well as the mind behind it would be better if uncreated). All art in any form is perversion. Man has worked out a multifariously complex camouflage of worthless mental playtoys with which he tries to impress upon practical (or ignorant) people, the scope and significance of his visionary meanderings. Literature has no place in a society of normal reasoning animals; it retards basic and elemental growth; it permits unbalanced minds with a knack of the dramatic emphasis of the right words at precisely the correct time and place to cloud the public horizon with the mists of petty maladjustment and chronic inability; it destroys our sense of reality and gives birth to unnatural inhibitions; it is a destroyer of thought in any original sense and has made live, vital human brains mere filing cases where information that has no bearing upon the life of the individual is stored so that he may check any natural impulse he may have; literature has been termed a battle ground of wits but it is rather a cemetery wherein is buried the most valuable trait we can possess; our instinct.

There is no excuse for music, painting, etc. because we would be much happier living more nearly the life of the animal we cannot escape being. Damn all childish fondling of intellectual absurdities. Our world has become practically unbearable and we may thank our misty-eyed friends of the long hair, charming brows and smelly underclothing. We are being educated to fit into a scheme of life where to be adjusted is to be mechanized. Feed us from cans; shovel out entertainment as though we really enjoyed it; brutalize what little sensibilities we may have been endowed with; mechanized religion; mechanized breeding; mechanized thought and give us as disciples of enlightenment deformed recluses who would turn a Sultan's Harem into a Y.W.C.A. merely because as an individual the Sultan must be socialized. Let our self-commiserating "authors" snarl and leer at each other out of money-dimmed eyes; let them caress and suck each other; let them toss high-sounding nonentities to and fro about their stained lucre; let literature become worthless; let it rot and become infested with maggots; but for Christ's sake hasn't someone the courage to bury it. Put a bill before the people (fat, sloppy bourgeois morons) and let's condemn literature as a poison worse than alcohol, amend the constitution and make novel writing a capital offense, and put all the dramatists and poets on exhibition and set the money aside that we may live the lives that our hairy, uncleanly, lustful, brutal minds and bodies make most enjoyable for us. Let's take off this cursed veneer and get down and enjoy what little it is in our power to enjoy.

To hell with all pretense; to hell with literature, music, painting, sculpture, and the lowest depths of the hottest hell with all philosophy, science and religion. Give me a mate, a glass of water and an olive and I'll hie myself to a tropic isle and let the sun imbue me with all the laziness and energy needed to make use of my mate, the water and the olive; and oh sun—purify me of all the stench of falseness and allow me to face reality without a sentimental acceptance handed down by any sex-famished long beard of the intellectual stone ages!

You can imagine my sentiments concerning your "social life." Why don't you study a couple of texts concerned with etiquette and take a correspondence course in the life of the tree monkey found in Brazil and you will have all the tact necessary to pour a cup of tea and entertain "young gentlemen."

My life for the short time it will last will be spent in drifting around and trying to come to some conclusion as to how supposedly intelligent beings can be satisfied with playing all their lives with building blocks. Oh God, I'm fed up and the vomit is permeating everything I am concerned with.

In keeping with my general air of cheerfulness and optimism I'll quote these famed lines of U. Laugh Loud in his epic "Smile Bright,"

> "I hear my coffin scraping o'er the floor—
> But damn the varnish."

[Handwritten note added]
The above was written this morning between two and three o'clock after I'd spent the evening and early morning hours in a thirty mile walk about the lake. I was quite tired and sleepy and this morning some of my statements sound rather awkward, but they still stand. Refute them if you like and I know you can because it is a purely personal matter.

Haphazardly yours
Kenneth

To Isabel Smith-Stein from Kenneth Patchen

May 18, 1930

Dear Isabel,

Please forgive me for a number of things.
Looking back over the past month I hardly remember.
I had an interesting emotional experience—I've been doing some writing—my own medium at last—feel almost happy—I need only perfect it—I asked you a question—answer it—do you care to see me this summer? Don't be so damned school-girlish—To hell with horse shows—Never take anything I say seriously—I don't mean half of it—I'm just intellectually impersonal—I don't give a damn for any human being—and never will. I'm better left alone—I felt in a rather happy? mood when I started this but now—Wish you'd write me a letter—I haven't placed you as yet—please do—at once—I need the sound of a friendly voice—

Your friend
Kenneth

To Wayne Patchen from Alexander Meiklejohn (ECA)

June 16, 1930
2626 Youngstown Avenue
Warren, Ohio

Dear Mr. Patchen,

The advisors of the Experimental College have asked me to send to the parents of each of our students a statement of our impressions of his activities and development during the year. We shall be glad to add to these statements or answer questions, if you wish us to do so.

Your son has had a difficult year in terms of his social adjustment. He makes very heavy demands on himself and the result is a great deal of discouragement and loneliness. His work has shown at times really excellent ability, and there is no doubt that his mind is able and that his power of writing is first rate. We hope that next year he will be able to accept the routine of work and his relations with teachers and pupils with much less stress and strain. If he can do this, he will have a most satisfactory year, and his scholarly achievement should be one of the very best in his class.

Sincerely Yours,
[Alexander Meiklejohn]

Student Evaluation of Kenneth Patchen (ECA)

1930
Experimental College
Patchen, Kenneth
Fellow: Orr

Patchen was rather a lonely soul for a while, but has finally associated himself with the Saxe, Dmitrieff, Garfield group. He reads lots of poetry, and has written some. He plays the Victrola incessantly sometimes, playing "Pomp and Circumstance", "Fraulein Pardon" and some godawful jazz record until the hall goes mad. He isn't in too good health, keeps odd hours, and sometimes burns incense. I should say that his life is saner than it was, and that he'll probably be all right.

To Alexander Meiklejohn from Kenneth Patchen (ECA)

August 7, 1930
3371 Youngstown Ave.
Warren, Ohio

Dear Sir,

I am writing to you for advice. I am going to Russia in Sept. and expect to be gone about a year. Will it be possible for me to enroll in the fall of 1931 as a Sophomore? In short, will there be an Experimental College then?

I would appreciate a prompt reply.

Truly Yours
Kenneth Patchen

To Kenneth Patchen from Alexander Meiklejohn (ECA)

August 12, 1930
3371 Youngstown Avenue
Warren, Ohio

Dear Ken,

I was very much interested in your plan of going to Russia for a year. I know that it will be an interesting and profitable experience.

I think I can assure you that the Experimental College, at least the work of the sophomore year, will be carried on during the school year of 1931-32. By all means I hope you will come back to complete your course with us after your travels abroad.

With best wishes for a pleasant voyage, I am

Cordially yours,
[Alexander Meiklejohn]

To Experimental College, Wisconsin from Lucien Koch (ECA)

July 21, 1931
Commonwealth College "Independent Education for Workers"
Mena, Arkansas

Dear sirs:

Kenneth Patchen has applied for admittance to Commonwealth for the fall quarter, 1931. Although I understand that he spent some time at the Experimental College he has not given the college as a source of reference. Nevertheless, I should like very much to know the opinion of the college concerning him. Could you help by filling out the enclosed blank?

I do not know who is on the grounds during the summer, but I hope that it will be possible for someone to get up the desired information. I would be greatly obliged. Of course, since I know the college's method of evaluating students having participated in such evaluations myself, we will place some weight upon your recommendations.

Most sincerely,
Lucien Koch
Director

To Alexander Meiklejohn from Kenneth Patchen (ECA)

October 20, 1931
Commonwealth College, Mena, Arkansas

Dear Mr. Meiklejohn:

I am taking advantage of the invitation to write which you gave me some time ago.

I want to ask you two things.

Do you think I did a wise thing in coming here?

Would it be possible for me to enter the University of Wisconsin as a special student, working not for a degree but taking such courses in Psychology and Philosophy as interest me?

Can you suggest anything? Advise me?

There are certain aspects of Commonwealth which I dislike but the freedom and the feeling of earning my way offset them with a margin to spare.

I want to write you a letter describing myself and what I want in life but hesitate because it may be asking too much of your indulgence.

I am thanking you in advance for your reply—

Yours,
Kenneth Patchen

To Kenneth Patchen from Alexander Meiklejohn (ECA)

October 31, 1931
Commonwealth College, Mena, Arkansas

Dear Kenneth Patchen,

I am sorry that I have been so busy that your letter has been neglected. Let me answer your questions as quickly as I can.

I should think that going to Commonwealth may be very good for you. On the whole, I think I like it much better than your taking special courses in psychology and philosophy. The Commonwealth community experiment is a very vital thing, and I am sure that if you take advantage of it there is opportunity for lots of insights as well as the more direct advantages of study.

Do write me about yourself and what you want to do. I may again delay in answering, but I shall be much interested and will tell you whatever comes into my mind.

Sincerely yours,
[Alexander Meiklejohn]

To Alexander Meiklejohn from Kenneth Patchen (ECA)

1932
c/o Anatole Dmitrieff
736 Home Street
Bronx, N.Y.

Dear Mr. Meiklejohn:

The last time I wrote to you, in the summer, it was to ask your advice about the possibility of getting a job in Madison. You were pessimistic of any hope on that score but invited me to write again, expressing desire to help me if it should be within your power.

As you remember I enrolled in Commonwealth in September. At the end of the quarter I left Arkansas, coming to New York, where I have been since the first of the year. I have taken an active part in the Worker's Laboratory Theater, acting and writing short plays.

I find it impossible to get work and my health being poor to an irregular diet and bad living conditions, it is likely that I shall leave soon, visiting friends in Cleveland and Athens, Ohio. Before I go however, I am to see Wm. G. Simpson in Suffern, N.Y. regarding summer work as a gardener.

Today I am writing to Zona Gale. I wish most intensely to enroll in Madison next fall, taking courses in short story writing, German, Russian and if possible, philosophy. I am submitting specimens of my work to Zona Gale.

If you see fit to recommend me for a scholarship I will be deeply grateful to you.

Respectfully
Kenneth Patchen

(I am living on 14th St. in Manhatten but since the address above is permanent I give it.)

To Kenneth Patchen from Alexander Meiklejohn (ECA)

March 3, 1932
c/o Anatole Dmitrieff
736 Home Street
Bronx, New York

Dear Kenneth Patchen,

It is good to hear from you, though I am sorry to hear that your plans have gotten rather mixed up. I was hoping that conditions at Commonwealth would work out in such a way as to keep you busy and happy there. I am especially sorry to know that you are not feeling well. Do make sure of getting arrangements made with proper regard for your health. That is a primary matter which has to be taken into account.

I am not too hopeful about an arrangement through Zona Gale. My impression is that she has very much limited her activities within the last year or two with respect to providing scholarships. However I will drop her a note.

Hoping to see you if you come in this direction, I am

Sincerely Yours,
[Alexander Meiklejohn]

To Zona Gale from Alexander Meiklejohn (ECA)

March 3, 1932
Portage,
Wisconsin

Dear Zona Gale,

One of the boys in the College, who finished only the first year, has asked me to write you a note in his behalf. His name is Kenneth Patchen. When he left us he went to Commonwealth College but stayed only a short time. He is a rather a curious lad, much shut up in himself and having great difficulty in adjusting to the outside world. In addition to that he is not in good health and seems to be dependent on his own resources. He tells me that he has sent you some samples of his writing. You will be able to tell from them as to his quality better than I can access it. In terms of eagerness of purpose and sensitiveness, I can heartily recommend him. Beyond that, however, I am not able to go.

Hoping that all goes well with you, I am

Sincerely yours,
[Alexander Meiklejohn]

To Alexander Meiklejohn from Dean Sellery (ECA)
South Hall, University of Wisconsin

March 8, 1932
University of Wisconsin

Dear Dr. Meiklejohn,

Kenneth Patchen, who says he was in the Experimental College 1929-30 and then dropped out, and has "since been knocking about: Canada, southern U.S. and Mexico", is applying for a Zona Gale scholarship. Professor W.E. Leonard has asked me to help him reach a decision in the young man's application. Will you tell me what you know and think about this young man? Is he steady enough to bring back to the campus, etc? Any suggestions will be welcome.

Yours Very Truly,
(*signed by G.C. Sellery*)
Dean

To Dean Sellery from Alexander Meiklejohn (ECA)

March 10, 1932
University of Wisconsin

Dear Dean Sellery,

It is very hard to tell what to say about Kenneth Patchen. He is a fine fellow, eager in disposition and attitude, and yet he finds it practically impossible to settle down to any established regime. His health is not very good and he is always under financial strain. I am afraid I cannot give very strong assurance as to his success in the University work, though I should be glad to do so if I could. My impression is that he is able as well as earnest. It may be that his wanderings have gotten him ready for settling down.

Sincerely yours,
[Alexander Meiklejohn]

Letter to Alexander Meiklejohn from Kenneth Patchen (ECA)

July 10, 1932
c/o Anatole Dmitrieff
736 Home Street
Bronx, NY

Dear Mr. Meiklejohn:

Once again I write to you, this time not for advice but for help.

I failed to get a Zona Gale scholarship as you probably know. This Fall I should like terribly to go to school. Friends have suggested going to Germany since living expenses and tuition are so low. I am working this summer as assistant farmer at Manumit, 35 dollars the first month, 50 the second; at the end of the summer I will have about one hundred dollars. I feel confident that three hundred dollars (or a little more, which I may be able to muster), should carry me through the school year at the University of Berlin or Vienna.

If you know of someone who would make me such a loan, with the guarantee of payment within a year it would help me beyond measure.

I will furnish references and do anything at all. The year will be tremendously significant to me and if you can help me I will be eternally grateful.

If I am to go passports etc, must be attended to, application to the University made etc, so it is imperative that I know very soon.

I am enclosing some things written recently which you might like to read.

Respectfully yours,

***Note:** Enclosed poems are "Snow if Falling," "Inheritance," "For Richard," "Empty Dwelling Places," and "Devotional Nocturne."*

Letter to Scholarship Committee, Columbia College, New York City from Helen Powell (ECA)

August 16, 1932
The University of Wisconsin

Dear Sirs:

Kenneth Patchen, who was a first-year student in the Experimental College during 1929-30, has asked me to send a statement regarding him and his work, in connection with his application for a scholarship at Columbia.

His year in the Experimental College is very hard to evaluate. During that time he kept himself very much withdrawn, and went his own way as much as possible, both intellectually and socially. Consequently, as judged on the basis of required assignments, his work was very uneven in quality. Some of his writing was beautifully done, and he continued to develop a strong literary interest and activity. But he seemed unable to accept any settled regime of work or study and dealt casually with those parts of the curriculum for which he felt little sympathy. One of his teachers reports that he did read "very extensively: poems, novels, plays, philosophy, and history."

It may be that in the two years since leaving Madison he has overcome the difficulties which hampered him here. There was never any doubt of his ability or of his earnestness.

His mark, as determined by the final paper and oral examination, was B+.

Sincerely yours,
Helen Powell
Secretary

Letter to Malcolm Sharp from Frank H. Bowles Assistant to the Director, Columbia University, New York City (ECA)

August 25, 1932
The University of Wisconsin, Madison

Dear Sir:
Please accept our thanks for your letter in regard to Mr. Kenneth Patchen.

It is my impression that Mr. Patchen has called at this office to discuss with us the possibility of making transfer to Columbia College, but apparently he has not filed formal application. I believe that the conversation indicated that he would probably have considerable difficulty in effecting a transfer.

Very truly yours
Frank H. Bowles

To Harriet Monroe from Kenneth Patchen (PAP)

April 10, 1933
Manumit School
Pauling, New York

Dear Editor,

I was born in Ohio twenty one years ago. My formal education has been limited to a year in Meiklejohn's Experimental College and some months in a small college in Arkansas. However in a somewhat sterner sense I have been educated. I have spent in all about eight months on "the road"; severe hardship and paralyzing disappointment have haunted my steps through the haunts of the homeless in the south and west. I am in a peculiar sense without a home. I have never had the security necessary to work.

My feeling for art has made it possible for me to endure and hope but I am growing bitter and discouraged for unless something develops soon another winter (and another) aimless misery is before me. I have the seed-conception of a major vision and it is agony not to be able to realize even the most essential and primary requisits of human living which are necessary for its consummation. I want so little: is there no help anywhere? I want nothing that I am unable to pay for in some way.

I write to you in hope that you (or some member of your staff) will see fit to advise or make suggestions. It is possible that there are student scholarships, loans etc. To which you can direct me. Or perhaps someone you know who could aid me in getting a job –I have had experience as gardener, clerk, laborer, odd-jobs-man, steel mill worker and other work. I can drive a car, do landscape gardening and could do professional cooking with a little more experience.

I should like to do reporting for a paper (although I have but a meager background for that) or write book reviews, edit, write publicity: in short, I feel confident of being able to do anything after a brief probation period.

(I have made no effort at publication until now and you are free to use any of these pieces.)

I am willing to go anywhere, live anywhere, do anything in order that I may write.

Can you advise me?

Truly,
Kenneth Patchen

P.S. I am unable to provide postage for the return of these pieces–have no scruples about destroying them.

Note: *Harriet Monroe was the editor of* ***Poetry*** *magazine at the time.*

Chapter Two: *Poetry* and Random House (1933-1934)

To Harriet Monroe from Kenneth Patchen (PAP)

Early May, 1933
228 West 13th St.
New York City

Dear Harriet Monroe,

With its face filled with forwarding addresses, your letter has just reached me. I am now janitor of two apartment houses, one on West 13th and the other on West 12th; the pay is $25 a month with a room. I am up at 6 thirty and am kept busy until about 8 P.M.

Starting at scratch something over a week ago I will not be paid until about the 10th of May so I can assure you that the $15 will be in the nature of a life-saver.

The work is wretched and hopelessly confining but I shall write if I must forego sleep to do it. I look forward to two or three hours of work each day for this summer and next winter.

Perhaps after a long time I shall be in a position to send you proof of this thing which I have called a "major vision" for want of a better expression.

Tell me: shall I destroy or put out of sight those pieces of mine which you are returning to me or shall I make an effort to publish them. As you say I do need criticism for I have been very much alone in trying to find a way.

My name is spelled PATCHEN not Patch<u>in</u>.
I am grateful to you.

Kenneth Patchen

***Note:** The date of this letter cannot be exactly pinpointed. There is an indication on the letter itself that it was answered by Harriet Monroe on May 20, 1933.*

To Alexander Meiklejohn from Kenneth Patchen (ECA)

July (?) 1933
c/o John Parke
Austerlitz, New York

Dear Mr. Meiklejohn,

I spent last winter with the forgotten in freights in the south, I suffered far too much. The heart is at the most bitter food.

I wrote to you last summer about this time, asking if you knew of anything for me. You were so very kind and sympathetic that I am again writing to you with the same hope.

Harriet Monroe (Poetry-Chicago) is publishing some poems of mine soon as is the Hound and Horn.

But I am so cut off and I want so to write.

Do you know of anything or anyone?

Respectfully,
Kenneth Patchen

To Alexander Meiklejohn from Kenneth Patchen (ECA)

July 26, 1933
c/o John Parke
Austerlitz, New York

Dear Mr. Meiklejohn,

I want to get a little house somewhere near enough to a village, farm or something so that I may support myself with odd jobs, or work of any sort. Do you know of any such place or of anyone who does.

Is there any hope of work in California. I have goodwill letters to people there (San Francisco) from friends here, but am afraid of going there and finding myself stranded.

I only need about four months (with a little leisure) and I shall be, able, I believe, to establish myself by the publication of a volume. I'd shoot straight for a Fellowship on the Guggenheim Foundation. All I want is a chance.

What is it that you are at work on?

I met Lewis Mumford last week. A fine man. He lives in America, N.Y.

You must be very busy, so forgive me for again bothering you.

Truly yours,
Kenneth Patchen

To Harriet Monroe from Kenneth Patchen (PAP)

September 4, 1933
c/o John Parke
Hanover, New Hampshire

Dear Harriet Monroe,

I lost my janitoring job some months ago; since then I have been working on a farm in upstate New York (for room and board); just now I am caretaker in a hiker's shelter on the Long Trail, here too I make nothing but my keep. The season for hiking ends with today (Labor Day) and I must move on. I am at a loss, not knowing where to go.

Lewis Mumford thinks that there is a possibility of my carving out an existence in Hanover: cutting and selling wood to the students at Dartmouth, building my own house; (working hard at getting established) perhaps I shall be able to carry this through. I must write next winter—

Do you know any people in Boston? I should like to get a job there. Anyone in New England.

These poems are written in Austerlitz, New York. Tell me of any leads anywhere. I am hard-pressed and discouraged.

Respectfully,
Kenneth Patchen

To Lincoln Kirstein from Kenneth Patchen (KPA)

Probably early in 1934
c/o Creighton Hill
64 Pemberton Square
Boston, Mass.

Dear Lincoln Kirstein,

I am working in the Cambridge Rubber Co. My job is to unload drums of crude rubber from a conveyor—two men to a drum; the drums weigh 500 lbs. Thirty five cents an hour. Seven thirty until five.

What do you wish changed in the review? Wheelwright objected to certain sections of it on the grounds that they were obscure. I shall rewrite it according to your suggestions.

I am utterly done in at the close of each working day but in spite of this I shall write.

I am grateful to you for your kindness and interest. It helps like the devil at a time like this.

Do you have any suggestions.

Sincerely yours,
Kenneth Patchen

P.S. Later I shall repay you the ten. At the moment I cannot.

To Lincoln Kirstein from Kenneth Patchen (KPA)

Around March, 1934

43 Allston Street
Boston, Mass.

Dear Lincoln Kirstein,

I have a little attic-room (two dollars the week) and I am working away against time.

I like Boston very much. Harry Murray hopes to get me placed somewhere soon.

I worked Monday of this week on a construction job in Belmont. The carpenters were to have begun work on the following day.

Conraid Aiken encouraged me to go on in the development of the review-idea. He thought it good.

Please let me hear from you concerning it.

Did The Story of My Death ever get across from England? I'd like very much to see it.

Sincerely yours,
Kenneth Patchen

To Amos Wilder from Kenneth Patchen

April 1934
68 Pemberton Square
(top floor front) Boston

Dear Wilder:

I plan to leave Boston for Ohio either Saturday of this week or on Monday next. I should like to see you very much before I go. If you can manage to get in—the Blake prints belong to—; I wish to return them to her before leaving. I hope to see you—if not, sincere thanks for everything. I shall write you.

Sincerely,
Kenneth

To Amos Wilder from Kenneth Patchen

April 24, 1934
Edgehill Drive
Warren, Ohio

Dear Wilder:

Hell getting here; very hell, here. I must get to Virginia! I have found the girl. (If anyone is to do it) I wish to have you marry us.

I hope to remodel an old house—I can get the land for a garden—I need money to swing it. I have so much at stake.

(*The Magazine*, Beverly Hills, Calif., has accepted some things of mine.)

If I believed in God I'd pray. Everything is wrong here; I'll be leaving soon.

Sincerely,
Kenneth

To Amos Wilder from Kenneth Patchen

June 12, 1934
Edgehill Drive
Warren, Ohio

Dear Amos Wilder:

I hope not to trouble you with my troubles...I have just returned to Ohio from New York City—with a wife. I have no plans...I am trapped here, don't know where to turn.

K.F.P

To Lewis Mumford from Kenneth Patchen (KPA)

August 4, 1934
Edgehill Drive,
Warren, Ohio

Dear Lewis Mumford,

You cannot understand what a hope's send your letter was to me. I seem to be completely at the mercy of this Mid-West tomb. I have a wife now and it is torment for me to remain under my father's roof—but how get away?

My one hope (I suppose) is to do a novel; but for that I need a job and some security. I have it well in mind, even drew up an outline of it (which somehow I lost). Yaddo, now that I am no longer alone, is out of the question—besides, no word of any kind has reached me from them since June.

I should appreciate any word you may have concerning these poems. In them you may find something worthwhile—I have worked hard on them. Perhaps you will know as you read them how anxious I am to realize myself in a prolonged work: these, with one or two exceptions, were written within a period of three weeks. (I sent some of them to Mr. MacLeish—no word from him.) New Masses has accepted all but one of everything sent them. At the moment they have four pieces waiting print. Malcolm Cowley has been most kind and encouraging—gave me two books for review.

The "big" magazines are ever ready with polite notes. The Magazine (Beverly Hills, Calif.) has taken several things. Recently I sent some things to England—Adelphi and New Verse—I have not heard from them. John Wheelwright has printed me in his new, Poems for A Dime, also, he has been interested to the extent of sending poems to Broom and American Poetry Journal—(no word from that quarter.) Conrad Aiken asked me to send things to him, in England.

The difficulty, as you can see, is that aside from the pleasure of seeing my stuff in print there is no benefit to me in this. Perhaps if I could get a book of verse published there would be a publisher to take interest in my proposed novel. In the novel I plan two independent themes—straight narrative and a "voice utterance".

With a job or some money (to start) I could swing the novel by placing short stories. I know you to be tired and on vacation but, can you advise me; this, after a fashion, is a matter of life and death with me.

Harry Murray was very kind to me in Boston.

I have heard nothing from John Parke.

I hoped for Virginia—a home there, garden, etc. I have no money to start. A friend in San Antonio, Texas, has advised me of houses there which may be had for $100 the year.

Do you think it advisable that I try a publishing house with the idea of getting out a volume of poetry?

Thank you for your kind note.

Sincerely,
Kenneth Patchen

***Note:** All hand written on three pages. Lewis Mumford was a respected critic and educator who had taken an interest in Patchen.*

To Amos Wilder from Kenneth Patchen

September 7, 1934
Edgehill Drive
Warren, Ohio

Dear Wilder:

I was indeed puzzled by your silence.

MacLeish and Mumford have made advances to publishers with a book of verse, in my name, as the subject of their efforts. I have scant hope in that direction.

I wrote some thirty odd pieces in the margin of three weeks. No short stories. Yaddo, for some reason unknown to me, fell through. Thank you for allowing me to see "1934"; I like it with this reservation; your particular language pattern, in my opinion fails of effectiveness precisely at the point of most stress; tropes, rhymes, etc. should be rugged in character, with "color"—a *real* subject should trample under foot the poet and his poem—I want more of the ache in wanting, not the wanted thing, however perfectly captured on the paper that thing may be.

The most beautiful vision of Christ is that of a shaggy Christ, bareheaded under great trees.

...I dread the thought of coming winter; the fall holds out nothing but a closed fist for me. I have tried (via U.S. Mail) to get a job in both Boston and New York. Nothing. Need I say that I am nearly mad with worry. I seem rooted here. Miriam, my wife, has been a real trouper...The enclosed two poems are of today's vintage.

Sincerely,
Kenneth

To Miriam Patchen from Saxe Cummins (KPA)

November 30, 1934
Random House
20 E 57 New York

Dear Mrs. Patchen,

I know you will be delighted to learn that Random House and your husband have come to an agreement today. This is <u>not</u> a triangle; we hope it will be an arrangement bringing great happiness to you, your husband and us.

Congratulations and good wishes!

Saxe Cummins

Random House Contract to Kenneth Patchen from Bennett Cerf (KPA)

RANDOM HOUSE 20 E 57 · NEW YORK

The American Selling Agent for the NONESUCH PRESS Limited Editions

December 6, 1934.

Mr. Kenneth Patchen,
c/o Walsh,
21 Bank Street,
New York City.

Dear Mr. Patchen:

I am enclosing two copies of our regular contract, which I think will cover the ground in exact accordance with the conversation that we had at this office a few days ago.

As I told you at that time, we are extremely enthusiastic about some of the poems that you have submitted to us, but think you will agree that others of them are unworthy of perpetuation in book form, and to include these inferior poems in the first volume would be a grievous mistake for everybody concerned and particularly yourself. The contract that we are signing with you and the modest advance that we are giving you, are simply to clinch the fact that we want to be the publishers of your book -- but only when it is ready for publication. I hope that by the Spring of 1935 you will come up and see me again with a collection that is ready to be brought out in book form. I want to emphasize again that there is absolutely no need to hurry in this affair. If necessary, the book need not come out until the Fall of next year, or even later for that matter. The point I am trying to make is that it is to your interest and to ours to bring out this book only when everybody is satisfied that it is ready for publication.

As I told you before, we will be willing to advance you more money from time to time if you find yourself in need of it. We believe whole-heartedly in your future and will be proud to have you on our Random House list.

When you have returned one copy of this contract duly signed and witnessed, we will consider the matter settled. If any points in it bother you, however, please do not hesitate to call upon me.

Cordially yours,

Bennett A. Cerf
RANDOM HOUSE

RANDOM HOUSE IS A SUBSIDIARY OF THE MODERN LIBRARY, INC.

bac:ok

Chapter Three: Before the War & The Guggenheim (1935-1937)

To Amos Wilder from Kenneth Patchen
[written on yellow onion-skin paper]

1935
Rhinebeck, N.Y.

We have been very happy here, though the problem of food has been, and is, unmanageable. We are hopeful of holding the fort until our garden shows signs of productivity—though not for months in the future. I get no books to review here; editors seldom send books out of the city. We are without income of any description....The trees are lovely with new leaves, the sky is like a great hand flexing and unflexing, clouds are peopled with cities, the wind is the wonder of something unreal....

Sincerely,
Kenneth

Note: *Included with this letter were two poems which later appeared in* ***Before the Brave.***

To Lewis Mumford from Kenneth Patchen (KPA)

June 22, 1935
Rhinebeck, New York
Dear Lewis Mumford:

We are very happy here. Our cottage is delightful, the country is very beautiful, the days are long and crowded with work and enjoyment—however (and I feel so absolutely strapped and tired in this). There is one thing wrong: we are without income of any description. I do everything possible but it doesn't work out. My stories come back; I get no books for review; nothing comes in.

Naturally we do everything to keep this condition secret from Mr. and Mrs. Billings; we are extremely grateful to them for making this summer possible and we wish to keep our relationship strictly to that of neighbors and friends, without any undue inconvenience to them or to us.

My work is planned for at least four months ahead—I hope to use no old poems in my book (to appear in January). The one way out, as I see it now, (and I hate this utterly) is to borrow enough money to see the summer through in food and essentials. It is very important to me to do this book well. Perhaps I can get a decent job in the fall, even a Guggenheim—I shall be in a position to pay back. I trust that you understand. Now, do you know of any individual who would, with these things in mind, make me a loan? (We do not need much.) Random House is out of the question.

This is in the nature of a drowning man and straw affair—there must be people somewhere who could do this thing without strain.

I look forward to seeing you again (I am hopeful of being able to give you that ten dollars—I do not wish to have money between us) and I shall have new poems to show you.

Miriam extends her regards.
Sincerely
Kenneth Patchen

***Note:** Josh Billings and wife offered the Patchens use of the cottage.*

To John Simon Guggenheim Memorial Foundation from Kenneth Patchen (GUG)

August 23, 1935
Rhinebeck, N.Y.
Dear Sirs:

Kindly send me your Fellowship Application Form.
Sincerely,
Kenneth Patchen

***Note:** This was the first of Patchen's many application to the Guggenheim Foundation. He would continue to apply on a yearly basis till shortly before his death.*

Kenneth Patchen's first Application for a Guggenheim Fellowship (GUG)

October 28, 1935
361 West 20th Street,
New York City

FELLOWSHIP APPLICATION FORM

JOHN SIMON GUGGENHEIM MEMORIAL FOUNDATION
551 FIFTH AVENUE · NEW YORK · N · Y ·
1936

RECEIVED

APPLICATIONS and accompanying documents must reach the Secretary of the Foundation not later than November 1, 1935. They are desired, for the convenience of the Committee of Selection, as early as possible.

In what field of learning, or of art, does your project lie? Poetry

Concise statement of project I wish to complete a book of poems.

PERSONAL HISTORY:

Name in full Kenneth Patchen

Present address 361 West 20th Street, New York City.

Telephone

A permanent address % Random House... 20 East 57th Street, New York City.

Present occupation Writer (unemployed)

Place of birth Niles, Ohio Date of birth August 13, 1911

If not a native-born American citizen, date and place of naturalization

Single, Married, Widowed, Divorced Married

Name and address of wife or husband Miriam Patchen, 361 West 20th Street, N. Y.

Name and address of nearest kin, if unmarried

Ages of children, if any

Have you any constitutional disorder or physical disability?

With this application please submit a small recent photograph.

***Note:** Also accompanying the application were two sheets of paper with additional material written by Patchen, as follows:*

3.
Random House will publish my first book of poems, BEFORE THE BRAVE, in January (1936).
I have published verse and criticism in Scribner's, Harpers Poetry: A Magazine of Verse, The New Republic, Herald-Tribune, New York Times, New Masses, Nation, Saturday Review of Literature, The Magazine, and in many little magazines.
Selections from my work have appeared in two anthologies: Proletarian Literature in the United States, and Westminster Anthology of English and American Poets.

PLANS FOR WORK
It is extremely difficult to determine in advance the direction of one's poetry: however, I am tempted to say that my future work will bear close resemblance to the chronicle of a journey through this present day. The start was made in BEFORE THE BRAVE (to be published in January by Random House). The writing would be done in this country; preferably in the South. I am under long-term contract to Random House.

To Henry Moe/ John Simon Guggenheim Memorial Foundation from Kenneth Patchen (GUG)

March 17, 1936
46 Perry Street,
New York City

Dear Henry Allen Moe:

I am very pleased to accept the Fellowship under the terms of your letter.
My gratitude is great.

Sincerely yours,
Kenneth Patchen

To Amos Wilder from Kenneth Patchen

September 3, 1936
3 Placita Rafaela
Santa Fe, N. M.

Dear Wilder:

Terribly pleased to hear from you...I am just back from a very tiring trip to New York City; saw a head specialist there about the sinus—got a prescription calling for cocaine. It seems that the ammonia in the rubber plant had eaten away certain tissues in my nasal tract; rather serious condition.

Miriam and I spent a month in Phoenix, Arizona. It was too hot and the town is bad. Santa Fe is better, though quite damp at times. Maine must have been great: rugged, lovely "—with human life not angels'." That to me is all that is best in what we so loosely call religious thought and feeling. Jesus, the "idea" of Christ, to me, again, is simply the aspiration of the common man (as opposed to the "Man of God") to realize himself on an earth that is of flowers and of rifles made. We must extract the concept of the gun and the sword from the mind-world in which too many of us live. It is necessary to quit a brain grown in a wrong womb of experience. The fault lies not in what we are, but in that thing which we would become. We must make over not the present world of sham and hypocrisy, but ourselves; this means time will leave us when we leave it. And we must get away with a fuller heart than was ever permitted us. All art will follow the art of the living—Jesus was master there, thus his value.

Thank you for telling me the important news. Please extend our best wishes to your wife.

Kenneth

To Henry Moe from Kenneth Patchen (GUG)

January 1, 1937
3 Placita Rafaela,
Santa Fe, New Mexico.

Dear Mr. Moe:

Yesterday I mailed to you the manuscript of my book of poems, FIRST WILL AND TESTAMENT; this work constitutes an expression of the uses to which I have put the Fellowship granted me.
I am engaged now on a new book which will consist of a poem-sequence and two poem-dramas—I request that a renewal be granted in order that the above project shall be realized.
(I am hopeful of creating a poetry for the theatre which will be good poetry and good theatre, not a bastard form of either.)

Sincerely,
Kenneth Patchen

To Amos Wilder from Kenneth Patchen

January 1, 1937
[Address assumed to be Hollywood]

. . . I sent the manuscript of my new book of poems in to Random House yesterday. Title: *First Will and Testament*. It is a good book: at least, good enough in this year before the war which frightens me. I am here to make money: lots of money for my books. It is a very bad place, cheap and shoddy; but one can be here without living here.

Sincerely,
Kenneth

To Henry Moe from Kenneth Patchen (KPA)

January 31, 1937.

3 Placita Rafaela,
Santa Fé, New Mexico.

RECEIVED
FEB -2 1937

Dear Mr. Moe:

I am at a loss to account for the miscarriage of the letter sent you together with the manuscript, First Will And Testament.

In that letter I said this: I wish to have the Fellowship extended another twelve-month period — this is my project for work under such an arrangement: to complete a book upon which I am now at work. This book will consist of a sequence of poems and two poem-dramas. I am eager to effect a marriage of poetry and theatre; it is my belief that good poetry can be good theatre.

Sincerely,
Kenneth Patchen

To Thomas Wolfe from Kenneth Patchen (HAR)

April 1937
[Assumed address: 2488 Cheremoya Avenue; Hollywood, CA.]

This century has been a black pit and a cancer for the artist. The young writer must equip himself with a sturdy light and a cure for incessant poverty. To survive he must make use of every weapon at hand. This letter represents my use of an age-old device of the artist. The annals of literature are studded with missives similar to this one—letters of D. H. Lawrence, Herman Melville, Francior Villon, Dostoievsky [sic], Edgar Allan Poe, John Keats, and many others. I wish desperately to continue my career as a writer and I have not the wherewithal for existence itself. . . .

Present situation: pennyless—doing hack writing.

Health: suffer with Sinusitis; weak heart.

Immediate plan and ambition: to secure the security necessary to the production of two plays.

Sometime plan: a long novel which will deal with present-day. America; more novels; further plays; books of poetry.

Item: I am ambitious in a large sense.

What I want of you: I wish to borrow 2,500 dollars on an 18-month, personal note basis.

What this would mean to me: 1) an opportunity to remedy my rapidly-becoming-dangerous physical condition....2) an immediate start on my plays (I would go to Boston to work)...

What this would mean to you: 1) you would have the satisfaction of knowing that you had made possible the further activity of a determined young creator...2) it would mean what you made it mean.

What assurance have you that this money will be returned? 1) My play will go on Broadway...2) my word.

I can do many fine things if I can escape this horrible house of want and poverty. These words are not written lightly.

Sincerely yours,
Kenneth Patchen

Note: *There is clear indication that this letter was sent to several writers as possible patrons.*

Chapter Four: The Hunted City (1938)

To Leon Trotsky from Kenneth Patchen and Harvey Breit(KPA)

January 24, 1938
2488 Cheremoya Avenue;
Hollywood, California

Dear Leon Trotsky:

We are two young men interested in literature and people; above all, in people. Writing, to us, in its highest sphere, has always meant the expression of man's desire to live well (that is to say, beautifully). It follows that the finest creators extend the horizon of human dignity and worth—and it is to one of these that we now address ourselves. To you, then, not as specialist or scholar, but as a man whose persevering and all-embracing honesty has enriched human kind, we do now come with inquiry regarding certain doubts with which we are deeply troubled.

It is our belief that we shall shortly be witness to a revitalization of magazine influence, an influence which has been subject to innumerable shipwrecks since the publication of Literature and Revolution; and, to use a faulty but definitive analogy, we wish rather to be the Lead-Goat than the sheep which follow him to their doom. In our present perplexity, one word from you will have the worth of volumes—and a connection with greatness will have instilled in us a flowering confidence.

It would simplify things to state that as men and as editors we could be compared to the patient suffering a split personality; however, we know that we could not long endure in an editorial capacity did we not adhere to a policy of attempting to publish all that is valid in literature, all that is tenable in some respect; it is not too much to suppose that the advancing the cause of understanding, we contribute, in however small a part, to the cause of international revolution...knowing these things, can we be satisfied with this identity? Obviously, this leads nowhere. What, then, specifically, is the relationship between an organ (the roof-supporting timbers of which are truth and excellence of accomplishment) and the revolution? We are not, speaking frankly, a Marxist journal: thus the horns of our dilemma.

Permit us to particularize with this one question, the answer to which has apparently eluded contemporaries of ours. Is it consistent with our intention to preoccupy ourselves concerning our contributor's beliefs in the arena of politics and affairs, if such beliefs are not apparent in the work under consideration? In point, should we print inferior pieces by those whose opinion we share in preference to better ones by those with whom we disagree? Again, in the critical sphere and that of polemics must our partisanism dictate an editorial judgment? At what point does the freest expression of ideas become reaction?

Possibly we have been unfair to you in asking for what will of necessity be a Marxian evaluation of what is, in essence, a liberal journal. This does not detract from our eagerness as we await your reply.

Yours for the advancement of revolution,
we are, sincerely yours,
(signed)
Kenneth Patchen

A N N O U N C I N G :

P U L S E will publish the best that is available in w o r l d literature.
Through **PULSE** all creative art forms will find untrammeled expression.
The credo of **PULSE** will be a truthful examination of experience.
We shall attempt in **PULSE** to properly evaluate all human activity.
Besides creative material **PULSE** will publish critiques of all the arts.
Judgment without fear or prejudice: **PULSE** will have no axe to grind.
Honest social conviction will achieve through **PULSE** impartial hearing.
To be non-partisan yet comprehensive shall be **PULSE's** endeavor.
We shall respect the artist's conscience, and reflect the world's **P U L S E.**

A MAGAZINE OF LITERATURE AND AFFAIRS

Price Twenty-Five Cents An Issue, $2.00 A Year — 1733½ North Dillon Street, Los Angeles, Calif.

Telegram to Amos Wilder from Kenneth Patchen

February 13, 1938
2488 Cheremoya Ave.
Los Angeles

Remembering your earnest kindness in the past and with terrible reluctance to request this final favor but have no choice whatever illness and bad happenings however now cloud beginning to lift ask you can you wire me fifty dollars on thirty day loan aware fully of your new responsibilities settle all soon.

To Amos Wilder from Kenneth Patchen

February 18, 1938
2488 Cheremoya Ave.
Los Angeles

I cannot begin to tell you what the money means to me; enough that I am wonderfully grateful. I am on the eve of success here. I shall write you in another connection within a day or two.

Ever yours,
Kenneth

To Amos Wilder from Kenneth Patchen

Winter, 1938

Dear Wilder,

You must believe that I am unhappy not to be able to meet my obligation to you at this time...Please have faith...I lost a "ghost-writing" job in December: no income since; we have sold everything we possessed, books, clothing, everything. I have walked the streets for any kind of job, nothing. We have often been without food for days at a time: no tobacco even and I have the habit very strongly; no carfare to get about—I've had to walk from L.A. to Beverly Hills to see a writer's agent...At this moment six of my movie stories are in the studio, stories which the agent hopes to sell for prices ranging from $3,000 to $5,000; (you must see I have reason to feel bitter): and I continue to work—at night, now that things are so horrible during the day: when I wrote to you last, one of the scenarios was on the point of selling—and the producer who wanted it was discharged unexpectedly! Three years residence is required by the relief authorities: I don't know what to do; can you think of anyone who would be willing to lend me some money so that I may be able to hold out? Every passway is barred.

I have worked so damn hard. It's months now at this.

If not, don't worry about this situation: I am determined to go on until I get on my feet once and for all.

Ever,
Kenneth

***Note:** This letter was written on the back of a PULSE magazine flyer*

To James Laughlin from Kenneth Patchen (NDA)

March 12, 1938
2488 Cheremoya Ave.
Hollywood

Dear Laughlin:

Yes, it is raining here—bad for the poor. A large part of my work is tied up in one way or another; however, find a few poems enclosed. Delighted that you like those already in your hands.
I'm having a shot at writing movie stories—hope to make enough of that filthy stuff called money to live a long while nicely and quietly in Boston, the only city I like so far.
A very long book is stirring within me; my 'Bridge'. I don't think Crane got very far really. Thank you for your exceptional promptness and good will.

Sincerely,
Kenneth Patchen

Would you be interested in publishing a volume of my poems in your New Directions Press?

***Note:** Reference is made to Hart Crane's poem, 'The Bridge.'*

To Amos Wilder from Kenneth Patchen

March 1938
1414 North Las Palmas St.

I am working hard, with little result to date. It is difficult to create a place for myself here; and possibly wrong to try.

I think I have learned some things since I last saw you. The "Moscow Trials" episode has not made me happy about the world. I do believe in change; but not at the risk of losing all things that men have fought for in the past. Love is greater than murder; faith finer than blind hate.

Kenneth

To Sherry Mangan from Kenneth Patchen (KPA)

March 26, 1938

Dear Mangan:

This is hard to say: I'm having a hell of a time trying to get the magazine started; its birth is on the doubtful side at this moment. I must return your poems. They gave me tremendous pleasure, like Irish whiskey. (I feel that I have no right to hold them longer.)

It may be that the magazine will go—may I print you if that happens?

All my good wishes,
Sincerely,
Kenneth Patchen

Everything is crazy in Hollywood.
Address me:
5526½ Virginia Avenue
Los Angeles

To James T. Farrell from Kenneth Patchen (UPA)

June 14, 1938
5526½ Virginia Ave.
Los Angeles, California

Dear Farrell:

I was greatly pleased to receive your letter: particularly to hear of the amount of writing which you have been doing.

I've been working like holy hell, but the returns are so many peanuts at the moment. Re the matter of my last communication to you: I have a job now—in the State Employment Service—at the intake desk—7 hrs. a day—35 dollars (app.) per month. And it's a foul job—turning away hundreds of skilled men every day. But it's bread and margarine. The movie writing goes on at night: mid-way in a big story now. My book (mss.) is a Jonah. Four months ago (after it had been held by MacMillan for 5 months) I sent it to Harper's: got a rejection: instructed them to send it on to Knopf: that was something over three months ago: yesterday, after sending in 'change of address', I was informed that Knopf had never received the mss.: I immediately sent off a god damn-you-note to Harper's: a whole year shot in just that sort of thing. I am beginning to suspect very seriously that there may be something behind all this: (there are some who would be happy if I never published again): just now I am sitting on my fists, and cursing.

My book completely edited, revised, new; I think that you will find it much better than the book you saw.

Thanks for the Globe lead. I shall see what can be done with it.

If there is anything in the world that you can do to help me get a publisher for First Will and Testament I shall be eternally grateful. It's hard to press anything from California.

I am trying to start a magazine—a good magazine—and I have reason to believe that it may come to something.

My very best to you and good fortune to your work

Kenneth

To Henry Moe/ John Simon Guggenheim Memorial Foundation from Kenneth Patchen (GUG)

July 23, 1938
5526 ½ Virginia Ave
Los Angeles, California

Dear Mr. Moe:

I wish to apply again for a Guggenheim Fellowship: I am ready to set forth on a rather ambitious work of six volumes which may amount to a contemporary 'Paradise Lost'. I have been working very hard on the plan of the poem and just now its parts are beginning to fit into the framework of the whole. Title: THE HUNTED CITY.
A publisher is interested in printing the six books; each title would see publication when finished and a single book made of the completed work.
I should like to present my plan to your committee (together with a portion of the first section of the poem): when is the closing date for this?
My second book, FIRST WILL AND TESTAMENT, will be published early next year.

With every personal good wish.
Sincerely yours,
Kenneth Patchen

To Amos Wilder from Kenneth Patchen

September 24, 1938
427 S. Figueroa
Los Angeles, CA

Dear Wilder:

It is not easy for me to formulate a credo in regard to "the poet and the class struggle." No contemporary poet (or artist) has evidenced a consistent attitude towards any major human problem; he has occupied himself with literary and political jockeying for position— not content with changing horses in the middle of the stream, he must change the stream as well; he has spent his energies baying at

the moon and mooning at the bay. There is little to go on.
No poet can write "for the people" without realizing that current literary taste (In the hands of the money-changers) has little to do with literature: ie., Burns, Heine, Homer, etc.
Jesus Christ is still a better subject for the poet than the emasculated Lenin of the Stalinists.
Auden, and all the baby Audens, male and female, over here, is the super-salesman of bourgeois taste.
Eliot was born sleepy, and his own work has done little to keep him awake—particularly his verse.

A Program:

Let the poet be at one with his own life.

Let him read more Dante and Burns and less political mouth-frothing.

Let there be an end to boot-licking down the line.

Influences of my life in a steel-worker's home on my work and outlook:

> In the beginning, at least, it gave me a contempt for intellectual writers who intellectualized but did not write—still have it.
>
> Made me suspicious of people who "loved the working class." The working class, by reason of its position in this society, is base, treacherous, ignorant and *cheap*; to say otherwise is to enter upon a major contradiction. The middle class is worse, and still more so the upper.

Our betters: Melville, Poe and Stephen Crane.

These things will not be of much use to you. I am very much involved in my new six-volume poem, *The Hunted City*. I am afraid it doesn't have a great deal to do with "proletarian" writing. I am rather bitter about the present set-up in that direction.
...When will your book appear? I shall watch for it with considerable eagerness.

Sincerely,
Kenneth

***Note:** Amos Wilder, who had asked Patchen for a declaration of his credo, quoted from this letter in his book, **The Spiritual Aspects of the New Poetry,** 1940, by Harper & Brothers Publishers.*

Clipping from *The Hollywood Citizen-News*:

October 1938

Topsy-turvy conditions in the world force too many persons to concentrate on the job of earning money before they do the work they love best, take it from youthful Kenneth Patchen, author of a book of poems, *Before the Brave*, which caused some critics to acclaim him as the representative voice of his generation.

In Hollywood to look about for ideas, Patchen declared that he preferred Spain to moviedom..."Everyone must discover for himself in what way he can be effective in the war against Fascism and reaction...Recently I have thought of the theatre as a writing medium...It seems clear to me that poetry, to retain its vitality for communication, must assume leadership on the stage. I am not thinking of certain Broadway 'blank verse' plays, which seem to be compounded more of blankness than of verse."

To Amos Wilder from Kenneth Patchen (on a 3x5 card)

December 6, 1938
2488 Chermoya Ave
Los Angeles

This particular poet has been flat on his back for something worse than five weeks...Last year was the same. Semi-paralysis of my lower back and legs. But I have been hard at work on the "Argument" for my *The Hunted City* and the first poem of *Horrible Ghost, Holy Ghost*, the first book in septology. I shall send you some of it when I'm able to get around a bit.

All my affection,
Kenneth

To Henry Moe/ John Simon Guggenheim Memorial Foundation from Kenneth Patchen (GUG)

December 15, 1938
427 South Figueroa Street,
Los Angeles, California

Dear Mr. Moe:

Under this cover find documents which constitute my application for a renewal.

Thank you for your prompt consideration in the matter of my inability to submit this material before now. I am sorry that I cannot report on New Direction's decision in regard to my book, FIRST WILL AND TESTAMENT; they have not reached one as yet. I had hoped to be able with this writing to tell you that the manuscript had been accepted for publication.
During the past year I have occupied myself with research and planning for the poem-septology, THE HUNTED CITY, which I propose to advance during the period of renewal; also, I have revised and made extensive additions to FIRST WILL AND TESTAMENT. The introduction to my long poem has been begun, I am enclosing its first part—It develops apace and seems to have a positive will of its own.

With the season's best from my wife and me, I am
Sincerely yours,
Kenneth Patchen

Note: Mr. Patchen submitted the ms of "First Will and Testament: Poems," and plans for the composition of a long poem "The Hunted City."

***Note:** Above was Henry Moe's handwritten note on application.*

To Harry Roskolenko from Kenneth Patchen (Yale Univ.)

December 21, 1938
427 South Figueroa Street
Los Angeles, California

Dear Roskolenko:

Accept my sincere congratulations on the publication of a damn fine book!*

Sincerely yours,
Kenneth Patchen

I shall do what I can to publicize it out here: giving my copy to the public library and buying another for myself when that is possible...writing a review of it this week for a local mag.

*****You are a better poet than I had thought. But then I hadn't seen many of your poems.

Note:*Sequence on Violence *(NY: Signal 1938); Patchen had requested poems from Roskolenko for his PULSE magazine.*

Chapter Five: New Directions (1939)

To Kenneth Patchen from James Laughlin (NDA)

January 13, 1939
427 S. Figueroa Street
Los Angeles, Ca

Dear Patchen:

I like very much the start that you have made on your long poem and it convinces me of any doubts I had about publishing you. I shall be glad to do so.

It seems to me that you really have something. A combination of the imaginative imagery of the Surrealists, the cadences of Whitman, and the revolutionary feeling of whomever you want to set up as a paragon of that quality.

I don't mean that you are not original; I am just attempting to compass you with descriptive referents. The little pieces do not stick in my mind much.

Yes, I should certainly like to publish you, starting with the collection of short poems in the fall of this year. I can send you some contracts a little later on when I have the time to draw them up. It is quite a long labour as we have no printed forms.

About payments: our schedule on a two dollar book is ten cents a book sold till receipts equal costs of production and distribution and thereafter sixty cents a copy. If a second edition is required the initial rate comes into force again until it is paid for and so forth. The costs which are charged against the book are all production costs, circulars, advertising, share of catalogue and salesmen's

expenses, but no office expenses or editorial expenses. All those are my contribution to the joy of nations.
I shall be glad to hear what you think of these arrangements and what you are doing now.

Yours,
[James Laughlin]

To Harry Roskolenko from Kenneth Patchen (Yale Univ.)

January 16, 1939
427 So. Figueroa Street
Los Angeles, California

Dear Roskolenko:

I've been in and out of bed with a bum back...hard to get much done. Dropped temporarily my column in the local mag. Will get your book in it as soon as I get back to it. Fired too, you know. Voices review set. Talking about you to people around.
What of the Creative Project? Any chance for me? Have written to Alsberg about it. Anxious to get out of here.
Happy to send poems to your anthology. Shortly. When will Abel's Rimbaud appear? Harvey has spoken sketchily of your project. Is it to be a permanent publishing outfit? Who have you lined up for the anthology? Etc.
The C.P. is the original s b out here. Stinking. Fists beginning to itch. Hope to get in some body blows one way or other. The bastards like to think of themselves as Reds!
Look forward to seeing you in New York.
Seen Fearing's new book?* A wet fizzle.

Sincerely yours,
Kenneth Patchen

*Note: C.P. is Communist Party; *Leftist poet Kenneth Fearing's **Dead Reckoning: A Book of Poetry** (1938) followed Patchen's **Before the Brave** at Random House.*

To James Laughlin from Kenneth Patchen (NDA)

January 16, 1939
427 So. Figueroa St
Los Angeles, California

Dear Laughlin:

I am confident that you will appreciate the hub of this communication: it has been seven months since I sent you my manuscript: I have not been any more impatient than is normal under the circumstances: by no word have I indicated this to you...but that is a hell of a time to wait.

I write to you in all good faith: had I not had it, I should have requested a decision long ago. An acceptance would have helped me considerably when I made application for a renewal of my Guggenheim; it would, further, have facilitated my plan of getting East: I did not press you.

Now I must ask you to make your decision.

My new work grows. But it is damn hard to work out here. Hope to get to New York soon. Which is good to California's bad.

Several people have volunteered to write an introduction: not sure now that I want one. Better to let the work do its own talking.
Best for the new year.

Sincerely yours,
Kenneth Patchen (signed)

To Henry Moe/ John Simon Guggenheim Memorial Foundation from Kenneth Patchen (GUG)

427 So. Figueroa St.,
Los Angeles, California.
January 19, 1939.

Dear Mr. Moe:

In conversation yesterday Theodore Robinson informed me that he had, in a letter to you, injected certain information pertaining to a local situation in which I was involved recently. Mr. Robinson's good will and intention led him to take a somewhat alarmist view of my position in the matter; I have told him that I deeply regret his unauthorized use of my name in presenting this situation to you — it is my view that this job-difficulty offers its own channels for solution. I wish to repeat that Mr. Robinson acted in all good faith but I must, in conscience, object to the use of my name in this connection.

I hope to be able to communicate with you shortly re New Directions' decision on my manuscript: I have requested that a decision be reached (after seven months of waiting). Accept the very best wishes of my wife and me for your new year.

Sincerely yours,
Kenneth Patchen

Telegram to James Laughlin from Kenneth Patchen (NDA)
January 20, 1939

WESTERN UNION

Received at 52 Warren Street, Roxbury, Mass.

BAM149 56 8 EXTRA DUPE OF TEL TEL=LOSANGELES CALIF JAN 20
JAMES LAUGHLIN 4TH= VIA NORFOLK CONN 21
=DLR 229 PERKINS ST JAMAICAPLAIN MASS=

DELIGHTED BEYOND WORDS WITH YOUR ACCEPTANCE CANT THINK OF ANY BETTER INCENTIVE FOR WORK THAN THE INTEGRITY AND HIGH AIMS OF YOUR NEW DIRECTIONS= TERMS OK= ACCEPT WITHOUT RESERVATION= COMING EAST IN APRIL= LOOK FORWARD TO SEEING YOU= GOING TOUT TO DRINK A TOAST TO MY NEW PUBLISHER=
KENNETH PATCHEN=

To Henry Moe/ John Simon Guggenheim Memorial Foundation from Kenneth Patchen (GUG)

January 21, 1939
427 So. Figueroa Street
Los Angeles, California

Dear Mr. Moe:

NEW DIRECTIONS has accepted my book, First Will And Testament, for publication in the fall of this year; also, and this pleases me greatly, they have contracted for the printing of all seven volumes of my projected work, The Hunted City.

Sincerely yours,
Kenneth Patchen

To Amos Wilder from Kenneth Patchen

February 3, 1939
Los Angeles, California

New Directions accepted my new book, *First Will and Testament*, for fall publication; also, and this pleases me greatly, they have contracted for the printing of all seven volumes of my *The Hunted City*. (No advance.)
My wife's parents just traded their house in the city for a farm in Acton, Mass.—and we get put in there, our keep being taken care of by the work I can do about the place, building coops for the chickens, etc.
You probably know about the Harvard scholarship for a young poet that Wheelwright is working on—I understand that I am first in line for it. My plan: use Acton as my base of operations; apply for jobs in Boston and New York, publishing houses, advertising.
My problem: I haven't any way of getting there. You don't know by any God-given chance of any individual who could lend me something toward the fare? Sure that things will turn out right if we can only get out of here...On top of everything—I should be under a doctor's care with this mysterious back ailment...

Sincerely,
Kenneth

Have poems in the current FANTASY which may interest you. A long poem coming in TWICE A YEAR.

To James T. Farrell from Kenneth Patchen (UPA)

February 3, 1939
427 So. Figueroa
Los Angeles

Dear Farrell:

New Directions has accepted my book, First Will And Testament, for printing in the fall; also, and this pleases me greatly, they have contracted for the publication of all seven volumes of my The Hunted City. No advance.
I've lost my job. Just out of bed after 8 weeks—my back and legs on the fritz. Trying like hell to get East: Miriam's folks traded their house in city for a farm in Acton, Mass. (We can go there—help about the place as much as I can) further: possible scholarship at Harvard—if only I can get there to see about it.
Do you know of anyone who could lend me money—on a straight loan? Got to get out of here quickly—no dough whatever.

***Note:** At this point in the letter, there is the beginning of a sentence which has been crossed out. It goes, "If I were well I wouldn't be so damn".*

Sorry to bother you, but I must [tell] you everything I can think of.

Sincerely,
Kenneth
5's, 10's—anything will help.

To Harry Roskolenko from Kenneth Patchen (UPA)

February 9, 1939
427 So. Figueroa St
Los Angeles

Dear Roskolenko:

Sorry re delay on review: paper here just held it up—for reasons of their own—will appear either this Friday or next.
Bending every effort to get East now: several angles. Back soon, I think.
When does the Abel book come up? I'll take one.
Getting ready some stuff for the anthology—get it to you within a short time. Are you planning to print any English work?
No soap on WPA for me at the moment.
How is your book selling?
New Directions just signed to publish my new book, FIRST WILL AND TESTAMENT, in the fall.

Sincerely,
Kenneth Patchen

To Kenneth Patchen from James Laughlin (NDA)

March 20, 1939

Dear Patchen:

It was very good of you to send me that enthusiastic telegram. It was a pleasure to receive it. I am sorry to have been so long in thanking you, but it's a busy life.
When do you come East? There will be a number of things for us to talk over in getting ready the book. I don't expect to start printing it before the summer (it will come out in the fall) but just as well to get the plans drawn up.
So let me know when you are heading this way and where you will be.
By the way, do you know a fellow named Roskolenko? If you do, please tell me, and I'll then tell you how you can assist me in a very troubling matter.
I don't know that there's much news here. Things creep along. The Schwartz book is doing fairly well, the Williams and Pound keep moving.
I think we'll have a good list next fall to go with your book. Here are some of the things I have in mind. The second part of WHITE MULE. The 1939 collection. Kafka's AMERICA. A book of comic-symbolic drawings by William Steig. Pound's IMPOLITE ESSAYS. A book of literary essays by Schwartz. The poems of Dylan Thomas.

A mixed book by Elizabeth Bishop. It should make a lively group, don't you think?
What news in the West? How goes the long poem?
Sincerely,

To Kenneth Patchen from James Laughlin (NDA)

March 22, 1939

I guess our letters crossed. I'm very glad to hear that you are going to be in these parts. Concord is a very nice place in the Spring; often I go out there of a June evening and go boating on the little river.
The poems are OK, perhaps not as hard as some others you have done, but very rich in imagery and suggestion. I am sorry to see them wasted on FANTASY. I hope in future that you will consult me about where you appear. There is such a thing as keeping up face, you know. Had you tried the better places with these?
Yes, I want something good from you for NEW DIRECTIONS 1939, certainly and by all means. The book will come out in next October and we'll likely print in July.
My thought had been the Argument for THE HUNTED CITY, but I see you have given that to Norman. Well that's just as well. That will bring you in some extra money and also be a sort of advertisement. Be sure to have her mention who will do the book.
Some of your friends have approached me for contributions toward your fare East. I think I should make clear to you how I feel about that. This is not an unusual situation; several others of the group are hard up and operating at a deficit so to speak.
My feeling in the matter is this; since I am to lose money doing their books I think that may properly be considered my contribution and let other friends meet the operating expenses. I don't mean to discourage you, but I believe in facing facts. I shall lose at least two hundred dollars on your book and probably more. I'm glad to do it because I like your work and believe in it, but I would much prefer that there were no illusions. You will, of course, take in a royalty of a few cents a book (I think I have already told you our customary arrangement) and in an extreme emergency you could count on drawing against that.
This is hardly a cheerful letter but then what in Christ's name is there to be cheerful about? I hold the poems here to show to people.

To Kenneth Patchen from James Laughlin (NDA)

May 3, 1939

Dear Patchen:

I'm sending the manuscript right on to you by express and please try to get it fixed into final shape and back to me as soon as you can. Send to 229 Perkins Street, Jamaica Plain, Mass.

If you get here later in this month you'll be here in time for proofs and such like.

We can draw up the contract when you get here. It's always a hell of a job.

The last batch you sent—I don't know just what to call them—have some swell things in them and also some quite weak spots. I can think they can be fixed readily. Did you mean them to go in the book as well as in the anthology? It makes little difference. Maybe good to get something very strong in the anthology as it feeds toward the book.

I thought we would print about 750. Do you think that's enough? Have you any idea what Random sold of the first one before they remaindered? We have done about 600 so far with the Collected Williams. The Schwartz is in the 500's but of course he is the critic's darling.

I have the look of the book pretty well in mind. Quite large. Nine inches tall, and seven wide instead of six because of your long lines. A fairly white paper. A strong face of type in 12 point size, maybe Granjon or Janson or something like that. For the headings I wanted to use one of those new scripts, but that wouldn't look well for those very long titles. So we'll try a 14 pt italic for those, I think. Do you prefer left flush or center? I thought of a dark blue winco natural finish with a box-flat back. The jacket will be cooked up in August when the catalogue is made. I know that stuff you have sent the drawing of and don't like it. It's stagey. I would rather work with conservative faces & get my punch by generous whites. OK?

Ok

To Kenneth Patchen from James Laughlin (NDA)

July 7, 1939

Dear Kenneth:

Thank you for your various messages and sendings. I'm sorry to have been so long silent, but things have been very busy here.

As to the poems you have added to your book: you know my feelings on that subject. I think you are a plumb damn fool to make such a long book. But it's your book and I shan't interfere. But let me give you the best advice, I can: put more intellectual fibre and framework under your words. Your words are beautiful, gorgeous, but I'm afraid you'll find people saying it's just verbiage and doesn't mean anything. I don't think this is so, but I beg you to curb your output, concentrate your good lines and phrases and not let any poem go out until you can tell in basic English exactly what it means. Basta.

I am sending back the note to the argument. Will you fill it out a little. You know what I mean. Give a little spiel about how the CITY is your big life work, or something, and what it is driving at, and what you think about it. You know, make something people can get their teeth into and begin to feel ownership in. Let me see what you write and I'll forward to printer.

I hope you'll have a section of the Argument for ND39. That's part of my general plan of development. Need it soon, too.

About the story*: it's a real piece of writing, but it needs to have the nuts and bolts tightened. I suggest that you do some more work on it. The cinematic fade-ins and fade-outs are good. More a matter of proportion at fault. Shouldn't there be a bit more development of the details of the original incident—the funeral and the kid's feelings. Also, cut down on the conversation with the Swanson bird. That spoils from too much. It's one of the best themes in the story—a good theme in general—but there's too much of it. You can indicate that whole thing much more forcefully in half the space. I would like very much to have the story in ND if you can bring it up to its potential. There again, need it soon.

Now another thing: I have got to have somebody here this Fall to replace Higgins and I want to offer you the job first, if you want it. It's a lousy job—but it's a job. It pays 100 a month and a month consists of 25 days of eight hours each. You would have to live in

Norfolk and not go batting all around whenever you felt like it, except during the five or six day vacation at the end of each month. You'd have to find some place to live in the village and count on the mile walk up to the office in the morning and back at night.
Please let me know what you think about the idea. There are six other applicants, but I want to take care of my own first, so to speak. The work is shipping, book-keeping, letters, addressing, filing, etc. Lousy work, but a job. So let me know.
The acknowledgement page ought to be sent in now.
I can't let you have the BLACK BOOK till we've printed out of it, I mean, till they've set up the part we're going to use.
What have I forgotten to mention? Oh well, get it in the next one.

Regards to all,

* *Patchen's "Bury Them in God"*

To Amos Wilder from Kenneth Patchen

July 12, 1939
Concord Mass.

Dear Wilder:

Work here (hoeing potatoes, beans, peas, etc.) has prevented me from making the short trip to Boston—though I want to see you very much. My book should be under the presses within a fortnight, available to show friends late this month or early next. I shall try to bring it to you—much of it you won't like: I was inclined to write anger. I have written an autobiography which is my own only superficially. It is pre-war poetry. It's religion against God. Is it possible you can drive out here? I am eager to have Miriam meet you.
Have you been able to work on your revision?
Edward Dahlberg, whose novel, *Bottom Dogs*, you may know, is working on a book which deals with the currents of American letters: it pleases me to learn that he is going to include discussion of my work.

Ever yours,
Kenneth

Note:** Referring to Wilder's upcoming book,* ***Spiritual Aspects of the New Poetry.

Kenneth Patchen's artist's statement for *First Will & Testament.* 1939. (KPA)

FIRST WILL & TESTAMENT
Kenneth Patchen

Kenneth Patchen's rise to a foremost position among poets writing in English has been spectacular and exciting. No poet since Hart Crane has aroused such violent partisanship. It is to be doubted that any young writer has a more loyal following in the colleges than Patchen. His savagery and power have become almost legendary; but it is in his native command of language that his real mastery and importance are most apparent. One critic has said that he writes "like an angel who has mastered the speech of the devil."

FIRST WILL & TESTAMENT's reception by the reviewers was a veritable landslide of approval: it was by far the best reviewed book of poetry released in many a year. Louis Untermeyer, in an article on American poetry in *The Virginia Quarterly Review,* said of it: "FIRST WILL & TESTAMENT is like no book that has been published in these states...Not since the first appearance of Robinson Jeffers has there been so fierce a rush of words—words in action—as the furious welter in Patchen's second book...it is bitter and tender, sadistic and sentimental, unbearably noisy and incredibly delicate."

A few copies of the first printing remain. We are considering the publication of a dollar reprint edition, perhaps for next Fall when Patchen's next book of poems will be ready.

$2.50

To Henry Moe/ John Simon Guggenheim Memorial Foundation from Kenneth Patchen (GUG)

November 6, 1939

Dear Mr Moe:

I had hoped to take advantage of your invitation to drop in on you when I came East; however, this has not been possible.

I was doing farm work in Massachusetts until about three months ago, at which time I was offered a job with New Directions; I have been working here since then — bookkeeping, wrapping and shipping orders, and making myself useful in the odd tasks that arise in a publishing house. At this moment, with the fall season getting into swing, I am often busy until the wee hours of the morning.

Miriam and I are hopeful of capitalizing on this present experience to the extent of getting a small position with a New York publisher. My new writing requires research beyond the facilities of the local library. All this by way of acquainting you with our doings of the moment. I am beginning to realize new potentialities in my long work, THE HUNTED CITY. I am forced to add to my plan almost daily. It seems to have a life of its own.

It is possible that we shall be in New York sometime this winter. May I call on you.

My wife wishes to be remembered to you.

Sincerely yours,
Kenneth Patchen
Kenneth Patchen.

Mr. Henry Allen Moe
in care of
The Guggenheim Foundation
551 Fifth Avenue
New York, N.Y.

To Kenneth Patchen from James Laughlin (NDA)

End of 1939

Kenneth, what in Christ's sweet name is going on. You're breaking me down. I've just received another complaint from a store that no books have arrived. WHAT IS THE MATTER? It gives me nightmares. If this goes on my business will be ruined. People will not put up with such service. This complaint comes from Milwaukee—the Bksp of Harry Schwartz—that order went in two weeks ago and they have gotten no books. Now WHAT IS THE TROUBLE? I can't dope it out. Are you eating the orders? Are you using them to paper the walls of your private megalomaniacal world? Or what?
If you sent out that order, and the ones for Doubleday and Goldman in St Louis, (check back in your records to see) then get after Fields and have him put a tracer on them right away.
Or do I have to come home and unscramble things? Are there dozens of orders that you have overlooked that I haven't heard about?
You just can't do this to me. It isn't right. You say you believe in good writing and then you stick a knife in it by not sending out the books. Jesus, it ties me in knots.
Maybe your system is balled up. You remember what I told you to do. Put all stock orders (orders for more than one title) in a file and every time a new book arrives in the shop go through them and send the new book out to every place that ordered. Now that ought to be easy as falling off a log.
The only thing I can think of is that you may have been waiting for some of the other books.
If that's the case, all is lost. Just put a match under the stable and burn the whole place up. If those Miller books and the NDs and FWTs haven't been in the stores these past weeks—when the ads broke and the reviews started to appear—then I can just kiss goodbye to my investment and fold up and quit.

Well, let me know the worst.

****

***Note:** The underlining was done later by Patchen*

To James Laughlin from Kenneth Patchen (NDA)
[Note: This was typed on the back of Laughlin's previous letter]

Norfolk, Connecticut

I can say a few Christs and Hells, too. What do you think I've been squealing like a stuck pig for? Because I've nothing to do but get a fat ass from sitting? If your books are weeks late in coming out and hundreds of orders pile up, can I make that up? We've been working until two and three every morning, hours on our own time because we feel you're entitled to a break on this. Mr & Mrs Carlisle tell us to go off for trips, to forget the work, that no one has a right to keep anyone working like we are. Trips! The only trips we take are to buy stamps (on our time) and to beg for newspapers and boxes from the townsmen. Do you know how many mailings are in the book? Far more than the orders you've sent in: TEN OVER A THOUSAND SINCE YOU'VE LEFT. Do you think that is done to tease you, to slow up your business? Do you know how much your "sales time sugar" and gifts to personal friends takes? Do you know that we have to eat and sleep sometimes? As for the orders you're worried about, I've got everything cleared up so that I'm doing day-to-day orders now, but that took time. It was only about a week ago that I finally managed to get that far. Do you know that there are at least a thousand more mailings to go out before the first of the year? Do you know that your book showed only four thousand mailings in four years up to now? Do you know how much time it took to get the Miller store and individual letters out? How much time it took on the catalogues? Time to answer questions that are imperative to handle? How much help have I gotten from you: waiting weeks for answers for the gummed paper address, to the EXAGMINATION [sic] disposal? etc. A skeleton staff of five people would be rushed here, even if the books were on time. Think about it a little bit before you say such unintelligent things as you've been saying. I've tried my best, Miriam has. She worked two weeks with a sprained ankle. I've been working with my back strapped up. Where's the balance in this?

Note: *Handwritten note*:
Don't you think you're old enough not to indulge in cheap, below-the-belt, personal cracks as the underlined on the other side—even if you have the money to pay for someone to take them?

To James Laughlin from Kenneth Patchen (NDA)

Thanksgiving, November 23, 1939

Laughlin:

I can't hold up anymore. The months before you left were hard, harder than you can know. Those since have been positive hell. It's not me to quit something I start; I don't feel that I am giving up. IT'S SIMPLY IMPOSSIBLE TO GO ON. You know what I put into this job: I came here cold, no experience at all for the work required of me, little aptitude for it...I got by on sheer grit and effort. But the old thing is coming up again. My back has been giving warnings for the last couple weeks, but I have fought it off, hoping that somehow I could lick it this time. I can't. It's like a nightmare. Every day finds it tightening up a little more. Where will you be if I'm flat on my back and helpless and nothing done to take care of things? Where will I be if this happens to me up here? It's time I said something and I'm saying it. I'll do whatever is in my power to do. But I can't hold this thing up. It's a monster with a new head every day. You've got to see that somebody comes up to take over. I'll stay on to break them in; I'll do everything possible. But I refuse any longer to knock myself into a bed for months. I've got to stop it if it can humanly be done. I've given everything up here, haven't written a line...have just bent to. This morning the Carlisles came down and found Miriam too worn out to stir. The bookkeeping and invoicing has kept me chained to this table; Miriam has had to do all the packing, lugging of books out to be wrapped etc. I don't like that. I don't think it's a place for me to be in. I've held all the jobs before now; I never thought that when she did work she'd be doing the work of two or three men, making up big orders with makeshift cardboard boxes...I went in town at 8 this morning to bum boxes at the stores. I'm slow on the ledger, that I know. I also know that we are handling a much bigger volume on this year's list together with orders for most of the titles for last year. Maybe it could be done by a handful of experienced people. But it's beyond me now. With the back-business hanging over me it would be the devil anywhere, doing anything; it's madness to try to buck it under these conditions. I came up because I needed a job; I need it even more now. We can't go back to Concord. It's got to be New York in midwinter. We haven't been able to save enough to take away the fear of going away from this house and this job. We've had pressing debts; living conditions (food mainly) have been unbelievably high. It's not that we go to anything better. God knows what it will be...particularly if I find myself laid up for 8 or 9 weeks. All that. But this, no. I'm leaving as soon as things are fixed in such a way that my leave taking can never by any stretch of the imagination be considered a walking out. That's about the size of it. That's the way I don't know what to say about not leaving here before January something. You've been damn swell about the whole thing and I'm going to buckle in and have a go at putting this job to bed in style. Figured out a new system of ledgering which cuts down on the time, but I'm just plain slow with figures and the rest of it. My mind just stops somewhere this side of these things. Further, my book is tugging away inside me and that more than any other thing balls me up. I've got such a good start with you as my publisher that I want my next book to put me over for keeps. And I can do it if I have time at it. The Fall deadline bothers me. This job is far from being preparation for the intense sort of writing that will be my new book. I'll have to inch my way into the image of myself needed for the kind of thing I want to do. Then, as with every one, bread & butter getting will throw me around a lot. (Uncle Dicky is a bit mixed up about my job prospects. I tell them almost anything so they won't fuss. For some reason they've taken a fancy to us..mainly to Miriam, I think. Wait until they see my book...Anyway, as I told you originally, I have nothing lined-up whatever; only the notion of dogging around until something opened up. I wouldn't leave this job for a better one, I mean I wouldn't let the consideration of a better job influence me in leaving here. It is as I told you: I'm in a sweat that the back business will set in again. But to hell with it. If it happens: Miriam can take care of anything; she can see that anyone I bring in to work knows what to do and how to do it. Leave it at that. I'll keep it off if I can and if it happens the job will be safe anyway. We don't want to bring people in if we can help it. If the Miller gets tough and out of hand we'll take whatever steps are necessary to handle it. Otherwise we'll manage the show ourselves. Maybe in the Spring you can suggest someone I can see about a job in New York.) Will you stop over here before going South? The Carlisles have invited us to have Thanksgiving with them tonight. Breit is going to help out for a few days next week. He can't do bookkeeping but he can do odds and ends and there are a lot of little things which he can do. I've told him that the pay is 50¢ an hour.

To Henry Moe /The John Simon Guggenheim Memorial Foundation from Kenneth Patchen (GUG)

November 27, 1939
Norfolk, Conn.

Dear Mr. Moe:

This is my application for renewal of the Guggenheim Fellowship. The project which I have set for myself is outlined briefly in the following:
It is my intention to write a long poem based on The Children's Crusade which occurred in the early 13th century. Perhaps the most poignant and horrible event in all recorded history, this continent-wide march of little children toward Jerusalem and possession of the Holy Sepulchre, is, in my estimation, a theme natural to the fullest exploration of the human spirit. That parallels of meaning can be drawn between that time and our own—what terrible hungers beset mankind now!—does not lessen the task's attractiveness, neither does it decrease my obligation; instead, and I say this humbly, here is a challenge adequate to all the resources of language and the powers of Art. Before the poem can be begun, it will be necessary to spend several months in intensive research: I wish to familiarize myself with every aspect of that period; it shall be my earnest endeavor to live then during the course of this work. Further, I have a number of problems of conception: what shall be the real character of the homeless minstrel in whose person The Christ is first born to the little boy whose consummate faith leads these thousands of children into slavery and ignominious death? Shall he encompass the being of The Savior? or shall he symbolize man's ignorance before the very presences of his own nature? What construction shall be placed on the child leader's death in the tent of the unbeliever? A little child shall lead them. Why has the legend of The Pied Piper (whose original is the minstrel) so captured the imaginations of men? Is there something secret and hidden in the figure of the little shepherd boy, whose vision in the field at night precipitates one of the greatest mass movements in human story? Why should Christ search for His Own corporal remains? By what miracle, what design, did it happen that an ignorant peasant boy in one of the darkest centuries should see the Golden Fleece and The

Great White Whale? These are, of course, only a few of the questions which confront anyone who would deal with this theme. Their answers constitute a large part of our heritage. Each age furnishes its own contribution. Every man brings his own proof and contradiction.

HORRIBLE GHOST, HOLY GHOST, the title I have taken for this poem, is the first part of a projected seven-book work, THE HUNTED CITY. If a renewal is granted me, I shall be able to carry out to the letter my plan of work for this long poem.

Sincerely yours,
Kenneth Patchen

Under separate cover I am sending a copy of my new book, FIRST WILL & TESTAMENT.

To Kenneth Patchen from Dylan Thomas (KPA)

(12th week of the war to
end war to
save my democramatic Aunty Titty.)

November 27, 1939

Dear Kenneth Patchen: I'd have written before, long before, I've been meaning to write, everyday I sit down, etcetera, but my troubles as one of those who is always with us and as one who tries in a temper always to live up to a standard of comfort and pleasure I have never been used to—in my poorest and most ragged days it's my only wealth to remember, with self-deception and envy, those rich days past which never were—have spoiled my natural politeness (another imagined quality of the unborn, never-forgotten past) and pinned me down, like a frog with ideas above his suction, on to a tableful of halfmade stories, semi white pages waiting for wheedle—"Dear—, I'm hoping that this may move you (though nothing will, I know, but the last dynamite trumpet) to help me, in my present desperate, with a small (big, big, damn your breath) which I will instantly, as soon as my ship (if it came home with a deck of poundnotes and a golden captain, I'd blow it up to the sky rather than let you put your Hongkong foot or Hottentot apron on the gangway")—old poems, flies-by-night, hack-to–come. With neither faith nor hope, and despising the charity I seek, I'm working quickly and mostly badly on a book of stories so that I may work slowly on poems, and, at the same time, whining, with my tongue in their cheeks, to a few old fashioned humbugs for enough money to live better than they do. I'm not angry because the large public does not support me; I give the large public very little, probably nothing, and there is every reason against them supporting me. As a public entertainer who entertains very few, I cannot grumble—or, rather, I can grumble but only for the pleasure of grumbling—and must either change my entertainment, take up some other occupation or be angrily content (which I am) with my present one. And I don't want you to imagine me—thank God none of us knows how extremely little the other one ever thinks of him at all, let alone imagines him as this or that—as a whiner against people with money; I whine, among other noises, for their money, which is quite different. The Welsh have money under their skins and that's all you see of it, their dried and stunted bodies rustle when they squat, their bad teeth chink when they bite on a pinched turnip, they piss a stream of coins which they at once suck down again. (This last cheapness is what I think the boiled string and lobster on my colonel school might say about the Welsh, or about anybody else, at length and with suet pictures. I remember somewhere in Miller's Tropic of Cancer, a man pissing gold coins at a wall, but I've plenty of cracks to grind with Miller.) They're mean. This morning I asked a Welsh farmer to lend me half a crown for a lying purpose and my expectations were realized: I got nothing and a long lie back. He said he had no money, he was very poor. He has two large farms, no wife, no good habits to waste anything on, lorries, a motorcar, and thousands of crinklers in God's hands (in the Bank.) His name, oddly or not oddly, was Henry James. I offered him a good lie for half a crown—not 'a good lay' as our American cousins put it, as they express themselves 'over the pond', and mind the inverted commas, Mrs. Ratface—and a good Welshman, that heavenly devil, should stump up readily. I could have told him the truth and he'd believed I was lying; we respect each other so much for our capacity for lying that we would never insult each other by imagining we were telling the truth. But the roguery, the wild eye (nearly always ingrowing), the sly and vicious tribalism, the imaginative deceits, the revivalist rhythms, the conscience—wallow, the occasional inverted miserdom ('having a good spend'), the comic religious hysterical churning together of false thoughts and genuine emotions (the Welsh equivalent of Irish blarney) are very lovable. You have to put up with them all, and smile, too, smile, if you still want to weep over the Celtic onion. That because Henry James refused me halfacrown to waste carefully. Money again. I'm smoking a halfpenny, writing with twopence on a sixpence, sitting on three and six—the chair was bought at a sale; the Welsh like sales almost as much as funerals; in either case you're getting something cheap, and in one case, brassbound, you're getting a lot for nothing, even if you get nothing after all, which is a matter of opinion, and that, in my opinion, is precisely what the hereafter is. In Welsh sales, by the way, I've seen farmers buy dirty and warped junk at twice or three times its doubtful value; a Welshman will buy a bargain at any price. When I lived in London a few years ago, in the bedsitting-room with the scribbled card on the door, cultivating a number of voices and obtaining at considerable cost the clap and the itch, first at the bottleparty and last to go, paying for the rent and the kippers on the gasfire with a pound a week from my parents, determined to get there, not knowing where 'there' was but having a very good idea, covering with crabs and cracks and wild dirt, with eccentricities I had long possessed but had never, until that moment, been frightened enough to expose and expand, my confusion at the shockingly liberated behaviour of other young men and women two stages further, from the provinces into another conventional life, than myself, enviously scorning the well-poised manner of the intelligent well-to-do, racing against time as though time were another young writer with a suburban home address, but always, in myself, naturally and fortunately thick-skinned and stubborn, I decided never to forget the importance of money and to devote all my spare time to gathering it from other than literary sources, and never to live below the imagined standard I had set myself, and always to live within those luxuries I enjoyably deceive myself into thinking I was born to enjoy. Although I have never forgotten the importance, the rest of my monetary decisions have come to little. Sometimes, indeed, I think I am living far above the standard I imagine myself to have been born to deserve; but that soon grows into an unworthy thought, and the wind again, blowing from penniless places, is thick with rich cigar smoke. Now I live only three times above my salary, & still badly, above, that is, what I earn through writing—an occasional drop of milk from life & letters To-Day, 10 shillings a poem from the New Curse, love and some stamps from the red monthlies—what I am fobbed off with by (as Charles Morgan would say) friendly conscience-smoothers, what I cajole, extract. I cannot, as Balzac wrote on the bare walls of his attic, write Rosewood Panels on the crumbling walls of this tall, then, nibbled & neglected, mousefull, sea-staring house, nor turn my water into wine, nor tear the invisible cigarbands off my Player's Weights. Angrily satisfied with the shape of things as they should not be, a man used to riches but born poor, I continue to think of money as it moves about beautifully beyond my reach, money that burns and multiplies and smells of hot food.

Interval for thinking of food and drink. Today it is indecently cold & I have no fire in this rotting room. Where are my London plans now? Gone up in smoke that should be going up the chimney. Now, through some dull work, I'm trying to move towards a respectable financial safety which I must immediately make perilous. I must be moving all the time, even if it's down. But that's more than enough of this. I've got some very thoughtful things to say about money, if I could only think of them.

I had a letter from you, dated Christ knows when, somebody tore off the top of the letter and I am the only one here who touches my papers—failing very very successfully to get enough money to live on (how am I living then? Anyone's hand to my mouth) is my excuse for never having answered it, and so the embroidered money-talk—in which you said that it might be interesting for us to exchange perhaps fifty letters about work and living and then publish them. Yes, I think it would be interesting; at any rate, I'd like to read them. Let's go on writing to each other for a bit and see what happens. When I read letters I nearly always whizz through the explanatory parts and the arguments and am really excited to know what the person writing has been doing with himself & with others lately, where he's been to, who he's met, what he feels like the moment he's writing, and, if I don't know him personally, what sort of person he actually is, what sort of face has he got, who he loves and doesn't, is his Sex Life a mystery, has he got any money and if so does he want to share it, where he comes from, what sort of parents did he have, what does he do most evenings, does he know anything about the private lives of film stars, even what he had for breakfast so that I can compare. So if I was reading, in a book, this letter I'm just writing, I'd say to the devil with all the twisted sentences and why doesn't he talk about the things that happened. Or an emotional gush is very nice too. It's like wanting paragraphs and conversations and a lot of moving about in stories, rather than studied settings, atmosphere, and morals expressed without people. I don't know what a reader of a letter like this could get out of it. But let's see what happens, write as we like, about anything or anybody, and if after some time we get letters together and find someone to sell them to the public—then let's hope he sells them well and we can buy another yacht. In that letter of yours you said too that if you get a renewal of your Guggenheim fellowship you'll be able to send me something for bread and potatoes, beer & cigarettes, bus-rides & cinemas, all the essentials, and thank you, thank you, and if I catch a rich widow or write a book in a trance and the Book Societies recommend it then I'll send you something that matters—I've never felt more worldly than today; I want to go on with a poem some time, but it will be all stocks and shares, even if it looks just zoological about bears & bulls; Anna Wickham, a large, frenzied poetess I used to know sold her little poems, & some of them were fine, as she wrote them, for a shilling each to a young relic called John Gawsworth, and once she rebelled and wrote a long, indignant poem about love entitled "Advance to 1/3d."—and you send me some cigarettes in a letter and I'll send you some cockles. But what I need right now is a lump of money to pay my fare and the fares of my family to Corfu where we want to live for a while with the Durrells and, if he remains there, Miller. I've got to get out of England before I'm called upon to join the army and see the next world or—and that's much more likely—before I object to fighting & having to fight and am sent either to jail or to a working camp (concentration camp, but run on British lines) with a lot of other jesusing, vegetarian, socialist, mother-stuck nancies and fanatics. I want to get out of the war: to America best of all but nobody, possibly quite rightly, will help me to. A man I wrote to recently about objections to fighting answered that, though he was, by nature & conviction, a coward and a pacifist, as I am, he would probably join up & fight—bayonetting included—because he believed that a writer should undergo contemporary experience to the uttermost. This seemed to me hysterical and pernicious misreasoning. To undergo contemporary experience to the uttermost, he would have to be bayonetted, he would have to starve to death, and as a dead man what use could he possibly be, either as a man or writer. He's a young man, and what's the good of dying for your writing before you've begun? And to call me an escapist is no insult. As far as a country at war goes, I'm hermetic. I want, among other things, to go on working, and I know I can work only in peace; I can't do a Brooke in a trench; mud shells shit and glory will make me swear & vomit, not write. So I want to be where there still is peace, peace at least from the propagating of hate, the enforcements of military discipline, the extraordinarily rapid growth of dictatorship all around me, and the immediate prospect of a noble death ha ha or ignoble detention ho ho as an antisocial shirker and—worse still—unrepentant individualist. At a recent London tribunal for conscientious objectors, the presiding Judge refused to register one man as an objector because he refused to fight "only on moral & ethical grounds." The only two men they totally exempted were: one "mentally retarded", and one who is already working in an aeroplane factory. Tribunals, in South Wales anyway, still ask: "What would you do if you saw a German...rape...kill...mother...sister?" If you come across, or can think of, any would-be patron who'd like to aid a poet's flight from war to work, mention (without success) my name. Wouldn't American Societies like me to come over, at their expense, and read poems to them in my passionate voice? I can't think why they should.

Now I know what you look like. I don't mean I know what you resemble: you look like a young man with a big nose and an open shirt, suspicious, broad, and rather angry, to me. I'm thanking you for the photograph. The only likenesses of me that I can find are tucked away, scowling, in groups. So, until someone appears with a camera, I'll just send on a photograph that was printed in some newspaper; I've lost the original, though not of myself: I wake up with that, with delight and repugnance, every morning or afternoon.

I'd like you to have this silly letter before Christmas; though again I don't know why. So I'll send it off now—without a word about your grand, exciting book which I liked more than any new book of poems for years. I want to write a lot to you about it, but it'll keep. Thank you for the copy. More, lots more, again.

Yours,
Dylan Thomas.

Note: *Four months later, Dylan Thomas wrote to James Laughlin*: March 5, 1940

"...Did Patchen ever get the long over-literary letter I sent him? I'd like to hear from him again. Is he still with you? I shall be

conscripted in about a month now, and am worried. I won't fight, and I don't want to object. Wish I was well out of it."
(From *The Collected Letters of Dylan Thomas*, edited by Paul Ferris, MacMillan Publishing Co, 1985.)

Sample of handwritten letter from Dylan Thomas to Kenneth Patchen (KPA)

7

patron who'd like to aid a poet's flight from war to work, mention (without success) my name. Wouldn't American Societies like me to come over, at their expense, and read poems to them in my passionate voice? I can't think why they should.
Now I know what you look like. I don't mean I know what you resemble: you look like a young man with a big nose and an open shirt, suspicious, broad, and rather angry, to me. I'm thanking you for the photograph. The only likenesses of me that I can find are tucked away, scowling, in groups. So, until someone appears with a camera, I'll just send on a photograph that was printed in some newspaper; I've lost the original, though not of myself: I wake up with that, with delight and repugnance, every morning or afternoon.

I'd like you to have this silly letter before Christmas; though again I don't know why. So I'll send it off now — without a word about your grand, exciting book which I liked more than any new book of poems for years. I want to write a lot to you about it, but it'll keep. Thank you for the copy.
More, lots more, again.

Yours,
Dylan Thomas.

Chapter Six: *Albion Moonlight* (1940-1941)

To Amos N. Wilder from Kenneth Patchen

January 14, 1940
From Norfolk, Conn. at New Directions

Dear Wilder:

Your letter gave me much pleasure. I believe that with the things you have to say about me in your book, my parents may finally realize that I am a writer of some tiny moment even I make no money at it. They are getting quite old, and I have not been a very attentive son; my mother will approve of you and be convinced that "nice people" are concerned with what I do. Is there any chance at this late stage of my seeing the chapter in which my poems figure? I should think not. What other person or matters do you treat of in that particular section? You are free to quote from *My First Will and Testament* if that would be of benefit to you...
Miriam and I hope to be released from this grind shortly. I've been working an average of ten hours a day since early July; Miriam and I conducting all of the business for more than three months—book keeping, shipping, etc...all of it...and New Directions is not small now.

To James Laughlin from Kenneth Patchen (NDA)

Sunday evening
Early 1940
c/o Benton
88 Horatio Street
NYC

Dear Laughlin:

The red order-number book was on the table with the white—possibly moved to little book cases beside my table.
Look in the pulpit (telephone stand) for blue invoice sheets.
Learn from D. Norman that you are planning a jaunt to Sun Valley this week (please send us our pay before you go.) Miriam found a place for us yesterday—quiet, roomy, clean, unheated—at 35 dollars a month; absolutely the best we can do in the way of living quarters!
You were right about staying away from colds and not getting them: we both got tough ones as soon as we hit the city. My back is still a danger, but I disregard it altogether.
Puzzled about the failure of the P.O. to send on direct the note from Enoch Pratt Library; all other mail came through straight.
You have become a legend in your lifetime in NY—great curiosity about your doings. I tell people that you are a very tall, lonely young fellow. I'm not as tall but I'll give you odds I'm as lonely. Been asked to read my poems at Cooper's Union for $25.00. Rosenfeld told me that P. Blair Rice came through town with the story that J.C Ransome [sic] is now lecturing about me to his classes at Kenyon. Give them time, and a broad heart.
Has my book sold any since we left? Thanks for telling us about The Living Age. Any others? Any reviews from colleges papers?
Are you going to lift stakes for Cambridge as planned?
Miriam says not to get hurt skiing.

Sincerely yours,
Kenneth

To Amos Wilder from Kenneth Patchen

1940
c/o Benton
88 Horatio St.
New York City

Dear Wilder:

Congratulations on the birth of your son. You must be very proud and happy.
We have found a place at last: a large sun-filled, fairly cheap 3-room apartment—81 Bleecker St. Miriam combed this section in the most complete way, and it was purely by chance that she happened to go through that part of Bleecker (near Broadway) which is largely filled

with warehouses. We shall receive mail there after Saturday. It is very quiet on that street and I hope to get a great deal of work under way. In what strange manner do things take their course. Just a few nights ago I visited Paul Rosenfeld, and he had this story to tell: he was commissioned by *Poetry* last October to write a review of my First Will and Testament; this he did (calling his review "The Divine Fire") —stating that my work was the finest he had seen in many years— developing the idea of the poet-within-the-poet whose hand is seen in all great art, etc., etc. He was extremely excited by the book. The review was sent in. In December he received proofs. What he had written was changed beyond recognition, sections deleted, paragraphs shifted about—in short it was now a hopeless botch. Puzzled, angry, hurt, he telephoned Chicago, getting [one of the staff] who said— "We think it bad for a young writer to be acclaimed without reservations." Rosenfeld hung up in disgust, withdrawing the review—to learn later that the review had been entrusted to another (a person who is calcu-lated to find little if anything in my poetry). A very curious business. I was very sorry that this had happened to Rosenfeld, a man whose unspoiled devotion to my letters has few equals in this country...
And now comes this fine news from you! [i.e. about the piece on Patchen in *Poetry*]. I am delighted that Dillon put his foot down on the "negative" review, and delighted that your article on my work is to appear.

To Amy Bonner from Kenneth Patchen (PAP)

April 10, 1940
81 Bleecker Street
New York City

Dear Amy Bonner:

Thank you for your very nice note to my wife and me. I am sorry not to have seen you before now. Won't you drop in on us any time that is convenient—we are home at all hours—look forward to seeing you.

Sincerely yours,
Kenneth Patchen

***Note:** Bonner was the East Coast representative for **Poetry** magazine.*

To Amy Bonner from Kenneth Patchen (PAP)

May 20, 1940
81 Bleecker Street
New York City

Dear Amy Bonner:

Won't you drop in here one evening soon for coffee? I haven't been getting around much recently—not exactly well.

Please let me know of an evening that will be convenient.

Sincerely yours,
Kenneth Patchen

To Amos Wilder from Kenneth Patchen

June 9, 1940
Bleecker Street, New York City

Dear Amos Wilder:

I have not the right to again inflict my problems on you, but...well, my new book is at stake (this is a horrible summer to be trying to write)—I have poured every energy into it and now I find myself with no way of paying the rent. I get fifteen dollars in royalties from Laughlin on the 1st of July—leaves me to raise at least $25 on rent, light, gas, etc. (I don't even think now of food.) Do you know of any way by which I can get this $25 within the next few days? If you don't, please don't think twice about it.

My book is called *The Journal of Albion Moonlight*, and it is about the world of this plague-summer...

I plan to get a job again in the Fall—determined (if possible) to use these months for writing. There may be little time left for creative work of any kind. All my good wishes.

Sincerely yours,
Kenneth

To Dorothy Norman (publisher of *Twice a Year*) from Henry Miller (UCLA)

July 5th, 1940

Last night I saw Kenneth Patchen and he confessed that it hurt him to ask you for aid, but that he was really desperate, and I believe him sincerely. I like him more and more every time I see him. I have great faith in his ability and believe without question that he will soon prove to be one of America's greatest writers, possibly the greatest writer. He is a real poet and a genuine person. He should be helped no matter how much it hurts. He is America in person, the best it has to offer—that's my honest feeling about him. I had the great pleasure and privilege last night of reading his coming book to be published this fall by Laughlin—title I am not sure of, though I think it is to be "Albion Moonlight". I am contributing a letter to the character, Albion Moonlight, which will be inserted into the body of the work. I know this book is of great value, one of the finest imaginative, one of the most sincere and honest books, ever written by an American. I am enchanted with it. It is unique and may make literary history. He has no copies of it, unfortunately, as he is writing it in long-hand, in a big dummy of an aborted deluxe edition of "Two Years Before the Mast". He doesn't know whether he will be able to get it typed, because of the money. This is no sly appeal to your sympathies—just honest fact. I feel very deeply about Kenneth Patchen's plight, but I also realize that he has sufficient genius to solve his personal as well as his artistic problems. But I repeat that I feel strongly for him—because I see myself in him, see my own miserable plight here twenty years ago. If there is a war and he is killed that will be the worst thing that can possibly happen to America. We can lose 100,000,000 people, but we can't afford to lose an individual like Patchen. If I have any financial success here, which is highly dubious, I am going to stake him to the limit. I believe in everything he says and does, even if that should entail our mutual destruction—yours and mine. There isn't another soul in America whom I would say that about. (I would have said it for Stieglitz and Marin, but they are beyond all that now—they are free and fully realized and they will be immortal.)

Henry Miller

To Henry Miller from Kenneth Patchen (UCLA)

July 25, 1940
81 Bleecker Street
New York City

Dear Henry Miller:

I can thank you for the wonderful spirit of your statement to Dorothy Norman: I do. And your tree has put forth fruit—she sent me 100 dollars. There are gods.

No, I am nowhere near the finish of THE JOURNAL OF ALBION MOONLIGHT—give myself until Sept. 1st.

Laughlin has seen nothing of it; hasn't come into town, and no recent word from him. I am anxious, too, to get his reaction to my journal. I quoted you (a bit from your Norman piece) in a letter to him.

Eager to see your letter to Albion Moonlight. Character: Jetter, the careless murderer; Billy Delian, in whose useless heart treachery and betrayal lie (Judas); Thomas Honey, the physical man, who has no endeavor worthy of his strength; Jackeen, the visible body of man's hunger on earth; Chrystle, the pure child who is in all of us; and Moonlight, whom you know—

I don't yet know how I shall end it: may have Moonlight tortured to death by the people of the journal; maybe not.

The heat ruined your photographs: Carson very unhappy about it.

Have had no word from Slocum.

I'd like to use a brief statement from you on the outside cover-face of the book—a few words in big letters.

I think of you often.

Always,
Kenneth

To James Laughlin from Kenneth Patchen (NDA)

August 9, 1940
81 Bleecker Street
New York City

Dear Laughlin:

Perhaps the best way to do this would be for me to take up in order the various questions you raise in your letter:

"I'm sorry if I hurt your feelings by my lack of enthusiasm for your book. After all, the best I can do for you is to give you my best judgment..." etc.

If you will bother to read what I said (not putting words in my mouth), you will find that what I objected to was not your lack of enthusiasm but your total unwillingness to spend any time whatever in a discussion of my work—what you think of it is your affair and could not in any way give me cause for hurt feelings. Surely you must know that I count my own opinion of the book at a rather high figure. I am not now in need of moral support, God knows.

"...This year we are going to understate in the catalogue, as many readers felt that we made too great claims last year."

Again your business. You asked me to assist you in this matter: obviously you know what you want better than I do. I was not aware that any claims advanced by you for FW&T could be considered extravagant: those claims concern me, the others do not.

"...I want a concise statement of the plan and meaning of your book."

I refer you back to what I said above concerning your failure to discuss this in person. If I knew more of what baffles you in the part you have read, I'd be in a better position to furnish clarification; as is, I may be shooting in the dark altogether. The book is a journal. This is important to remember. It is not a novel.

The plan: I attempt to write the spiritual account of this summer. I do so on several levels...I had, then, a number of very definite problems: I could have written it as a day-to-day statement of beliefs, relying on the name of Kenneth Patchen to give it the necessary dimensions; this was the obvious thing to do: I decided not to do this for two reasons—1) statements however wonderful have a way of boring the book-reading public, 2) there was the inescapable alternative of writing in the stated voice of K.P., and this I did not care to do because I wished absolute freedom of movement. I met these difficulties in the following way—what I spoke of as several levels of approach: realizing that I must give corporeal presence to the journal's narrator, I decided to surround him with semi-fictional characters, who would act in the capacity of lending definition and interest to the things which Albion Moonlight chose to record. Should these characters conform to the accustomed time-and-space machinery of the novel? No. I had no intention of writing either a murder-mystery or a love story, and even less to write a novel of ideas—it was my task to keep inviolate my intention of writing a journal of this summer—a summer when all the codes and ethics which men have lived by for centuries were subjected to the acid test of general war and universal disillusionment: I had to recreate that chaos—whether I have done so will define my success or failure.

Further, I have been aware very acutely of the necessity for a complete use of the narrative method when it served my purpose; when, in other words, it did not distract from the real action of the book—which action is the action of this summer: uncharted horror and suffering and complete loss of heart by most human beings. I have used the narrative method in this manner: it has been my weapon against the false and sterile reality of the story books—I have satirized the creaking framework of the whodidit and whatsto-happennext fairy tale; I have, I think, kept the reader on his toes—I have made him a participant—I have removed the obvious landmarks and encouraged him to accept the book for what it is...

"...I'm sure that we can turn good profit for you. We will give you all the right kind of promotion, you turn out a manuscript in which we can have confidence. But at the moment, I can't see my way to advancing you anything further on it, because, frankly, I'm not at all satisfied with its structure."

Read my letter again. I said I wanted a build-up because I was going to turn my hand to prose—to novels. I am not thinking of great sales with the Journal—it will sell well, or not: I don't know. At any rate, you won't lose any money on it. When you say that you can't advance more on it because you are not satisfied with its structure, you can only mean one thing: you are not sure that you will publish it at all; for otherwise, you would be anxious to assist me to make my book better, by giving me more in advance. Perhaps, as before, you were not thinking. I did not ask you for more advance. You know that.

I asked you if you could help me, if you knew anyone who could. And you answer:

"About raising money—I don't know, offhand, of anyone who is making any handouts."

'Handouts!' You better just sit down and work your head a bit before you say such richboy horseshit to me.

"What about Miller? He is getting an advance of $750 from Doubleday Doran. Perhaps he can help you some."

You know what I think of that. Miller is getting an advance to write his book, not mine. I'm not a jackal, nor is he a lion: we're both in the same leaky boat of trying to be artists in a country where even the most enlightened publishers are more interested in not giving one bad moment to the 'average, intelligent reader' than they are in opening up new veins in human consciousness.

I'll make out as best I can, as I have been doing. I do my job.

"...I don't want to see you put out a book that will hurt your reputation...You must think, not just emote. Think your book through. Give it a plan, a form. Make it communicate a hard and definite core of meaning..."

I made my reputation and I'll look after it very well.

"Think your book through..." My book has been thought through, lengthwise, sidewise and edgewise: that's exactly what bothers you in it—there isn't a lot of chewed-over sophomorisms which parade as 'ideas'—I am thinking out of my own head every minute. That's the value.

"A hard and definite core of meaning..." Now what? What is the hard and definite core of meaning in the New Testament? in Shakespeare's Hamlet or King Lear? in The Brothers Karamazov? I dislike such hazy, meaningless phrases. What did Kafka mean by 'the Castle'? what was 'The Castle'? what was the significance of 'Moby Dick'? is it Death? is it God? (What is god? what is life? what is Death? what is Birth?) Give me a line-by-line analysis of Tom of Bedlam's Song, of Wm Blake's Songs of Innocence, of anything by John Donne, Villon, Baudelaire, Nijinksy—they've done alright without your 'average intelligent reader.'

Well, anyway, I must get back to work. It will take me a little while to get back into the mood of my book. I have to have my wits about me—and everything else I've got.

I believe that what I have said to you is accurate and honest.

Sincerely yours,

To Kenneth Patchen from James Laughlin (NDA)

September 21, 1940

Dear Kenneth:

I have given a good deal of thought to your request for a further advance on THE JOURNAL and I'm sorry to have to tell you that I don't feel it is justified.

It is true that I have given larger advances to other writers but, in their cases, I felt that it was good business to do so. That isn't true of your case. I wish you as well as anyone does and nothing would please me more than to see you write a good book, but I must tell you that what I read of the JOURNAL seemed to me a hopeless mess and I can't see how it can possibly sell at all in its present state.

I think too that you must adjust your thinking to the idea of a job. Other people in your situation work at a job and write well in their spare time. Look at Williams. You can do it too if you want to try.

I'm sorry not to go along with you but as I see it you've got to get a job sometime and you might just as well do it now.

Good luck:

To Kenneth Patchen from Henry Miller (UCLA)
c/o General Delivery, Charleston, S.C.

81 Bleecker Street, New York City

Dear Patchen,

Just got back here Saturday, an hour after the post office had closed, and so only received your letter about Wilson this morning. Have just written him air mail and hope it will bring results. Am no good for a letter now as my stomach is on the bum—have had a steady pain in the guts for four days as a result of the bad food in these parts—was wandering about the environs of Charleston over the holidays, which explains also why I didn't answer your previous letter. As to collaborating with you—frankly, I don't know. I don't know if I'll have the energy required. I find it difficult to do any writing whatsoever. But you might try—make a beginning and I'll tell you whether it's possible or not.

All that about Laughlin is according to Hoyle. I don't think he'll come to the bat even if Wilson does sponsor the book, which is dubious. Every unusual book takes several years to get launched and another five or ten years to get properly reviewed and then, just when you're about ready to kick off, it finally finds favor with the public, i.e., with a rare few. I believe in making every effort, but it is well also to realize the nature of the situation. If the opposite were true, if you found favor immediately, met with no resistance, I think you would begin to have doubts about your own worth.

I notice that you used the word "command" in one of your letters. "We must command," you said. My dear fellow, if we were in a position to command we would not be in the position we are. That's merely a wish. I don't think you will ever be able to command, but you can lead—and then only indirectly. Beggars—and that's what we are—can't order people about, however right they may feel themselves to be. When you have stiff opposition it's no use butting your head against the wall; it's better to be flexible and fluid, to seep in wherever there's a leak. Sometimes you can play the lion, but sometimes it's necessary to be wily as a serpent or gentle as a dove. The choice of tactics doesn't imply loss of integrity. Did you ever, for instance, seriously and honestly play with the idea that you were, for a brief interval, God Almighty—and try to imagine what you would do with world if you were? It's worth trying, I assure you. Give yourself supreme powers; try to make the world over, in detail, according to your conception of justice. I wager that if you think about it profoundly—and it's not easy to do!—you will end by first desiring to alter your own way of life. Myself I have come to the conclusion that what the other fellow does is no concern of mine; the only way I can influence him, I think now, is by my own behavior, my own example. I think you're entering a new phase of your life; your metaphysical self is only just being born. Henceforth you will go two ways at once, and the artist in you will be the mediator and, if you live wisely, the saviour. Your real creative powers are only just beginning to burgeon. There will be a hell of a lot of confusion yet and most of it you will work out in creating. But in the creating you come face to face with the real person, the unalterable Kenneth Patchen, and that becomes more and more terrifying as you proceed. I hope I shall always be to you all the things you expect me to be, but whether I am or not doesn't matter—it's what you are to yourself, only that counts. Maybe you will not agree with me now, but later I think you will find it true, that part of the difficulties you now find yourself in are of your own making. These which are created by others, by the world, so to speak, are believe me, the lesser ones. All difficulties serve a purpose, usually hidden at the time. This can sound smug and complacent if said with indifference, but you know I am not indifferent. Finally I'd say something like this—if those whom you have a right to expect help from fail you it does not mean that you have been ditched or betrayed. Your judgment may be faulty. Help usually comes from unexpected sources. Help comes mostly from within, from one's own resources. Everything of any value was accomplished by individuals, was <u>a creation</u>, in short, and that only because of faith. The power to command lies only in the personality. Frankly, if you had the power I doubt that you would want to use it. When I read about the great Tibetan sages, who have gone into this question of power more profoundly than any other people, I realize that we talk about it like children.

Well, shit, you'll be thinking I'm trying to sermonize you. I'd better stop. I've written Wilson and I hope to Christ he responds. I'll go every step of the way with you, but you know that even with the best heart in the world I can't be Jesus Christ. If to-day I know more about my real powers than I did before I also must admit that I know more than ever about my limitations. Real evil, it seems to me, is only in the confusion of the planes or hierarchies or levels or functions. Does this make any sense to you?

Laughlin, by the way, is a truly evil person, for the very reason I give. With him it is all confusion. I have just glanced at the Kafka book on America. It should never have been published—it is a very bad book and should have been destroyed. Laughlin thinks only of the name, of exploiting it for his own good. And the real work, the thing of moment and of value, your own book, he ignores or rejects. Well, it means this—you've got to look beyond Laughlin. You ask—<u>to whom</u>? I can't give you the answer: that is <u>your</u> problem. Each new thing creates a new situation. If we could simply follow the rules it would be easy—but for men of genius there are no rules to follow. If you will accept this as an axiom and not as a deplorable plight you will discover in your own self the energy and resources with which to navigate in the uncharted seas.

My best to you and Miriam. Will be in Savannah from Wednesday or Thursday till Saturday, I expect.

[signed]
Henry Miller

Note:** Laughlin had commissioned critic Edmunc Wilson to read Patchen's manuscript for **The Journal of Albion Moonlight

Henry Miller
c/o General Delivery
Charleston, S. C.

CHARLESTON S.C. JAN 6 2 PM 1941

Mr. Kenneth Patchen
81 Bleecker Street
NewYork City, N. Y.

Air Mail

To Kenneth Patchen from James Laughlin (NDA)

January 21, 1941

Dear Kenneth,

I have the bad news for you that Wilson thinks badly of your book and so I feel more sure than ever that I shouldn't publish it as it stands.

But really, I see this as good news—in the long pull—because I think it would have damaged your reputation terribly.

In substance he says about what I did—that you are terribly talented, that parts of the book are very entertaining, but that it doesn't add up to a whole and that it is much, much too long. He says, for example, that he can't conceive of anyone but Miller reading more than 50 pages.

I will show you his letter sometime if you would like to see it. He is very fair to you and I hope you will not hold this against him. He says you are very talented and have a great facility.

Now Kenneth, I hope you will not be too dejected by this blow. Naturally you will suffer with it, but if you can use it as a step forward all will be well. I mean that. Everybody knows that there are many reversals to be met with in the best careers.

I still think that it would be worth your while to fix this book up—pulling it together and shortening it to about 80 pages.

But if you think you can't, then I suppose you can't. In that case I have no objection to your showing it to other publishers, but please don't make any deal with anyone affecting my other options without consulting me. As I said before, all I want is to see you get ahead, and will of course not stand in your way if you can sign up favorably with someone else. However, I do hope you won't publish that book as it now stands.

Don't be angry with me—I really wish you well—and keep in touch with me. Let me know what you decide and what you plan. There is a place for you in the poetry pamphlets in 1942 if you want it. Also I would be glad to have parts of Albion for ND41.

Best luck, J

To Christopher Morley from Kenneth Patchen

January 26, 1941
81 Bleecker Street
New York City

Dear Christopher Morley:

May I begin this by quoting from several statements which Henry Miller has made about my work, and in particular about my new book (not yet published) The Journal of Albion Moonlight:

"...for not only has nothing like it been written since the inception of our literature but in all English literature it stands unique. The fact is that it is different, and not only different but pure and poignant and mad in the true poetic sense of the word. A book such as this could not have been written in any other time but the present; it reflects the chaos, the horror, the insanity, the bewilderment, the anguish and the indifference of our time in a way which is almost unbearable to read. I say honestly and without fear of contradiction that I know of no other American writer capable of giving us such a naked, truthful, fearless and harrowing account of the psychological condition now prevalent in the world.

I welcome the opportunity to raise my voice in behalf of an American writer whose work I so greatly admire and esteem, hoping that in time it will be taken up by the great amplifiers to which alone the public's ear is attuned."

Henry Miller

Now, what I have to say, Mr. Morley:

I read in the paper that there had been a performance of your play for the purpose of raising money to assist needy young poets—God knows I am such a one at this moment, no money for rent, food, electric lights, etc.: my position is desperate at this hour; I have devoted every energy to my book and now I simply don't know where to turn for funds to carry me until I can get my ball rolling again. Well, that's about the size of it—I send this on to you with a little prayer, etc.

Sincerely yours,
Kenneth Patchen

Letter to Robert Duncan from Kenneth Patchen (KPA)

March 12, 1941
81 Bleecker St
NYC

Dear Robert:
Thanks for the two little rays of light.
We won't be able to get over tomorrow:
sorry: good of you to ask us.
Now (and I hate to do this) — I must
have my typewriter tomorrow; no
other course but to pawn it — must
get the money on it tomorrow* — I'll
try to get it out again within a week
or so and you can have it again. Please
drop by here with it sometime before 3
in the afternoon — say about 2 o'clock.
Don't fail me on this.
See you when you come.

* That is, Thursday — day you get this note.

Sincerely yours,
Kenneth

Note:** It was Robert Duncan and Virginia Admiral who helped type* ***The Journal of Albion Moonlight *from Kenneth's handwriting.*

Kenneth Patchen's press release of artist's statement for *The Journal of Albion Moonlight* (KPA)

THE JOURNAL OF ALBION MOONLIGHT
Kenneth Patchen

Henry Miller: "This book is of great value, one of the finest imaginative, one of the most sincere and honest books, ever written by an American. It is unique and should make literary history. I haven't read anything in years that stirred me so. I believe without question that Patchen will soon prove to be one of America's greatest prose writers, possibly the greatest."

So Kenneth Patchen, famous and brilliant young poet, moves into another field of creative activity—takes his name with the surety of great talent into yet another high place. *The Journal of Albion Moonlight* is perhaps the strangest book ever to be published in America. It is, in outward body at least, a record of the summer of 1940, what the author calls 'the summer of the plague.' But its purity of spirit, its amazing intensity, are without parallel in our literature: it is as though the conscience of the world spoke in these pages. Moving though a place of nightmare in an almost sepulchral calm, Albion Moonlight and his little band of scallywags and saints make sport of the rules and conventions of a society which has never so much as admitted their existence. Defying all the regulations of the too thoroughly exploited novel, Patchen yet manages to convey a sense of reality that is wellnigh breathtaking—a reality that suggests cold dynamite lying on a beautiful lawn where children play at croquet with iron mallets.

Not since the prophetic books of William Blake has a poet written a document of such strange and terrible power as Kenneth Patchen's *The Journal of Albion Moonlight.*

$2.50

To Wallace Stevens from Kenneth Patchen (HUN)

April 18, 1941
81 Bleecker Street
New York City

Dear Wallace Stevens:

This is the story in a word: as you know, we are having my book printed by subscription. Everything has been advancing smoothly (34 copies of the ten dollar edition sold at this date: no effort to sell the five dollar copies has yet been possible); but now certain aspects of our original plan must be altered. We had counted on getting James Laughlin's list for a mailing; also the Gotham Book Mart's: Laughlin is somewhere in the far West on his way to Mexico; Gotham's list, I discover, can under no circumstances be given out. Which means that our plan to sell the five dollar edition by direct mail is not possible. Then we have this course: to sell the books through Gotham Book Mart and Argus Book Store (Chicago) on a dollar commission per sale basis, using a formal mailing piece (printed at our expense) to sell the 200 copies. This can be done. <u>But</u>. We cannot expect that people ordering the book through a store will pay its purchase price until the book is delivered into their hands. By selling through letter direct (as we are doing on the ten dollar edition), it would have been possible to pay the printer out of returns as his work progressed. And the printer, of course, is a businessman; his break-down on the job is as follows: 100 dollars when the typescript is delivered to him; 300 when the galley proofs are ready; 300 when the book goes to press; 300 when it is dispatched to the binder; the balance (120 dollars) to be paid within thirty days. You will understand that the whole thought behind our scheme was to get the book to pay for itself as it came into being; we are, at this moment, church-mouse poor—we planned to use early returns of money on ten dollar sales to pay the costs involved in a mailing of some 2500 pieces. We cannot pay the printer right through and still conduct a campaign through the stores; we cannot meet the printer's demands with money in the pockets of people who are awaiting delivery of the book. Therefore, there seems to us no other course open but that of having the venture underwritten on a time basis. I am absolutely confident of our ability to sell every copy within a short time of the book's release date: 500 at ten dollars, 200 at five—1500 dollars (less commission to stores)—our realizable capital.

Now this is the proposition: an advance of one thousand dollars (payable to Peter Beilenson, Mount Vernon, N.Y., the printer): 500 to be returned by the end of May into a bank account taken in the loaner's name: balance to be repaid into account as money comes in through book stores, and our own direct efforts—all money returned by September 1st: 1500 dollars in books as security: all legally drawn-up and sworn to.

That's about it, I guess. I shall be happy to furnish you with any information which may have been lacking here—or to talk the matter over with you in Hartford. It means an awful lot to us now.

At any rate, we both want very much to see you when you come into New York.

Sincerely yours,
Kenneth Patchen

To Amos Wilder from Kenneth Patchen

April 19, 1941
Bleecker Street
New York City

Dear Amos Wilder:

Thank you for your good letter and your support of my book. I have no time now (We are, as you can imagine, up to our ears in the work of getting *The Journal* out) to answer the questions you raise in regard to the book; I think that you will discover that when you have read all of *The Journal* certain of your objections will be weakened. At any rate, I am deeply appreciative of your concern with my work; it makes my task at once easier and harder to know that I have readers such as yourself...*Albion Moonlight* goes to press Monday. We are getting splendid support in our effort.

Sincerely yours,
Kenneth

***Note: The Journal of Albion Moonlight** was launched at the Gotham Book Mart in New York; Francess Steloff the store's owner had bought out the trade edition of the book which sold for $5..*

To Wallace Stevens from Kenneth Patchen (HUN)

April 23, 1941
81 Bleecker Street
New York City

Dear Wallace Stevens:

I have delayed answering your letter until such time as I had something very definite to tell you: tomorrow I am seeing the printer and the talk then should prove fruitful. I am going forward with caution and industry. You may expect to hear from me on Friday—with most things smoothed out.

Sincerely yours,
Kenneth Patchen

To Wallace Stevens from Kenneth Patchen (HUN)

June 2, 1941
81 Bleecker Street
New York City

Dear Wallace Stevens:

I have waited until I had something to say: it is this: my book has been underwritten to the sum of one thousand dollars. On the press now—I'm receiving galley proofs—off the binder's machines end of this month. I near broke my neck dashing around about it, but it's done and over. And I can get back full steam to my writing. (Find a poem I wrote yesterday on other side—getting ready a book of poetry for Fall publication.)

You said that you would like to help—I can use the fifty dollars you mention for cost of printing mailing piece, postage, etc. It will be returned to you by the 1st of August—when book has been out a month.

Thank you for your patience in this matter. I hope you will like my poems of this summer.

Sincerely yours,
Kenneth Patchen

Note: *Included were two poems: "As We Are So Wonderfully Done With Each Other" and "Where My Stag-Antlered Love Moves" published in* ***The Dark Kingdom,*** *1942.*

As We Are So Wonderfully Done with Each Other

As we are so wonderfully done with each other
We can walk into our separate sleep
On floors of music where the milkwhite cloak of childhood lies.

O my lady, my fairest dear, my sweetest, loveliest one
Your lips have splashed my dull house with the speech of flowers.
My hands are hallowed where they touched over your
soft curving.

It is good to be weary from that brilliant work
It is being God to feel your breathing under me

A waterglass on the bureau fills with morning...
Don't let anyone in to wake us.

To E. E. Cummings from Kenneth Patchen (HAR)

June 4, 1941
81 Bleecker Street
New York City

Dear Cummings:

Just read your Speech From A Play in Furioso and want to tell you it's very exciting stuff to me. Guess you're my choice for the best poet now using English. All power and love to you.

Sincerely yours,
Kenneth Patchen

Jesus what lovely things you do

To Louis Untermeyer from Kenneth Patchen (IND)

August 3, 1941
81 Bleecker Street
New York City

Dear Louis Untermeyer:

Thank you for your card about THE JOURNAL OF ALBION MOONLIGHT.

The book is selling extremely well: Gotham Book Mart alone sold 60 copies in ten days. We are more than happy with the private response. Review copies have just been sent out.

You will find under this cover a batch of my recent poems. I believe that the length in all cases does not exceed the limit set by you; in some poems I have substituted a short title for a long one, the better to keep within your requirements. I shall look forward with great eagerness to your decision as to the usability of certain of these poems in MODERN AMERICAN POETRY.

All my good wishes.

Sincerely yours,
Kenneth Patchen

To Louis Untermeyer from Kenneth Patchen (IND)

August 13, 1941
81 Bleecker Street
New York City

Dear Louis Untermeyer:

In event that you use <u>Like A Mourningless Child</u>, please change the last line: 'I am so close to good. I have no <u>wish</u> to see God' to read: 'I am so close to good. I have no <u>need</u> to see God'. I am very anxious to know whether you are going to use any of the long-title poems from FIRST WILL AND TESTAMENT: in a way I hope to make long titles my signature, and of course it would please me mightily to have this innovation on permanent record in MODERN AMERICAN POETRY. The poems I am writing now are mainly too long for your present use—hence I didn't burden you with them now—, but I should like to show them to you before they appear in a book; may I send them on sometime in the early winter?

The enclosed poem I send you with a little prayer that it isn't too late for you to consider for printing in your anthology: I feel that it is one of my best.

My warmest good wishes—

Sincerely yours,
Kenneth Patchen

To Wallace Stevens from Kenneth Patchen (HUN)

December 22, 1941
265 Avenue A
NYC

Dear Wallace Stevens:

I write now at the close of the year with the morbid news that I cannot make good my debt to you at this time. The accounting includes the information that I am helpless in bed with a semi-paralysis of the lower back—I can look forward to about six more weeks of it (had it twice before). We are, of course, broke as buds.

Just finished a new book of poems, which will be released next month. Perhaps you will find it something to make a rain-check compensation for your extreme good kindness to me. Accept my assurance that I shall honor my obligation the moment I can; and my good wishes.

Sincerely yours,
Kenneth Patchen

Chapter Seven: One Who Knows (1942-1943)

Postcard to E. E. Cummings from Kenneth Patchen (HAR)

January 13, 1942
265 Ave. 'A'
NYC

Dear Cummings:

Understand that you have been down with your back: me too—for about 2 ½ months. Nasty stuff, isn't it? this is my 3th siege. Accept sympathy from "one who knows." Our best to both of you.

Sincerely yours,
Kenneth Patchen

Note: *The abbreviation for 3rd is exactly as Patchen wrote it.*

To E. E. Cummings from Kenneth Patchen (HAR)

January 28, 1942

Cummings—

You know, I am convinced more and more that this is exactly the best possible world. I love wine with all my heart: your gift went there.

Kenneth Patchen

Letter to Wallace Stevens from Kenneth Patchen (HUN)

April 2, 1942
265 Ave A
NYC

Dear Wallace Stevens:

I find I must ask you for one final favor: my wife and I have been offered use of a houseboat off Long Island for the summer — provided we can pay for certain needed repairs, gas, electric, etc., as well as assurance that we will have the wherewithal for food. It's damn important to me that it work out. If humanly possible I must get some things straightened out here this weekend, with a trip to Philadelphia likely—it would mean more than I can say if you should see fit to extend me fifty dollars (or less) by return mail, and I'll get it back to you if it kills me. I need not tell you that I am sorry to bother you in this way again, but an awful lot is at stake. I've spent half the winter in bed with a bad back and I figure the summer on the water in the sun will be good for me and my poems. So this note.

All my good wishes to you.

Sincerely
Kenneth Patchen

To Sherry Mangan from Kenneth Patchen

May 13, 1942
265 Avenue A
New York City

Dear Sherry Mangan:

Well here I'm in a hell of a spot: we were to have moved out to the houseboat Sunday, and I come down helpless in bed with a haywire back, doctor, drugs, etc.—and now up a tree all around. So I write asking you for a loan of ten or fifteen dollars (more if I can), payable to you within two weeks. Hope to heaven you can and right off.

Sincerely yours,
Kenneth Patchen

About other things another time.

To Wallace Stevens from Kenneth Patchen (HUN)

November 5, 1942
317 West 4th Street
New York City

Dear Wallace Stevens:

I am aware that it is unlikely that you will like to get this note and even more unlikely that I shall benefit in any way by incurring your displeasure; but I am a poet trying to get some work done and I don't know where my next day will find its payment. I am within three weeks of finishing a two hundred page book of poems which Harpers will publish in February and I have about eleven cents in the house and no idea whatever about adding to this sum. I've run up a store bill across the street and the worry is beginning to sap my head for poems. Now I know I should not be writing you again for assistance but by God I've got to. Any money I can get goes into poems and I feel that with fifty dollars I can write about fifty poems.

All my good wishes to you and I'm sure you must have an idea of me which I don't want you to have. But I must write my poems.

Sincerely yours,
Kenneth Patchen

Note: *The tone and construction of this letter gives rise to the conjecture that it might have been a form letter, similar ones perhaps having been sent to several people.*

To Henry Moe/ The John Simon Guggenheim Memorial Foundation from Kenneth Patchen (GUG)

November 29, 1942
317 West 4 Street
New York, NY

Dear Mr. Moe:

Accept this as my application for renewal of my Fellowship. It is my intention to devote myself to creative work in the field of poetry.

I have just finished a volume of poems, THE CLOTH OF THE TEMPEST, which Harper will publish in February.

THE TEETH OF THE LION, poems, has just been published by New Directions.

Translations of my work into Spanish and French have been underway for some time.

Sincerely yours,
Kenneth Patchen

To Henry Moe from Kenneth Patchen (GUG)

January 23, 1943
317 West Fourth Street
New York City, NY

Dear Mr. Moe:

With full realization of the great demands made upon you at this season, and with every expression of gratitude in advance for your efforts in my behalf, my present situation gives me no choice but to hope that an early solution to my Harper difficulty can be effected. You see, everything is at an absolute standstill with me (as it has been for the past six weeks): the income from the sale of the Limited Edition, which income I had planned to use for the writing of my contracted-for novel, is not available, and it is a mild statement to say that our situation has been desperate. I have had no guide at all as to my next activity, and the spring publishing season advances at an alarming rate. You will understand that I write to you out of no other desire but to acquaint you with my predicament as an artist at this hour.

Sincerely yours,
Kenneth Patchen

To Henry Moe from Kenneth Patchen (GUG)

March 10, 1943
317 West 4 Street
New York City

Dear Mr. Moe:

George Leighton has told me today that you are sending on to him the letters regarding my situation at Harper's which were exchanged by Mr. Saxton and yourself. With the full realization that the tremendous demands upon your time have made it impossible for you to continue activity in my behalf at this time (in this particular matter), I believe I should express to you now the deep sense of gratitude which your interest in me and my problem has caused me to feel; and also to say that I am confident in the belief that your moral presence in whatever will now ensue between myself and publisher shall go far to clarify and to overcome this difficulty. I shall consider it a privilege to acquaint you with what I am sure will be a happy solution for them and for me.

On Friday of this week I plan to see Mr. Leighton, and from him learn the particulars of your view of the matter as expressed in the letters you are sending him.

Sincerely yours,
Kenneth Patchen

To *Poetry* magazine editors from Kenneth Patchen (PAP)

To EDITORS, POETRY magazine

May 26, 1943
317 West 4 Street
New York City

POETRY
Editors:

Enclosed find six poems for your considered use.

Sincerely yours,
Kenneth Patchen

P.S.

I may say that I do not understand the very bad way in which my poem was printed by you: naturally I thought that the two poems would be printed together (not the one unheaded, crowded in, etc.). It does not seem too much for me to have thought that the poems could have been grouped in a decent manner.

K.P.

To E.E. Cummings from Kenneth Patchen (HAR)

317 West 4 St
New York City

Dear Cummings:
I will bother you to read this but nothing further if you don't know of anything right off. I've been counting on getting 125 dollars in this week, but I learned yesterday that I won't get it. This catches me bang. got 55 dollars store bill, 40 rent etc., and the book to finish and I don't know what next. Do you know of any really good person to whom I could appeal for money on the basis of my poems to do? I have mss. to sell but never got anywhere with that and I'd rather just cold ask for the money to do work. I don't know of anyone. I'll phone you at 5 tomorrow (Thursday) and if you have any leads for me I can hear them then and if not not and I'll say hello. I know you will understand that I've got to try every bet I can think of.

All good wishes

Sincerely yours,
Kenneth Patchen

Excerpted from *A Letter To God* by Kenneth Patchen

August 1943

God, we shall accept the terms of your world.
That we may not kill.
That we may not hate.
That the things of labor belong to all men.
That the things of spirit live in all men.
That the things of God are on earth for the use of all men.

None shall kill when all are completed.
None shall hate when all are at love.

To James Laughlin from Kenneth Patchen (NDA)

May 29, 1943
317 West 4 Street
New York City

Dear Laughlin:

Thank you for your letter to Miriam. You are right about some things, wrong about others. In the first place, my thinking, if any one color, is religious; in the second, my illness is of a kind puzzling to the doctors for reasons that they can't understand how I have managed to get about at all for so long—power of will alone. And my will is intact, untouched by the steady, unrelenting pain in my spine. I only mind not being able to walk. God knows it is not good to look helpless.
Cloth of the Tempest is on the press now—seen initial set-up proofs—release date: early fall. Getting down to the writing of the novel next week. Funny to be writing something I wouldn't ordinarily bother to read. Burning to write poems, my head full of them; but—later.
We have been offered a little house in the mountains—rent-free—Mt. Pleasant, New York. Go up as soon as I'm able to stir (this is a big problem now that gas-rationing has stopped private cars), and we get enough of that happy paper
[contents missing]
which were to have appeared in Ivan Goel's new magazine; I withdrew them after I got fed-up with the way he handled things. He reduced them too much in size, didn't tell me of some contributors until last minute, etc.
This is the reason I'm sending them to you: want you to see what they're like to maybe interest you in a POV booklet of similar experiments, some 'type-drawings' (which I make from already-printed things-magazines, ads, foundry catalogues, etc.), and some writing-and-drawing-poems—think it would make a very exciting, and saleable item. All done from line-cuts. I'd 'make' everything—title pg., everything. A hand-made job from beginning to end. I think that I'm opening up to something new; I can get wonderful strange effects that were impossible ever before. The cost of cuts above regular composition work I'd split with you out of royalties. Does the idea interest you? If so, when could you bring it out? I can get it ready for you anytime. Let me know. And please return enclosed proofs.

I hope that you are well and reasonable happy. And wife. And son.

Sincerely,
Kenneth

I'm working with the printed book itself as the key to a new medium in poetry. Creating for and with the page as the reader sees it. Beautiful freedom in.

To James Laughlin from Kenneth Patchen (NDA)

1943

Dear Laughlin: Congratulations on the addition to your family!
This week and last busy getting settled into a new place—a tiny house. Consider ourselves very fortunate to find anything livable in NY now—and this is really fine. One room upstairs, one down; and little garden in front. Back cottage, off the street, restful, should be good for work—have a lot lined up.

Memoirs of a Shy Pornographer is within days of being ready for final touches—will send it on to you.
Beginning to get letters from people in England who are excited by my poetry. Very encouraging.
About Moonlight: why not bring it out as a New Classics at 1.50? Miss Steloff will take 500, as I told you. Bookstore on 4th St., another 100. We could take a couple hundred to sell to people we know. If it should happen that you want to do The Shy Pornographer, a splendid job of exploitation could be worked out for all my books with you—Miss Steloff was talking about a folder which could be mailed out to her list, and you could work in on that.
One thing, Laughlin, and I'm sure you'll understand, I'm not able any more to cope very well with complicated troubles; and I'd rather forget the whole matter of reprinting Moonlight etc., if we can't work out something soon. It upsets me too much, and then it's really no good.
Heavy fall of some snow today. We've got a nice little fireplace. So far, only a mattress to sleep on—couple chairs as furniture. Miriam's [Missing rest of letter]

***Note:** Frances Steloff was owner of Gotham Book Mart in New York City.*

To Wallace Stevens from Kenneth Patchen (HUN)

November 16, 1943
331 West 22nd St
New York City (11)

Dear Wallace Stevens:

In an effort to spur sales on Cloth of the Tempest, I am planning a folder which Gotham Book Mart will sent out.

Actually, I have a double purpose in this: the first 'reviews' of the volume lift the hair on my scalp—I had known that there was hatred here for anything which did not conform to what was expected; but to have my experiments in drawing-and-type treated as some sort of slightly goofy joke ———! Like every other serious poet I ask only to be judged on the merit (or lack of it) to be found in my work; and I'll fight every effort to label me buffoon. I wonder if you have the feeling to give me a statement on my book which I can use in the folder.

Sincerely yours,
Kenneth Patchen

We had a good summer—beautiful mountains—and I wrote a novel. Working on another now. I wish to God I could be writing poetry. But trying to make money.

Note: *the misuse of the word 'sent' in the first sentence of this letter follows Patchen exactly.*

Chapter Eight: On the Side of the Angels (1944-1945)

To James Laughlin from Kenneth Patchen (NDA)

April 26, 1944
336 West 12 St
New York City (14)

Dear Laughlin:

You will probably never realize what I went through before I sent you that wire—I didn't want to. That's the sort of world we're in; but—what the hell—Thanks from the bottom of my heart. I knew that you would send it, and—somehow—that meant more to me than getting it. I won't bother you with a lot of details; but these are the high-spots in the present situation—Miriam's father left a very confused proposition for the three of us involved. (I believe that you know that Miriam was an only child.) There's the little farm—which you saw. It's not all paid for—mortgaged to boot. Miriam's mother, whom I like very much is an old woman—a woman who has worked too hard, suffered too much. So—I think that now Miriam and I will sort of have to step in, assume responsibility: God knows I never seem to make any money with my writing—guess I'll have to hit for it now; for, you see, it isn't just that we have this new thing to face, but it set me along the road of what it might be to get old and have nothing, and be nothing to anyone in the way that counts—I mean, to have some money when something comes up for those you love. Practically, we'll probably have to go to Concord to live and look out for things. Just as we were so wonderfully happy with our new home here—Miriam painted it—and what a job! without a ladder, proper brush—the rest of it. Worked like mad—happily.
These things come up.

Sincerely yours,
Kenneth

Miriam is there now, of course—don't know what will happen. I couldn't manage trip now.

Postcard to E. E. Cummings from Kenneth Patchen (HAR)

May 15, 1944
R.F.D., Concord, Mass.

The death of Miriam's father brought us here. We hope to show you our new house in NY before you go away for the summer. Back around 1st of month. Will phone.

Our best—Kenneth Patchen

To Jasper Wood from Kenneth Patchen (NOR)

September 12, 1944
336 West 12th St
New York City (14)

Dear Mr. Wood,

Your letter has just reached me at Mt. Pleasant. Thanks for the things you say about my work, and for your invitation to contribute to the new magazine.

Re Journal of Albion Moonlight: New Directions, 67 W. 44 St., NYC., is thinking of bringing out an edition for around three dollars—provided they get a goodly number of advance orders; so it would be a good service to the book if you would suggest to any interested people there that they send in their order now.

I may say that I was astonished to hear that something interesting was planned out of Cleveland; my "home town", Warren, is too near—and I remember what a bog-hole that part of the country used to be. Frankly, it was my impression that everyone had just curled up and died out in your Great State. I don't believe there's a decent book store in Cleveland—is there? Maybe it's not as bad as I think—it's probably worse. Not that anywhere else in the U.S. is much better. How big a magazine do you plan? Printed? What's the 12:30? Are you a group of college people? When exactly do you hope to get the first issue out? Do you have any backers? Any of you had any experience distributing a magazine?

You might write to Sanders Russell, c/o John Baxter, 425 Bonita St., Pasadena, Calif. He has an excellent paper on American and British poetry; and he's a good poet.

I think you'll come up against this pretty fast: there are only a handful of writers in this country whose work is even worth reading—I can think of four at the moment. So your main hope is to be lively—stir things up—deflate stuffed shirts—and pray for even one good new writer. Guard against provincialism. A magazine out on the coast, Circle, has the right spirit, but it prints too much tenth-rate junk by the editor's friends. That's all right for high schools. In my opinion, transion was a pretty decent job—until the last few issues.

Why not ask E. E. Cummings (4 Patchin Pl., NYC.) for poems?—tell him I suggested it. He's a good man.

Also Wallace Stevens (Hartford Accident and Indemnity Co., Hartford, Conn.). Fairly interesting poet. Which is saying a lot these days.

I'll type out some poems for you when I get back to the city this week-end.

Why not get some competent people to write 'informal' pieces on half a dozen writers you like. A nice cross-section of opinion might be had if you ask, say, 15 or 20 people around you to give a 50-100 word reaction to these writers. All of us know that there are no good critics in this country; I know that it would be of great interest to me to have just an honest view of my work by non-professionals. I'd like it if you started the series with me. (It's my hunch that you would be on the track of something alive.) Mix up your 15 or 20 people as much as possible—and get them to say only what they honestly think.

So—all the good fortune in the world! I hope your magazine knocks them dead.

Sincerely yours,
Kenneth Patchen

By the way, New Directions will bring out a new prose book of mine in January—Memoirs of a Shy Pornographer— 3 dollars.

***Note:** In the foregoing letter, the misspelling of the name of the magazine **transition** follows exactly that of Patchen.*

To Jasper Wood from Kenneth Patchen (NOR)

September 23, 1944
336 West 12 Street
New York 14, NY

Dear Jasper Wood,

Here are six poems for your magazine.

I have more, if you want more.

Would you like to see a couple of chapters from an unfinished prose book?

I hope that you will let me know how things go.

All the luck etc.

Sincerely yours,
Kenneth Patchen

By the way, I believe there is an Et Cetera already; a magazine of semantics.

To Jasper Wood from Kenneth Patchen (NOR)

October 2, 1944
336 W 12 St
NYC (14)

Dear Jasper Wood:

What a wonderful letter!

How is this for your magazine's name: OTSOTA (ON THE SIDE OF THE ANGELS)...?

Otsota has an archaic sound which I like: it's arresting, good to look at, short, and I think it covers what you stand for.

Maybe run it OTSOTA: On The Side Of The Angels.

Don't think twice about Wilson. He's afraid of his shadow and since he makes it I don't blame him: a thousand years old in the wrong direction, and bad manners (promiscuously like that) have no place anywhere. An old old woman, Wilson; a lot like the late pres. by that name.

For the others, well, let it go: they are Commercials, I think.

Reprint some Herman Melville instead. Or Blake.

The answer to how I make a living is that mostly I don't: my books never bring much in but chicken feed: I have arthritis of the spine and spend a big share of the time in bed; usually my wife has to be on hand to wait on me, so jobs are pretty well out for her too. On this score, know of any monied Cleveland people who might buy a ms. book? For instance, that of Cloth of the Tempest...100 dollars down, and as much more as they want to pay later. (I could sure use the 100.) I write the books in publishers' dummies...all in long hand, corrections, notes, etc.

I'll make a pleasant sum on the reissue of MOONLIGHT: but that's far off in January before it comes to payment.

What is your deadline on material for the first issue? I hope to get some more poems to you...and the prose piece.

Have you given much thought to format? What I like to see in a magazine is lots of punch in use of a good black type (Bodoni, say) on book-stock paper. transition was nice. No wood—or linoleum—or other nonsense cuts. Lots about contributors. Bold running-heads above poems and stories and articles. The whole thing neat and shipshape. Only three or four names of contributors on cover.

Do you plan ads? Query Gotham Book Mart, New Directions, all book stores in Cleveland, all such stores in Ohio and the Middle West, and maybe try to get 'exchange' ads with other Little Mags. Writing around if nothing else will make you known to people. And also try now to make arrangements to get your magazine handled by all the bksts that handle mags. Write to those listed in the 2nd issue of Circle, say; and Brentano's in the various cities. I think with a lot of work and pushing you can get it around.

After you get material set for first issue, print up an ad card...have a party in Cleveland (maybe now), admission price of a subscription. I wish I could tell you that I'd come to Cleveland to read in behalf of the magazine; but I can never tell whether I'll be able to get around or not. Do you think you could get any sort of crowd to hear me read poems? At 50¢ a head, perhaps. (I'd likely be broke (in November, say) and need trainfare back and forth out of it.) I have a steel harness and might swing it. Kill another bird by stopping to see my father and mother in Warren on the way.

If I can't come (or if you think it might not pan out anyway) I can let you have some ms. pages to auction off at your party...or a water color.

How old are you? Your wife?

We love jazz. Have a lot of good records which we can't play in our present place because the electric current is wrong for the machine.

Do you know Celine? Journey to the End of the Night and Death on the Installment Plan...wonderfully strong and bitter books. They are out of print: if you haven't them, we'll send on our copies, provided you guard them with your lives.

Like to know how you set up the symposium.

Sending you a copy of The Dark Kingdom. And couple photos which Publix might put up or whatever.

All our good wishes to both of you.

Sincerely yours,
Kenneth Patchen

By the way, I got a letter the other day from something The Ohioana Library (Columbus) telling me that Cloth of the Tempest has been chosed by their committee of judges (John Crowe Ransom, Ridgeley Torrance, Jean Starr Untermeyer) as the best book of poems published by an Ohion in '43, and I'm to receive a medal—made of clay, no less.

***Note:** The various misspellings and typographical errors which are in the original typed letter are retained.*

To Jasper Wood from Kenneth Patchen (NOR)

November 3, 1944
336 West 12 Street
New York City (14)

Dear Jasper Wood:

Two weeks ago my back took a turn to the bad. I am out of commission and, judging from past experience, shall remain so for some months. It's one of those things. My mother is not well and I could have stopped in Warren on the way back from Cleveland to see her...too bad, all around.

I don't remember anymore what things I touched on in my last letter to you; so I'd appreciate your answering that...the thread of the correspondence has slipped my hands, and I'd not care to repeat here what I said there.

All good wishes.
Sincerely yours,
Kenneth Patchen

To Jasper Wood from Kenneth Patchen (NOR)

November 30, 1944
336 West 12 St
New York City (14)

Dear Jasper Wood:

For the first time in weeks now I am able to turn to letters and work: I've had a pretty savage time of it...very ill and without money. By the way, are there any people in Cleveland who would buy a ms of mine...for almost any amount I'd sell. Actually I should be out in Arizona in the sun or such, but I realize that that is out of the question.

Now your letter of the 15th:

a) I suggest that you run the section of Moonlight which begins on pg 200 with the words To tell the truth and ends on pg 207 with the words if that would stop the war. (I have always refused to allow extracts of the book to be printed, but I feel that this piece will serve your purpose very well...and I don't want to let you down.) Please say that this is the first time that a magazine has printed anything from Moonlight, as the author's permission has been wanting heretofor.

b) Russell's review in Retort would be a mistake to reprint. I don't want it. Ask him for his general article on American and English poetry.

c) Today I've made a couple ink drawings for you. Use them as you can. The one which I have tagged 'x' on the back (the Christ head), you may find suitable as a cover for your magazine. I thought that three or four contributor's names might be printed in black on middle right side...OTSOTA being printed at top left. The face in red, as I have it. Please let me see the proof.

d) Are the 20 or 25 comments in...may I see what you have.

e) Why not get short reviews of each of my books in?

f) I suggest that on the last cover (that's back cover) a sort of ad page be drawn up of my books...and I'll supply you autobiographical matter for this.

g) I intend to send you some experiments and further poems...How much time do I have? I suggest that you use Bodoni 12 point type for your magazine...it's strong, clear and dignified.

I suggest that you use either a very good paper or ordinary 'novel' stock...which latter has the advantage of not having a shiny, slick surface.

And use a good, stiff paper for the cover, the magazine's name stamped on the back.

Please let me see what you have on the section on me... anxious now to get that set right off, as I may have another bad period when I won't be able to do anything about it.

Jamaica sounds pretty interesting.

I hope you'll answer this return mail and I'll pitch in to get my part of it done.

All my good wishes,
Sincerely yours,
Kenneth Patchen

To Jasper Wood from Kenneth Patchen (NOR)

December 24, 1944
336 West 12 Street
New York City (14)

Dear Jasper Wood:

What a wonderful thing to do! I can make the rent now...and get in some more work. I think that I don't have to tell you how deeply I appreciate your action. Thank both of you!

Your chapbook idea strikes me as splendid. First of all it has the advantage of being workable; a magazine at this time runs head-on into the fact that practically no one is doing anything of much interest or value, and the few who are somehow just never respond to a venture such as you proposed.

Several things have occurred to me since I received your letter this morning.

a) Make a true book of it; say, around 60-70 pages; price it at one dollar; use stiff covers; book paper (ordinary novel stock): give it a book title—ON THE SIDE OF THE ANGELS: KENNETH PATCHEN, published by The Otsota Press, Cleveland Ohio etc.: you can really hit the bookstores then and have a good chance of selling a lot of copies. And of making a permanent, important record... something even more interesting 25 years from now.

b) For I'd like to give my book the character of a record. I'll write a piece for it that will not only state my view regarding my work (and the work of others) but also take the reader into our house: I'll talk about my work habits, daily life etc: Miriam will write something of a nature calculated to give the whole picture; in other words, an honest picture of me at this time will be available...the sort of thing that was done now and then in Europe in the old days when artists had a place in the scheme of things.

c) I'll provide a section of new poems and experiments...a couple watercolors can be reproduced too. And for this section I'll write a little introduction. Actually it will make a little book inside the other.

d) And here, I think, is a good idea not only for the quality in interest of the book but also should provide fine publicity: ask people to contribute their opinions of my work...I enclose suggested copy for this—letters to papers and magazines and cards for use in bksts.

e) Also, I shall write to some people in England asking them to send me critical statements on my work. Doing that today. —— see h)

f) Print opinions of each of the books and short selections from them. I can supply chapters from MEMOIRS OF A SHY PORNOGRAPHER and the prose book I'm working on now—THE STORY OF A MAN.

g) Now this will take time to swing: so put the deadline for material assembling at, say, February 15th...giving time for statements from people and critical matter to get in and the things you'll get from your letters to the press and your cards in bksts. Meanwhile, of course, you can be drawing up the Sommer book and making plans for the others. That should put publication into May or June probably, unless you're lucky with your printer etc. And that is a good time to come out. And I'll then have time to ready new poems and marshal the personal data etc...and we can do an important job to start Otsota on its way. I'll bet even with a Feb 15 deadline we'll have to jump to get it setup.

h) Does all this seem right to you? I ask because it would be fatal of course to have the project advertised and then abandoned for any reason. You can understand that I want assurance that it will absolutely go through. Couple years ago some people sounded me out on a book which would concern itself with ALBION MOONLIGHT ...they got out advertising on it...I devoted a lot of time to it...and it just never came off. Making a bad smell all around. You and I don't need to draw up any documents signed in our lifeblood sort of thing, but I'd just like assurance that nothing in your situation there (like leaving the city for something else or whatever) will throw the thing out or delay it unduly. In line with this thought, I'll delay writing to England for contributions until I hear from you. Also, I'll hold back on giving NY bksts the cards until I hear from you. Let me know return mail. We'll have to move right along to hit that Feb 15 date...if all this is all right for you.

i) And I'll do a new cover...one more suited to the nature of this undertaking. (One thing I forgot to point out above: It will take time for the magazines to run anything on the lines of your open letter...and more time for people to respond to the invitation. Too: even if nobody of the lay-public answers, <u>it will have been good publicity</u>...and you can continue to line-up your Cleveland statements.)

j) It will cost money to do the thing but you may very well sell a couple-three thousand copies which will insure the rest of your books as well. Put it on a publishing house basis: send out review copies etc. And when it's ready put in little ads around: NATION, NEW REPUBLIC, SAT REV OF LIT, POETRY etc (cost maybe 15 dollars all told and in all the "little mags".) I think it's the sort of thing that will interest people...human interest.

(Come to think of it: you may get it ready by April.) Excuse jumpiness of this... many interruptions...leak in the gas stove and workmen in all day..

k) I'll devote my Sunday to getting my part of it ready. I have my prose book to work on...already lost so much time on it because of illness that every minute must be made to count now. Please thank John Phillips for inviting me in on the Jamaica thing ...we'll see what goes.

Cleveland is out for me...can't even get into the street here. Any chance of your getting into NY for a weekend? You can sleep on our floor...only one bed which I can't leave. It would be great to see you and have an opportunity at the same time of ironing out all the details of our book. But we can keep the mails busy.

Re your sending me 5 every other Wednesday...You know I would have refused the 25 if you had asked me about it...God I couldn't when the landlord was right there and it was right there too—gobblegobble...but people like you are completely out of my sights for money—there are people who can afford to part with it. You get what I mean.

I think you've hit on a marvelous idea with your chapbooks. It'll be a lot of work but let's show them something good.

All set at this end.

Our best to you and Nancy!

Sincerely yours,

Kenneth Patchen

By the way, these statements from people over the country can be printed in small type—get an awful lot in that way.

The new edition of Moonlight will be ready the 15th.

To Jasper Wood from Kenneth Patchen (NOR)

January 3, 1945
336 West 12 Street
New York City (14)

Dear Jasper Wood:

I was glad to get your good letter.

Did you send letter to POETRY (Chicago)?

I think we have a splendid chance to put this over in fine style.

I'd appreciate it if you send on the first reactions from people; I'll get them right back to you.

I should have all my material in shape by the time you come here. We hope the operation isn't anything serious—?

We have been Rouault fans a long time now. Great.

God! it'll be something if your lead on the mss. pays off! Sending you some of the books so your party can get an idea. Price?

I had thought once I wouldn't sell the MOONLIGHT under 2500 dollars...I'd like to get 1500 (1000 at the least). Thing is, the sale (in justice) should see me through the writing of another book. CLOTH OF THE TEMPEST: 7500 (500 at the lowest). See what you can swing. Wire me if it's hot. Consider 10% of what you get as a contribution to Otsota.

All our good wishes
Sincerely yours,
Kenneth Patchen

To Jasper Wood from Kenneth Patchen (NOR)

March 11, 1945

Dear Jasper Wood—

I had hoped that you would express in a letter some of the sentiments which you saw fit to express orally to us during your visit. I refer to your bitter criticism of me and my role as artist: you stated that books and the rest of it were quite unimportant beside an activity which you called "being a man of action"; you said that my position amounted to nonsense and that I had compromised all the things I claimed to believe in. You said many other things—but for me the foregoing statements were more than enough.

More than enough to cause me to decide to sever whatever relations I may have had with your press.

The fact that you were a guest in my house prevented me from saying what was in my mind and heart to say to you in answer to your amazing pronouncements.

No good purpose would be served either of us to go through with the project of my book in the face of your attitude.

Sincerely yours,
Kenneth Patchen

P.S.

I should appreciate your sending me my Ms. Book (MOONLIGHT) at your earliest convenience.

K.P.

Note: *A disastrous dinner meeting with Wood occurred at the Patchen's apartment on E. 12th Street at which E.E. Cummings had attended. The* ***Panels*** *book would be taken from Wood and later done by Bern Porter.*

Preface to the Waldport Pamphlet *An Astonished Eye Looks Out of the Air (1946)*; letter is dated July 1945. (KPA)

A WORD

THESE POEMS COVER THE TEN YEARS OF MY WRITING LIFE. THERE SHOULDN'T BE ANY POINT HERE IN TRYING TO ADD TO WHAT THE POEMS SAY; BUT PERHAPS A FEW FLAT STATEMENTS MIGHT NOT BE WASTED (PEOPLE SOMETIMES PROTEST THAT 'MODERN POETRY' IS TOO OBSCURE) SO, IN PLAIN ENGLISH:

I AM OPPOSED TO ALL WAR.

I DON'T BELIEVE HUMAN BEINGS SHOULD KILL EACH OTHER.

I AM OPPOSED TO ALL VIOLENCE — FOR WHATEVER REASON.

I BELIEVE THAT WARS WILL ONLY END WHEN MEN REFUSE TO MURDER ONE ANOTHER — FOR WHATEVER REASON. I BELIEVE THESE THINGS AS A MAN AND AS A REVOLUTIONIST. FOR I BELIEVE WARS WILL ONLY END WHEN THE PRESENT MURDEROUS FORMS OF SOCIETY ARE ALLOWED TO DIE — AND ALL MEN ARE AT LAST PERMITTED TO LIVE TOGETHER AS BROTHERS.

K.P. NEW YORK CITY JULY 1945

A PREFACE TO THE WALDPORT PAMPHLET
"AN ASTONISHED EYE LOOKS OUT OF THE AIR"

Note: *This book was done with poet and printer William Everson at the Untied Press of Waldport Conscientious Objectors' camp in Waldport, Oregon.*

To Henry Miller from Kenneth Patchen (UCLA)

December 27, 1945
336 West 12 Street
New York 14, New York

Dear Henry Miller

Congratulations on the birth of your daughter!

I'm just out of the hospital after an operation—appendix.

Someone told us that you were coming to NY soon; hope to see you.

The publishers in England won't risk bringing out my prose books because of the censorship laws there—I am thinking of having a shot at getting a volume of selections from Moonlight, Shy Pornographer and the new Sleepers Awake On The Precipice done over there; would you be interested in writing an introduction for such a book? An introduction by you would do much to get the book published. Someone else who understands British censorship could make the selections.

I'd like to clear the boards on these books so that my new prose The Surrender of the World can appear there when it appears here next November or so. I hope to hear from you soon on this.

All our good wishes to you.
Kenneth Patchen

To Jasper Wood from Kenneth Patchen (NOR)

December 27, 1945
336 West 12 St
New York City 14

Dear Jasper Wood:

What a beautiful gift!
Our best to Nancy and you—

Sincerely
Kenneth Patchen
Every wish for your New Year!

Chapter Nine: *Sleepers Awake* (1946)

To George Leite for publication in *Circle*, later withdrawn, from Kenneth Patchen (KPA)

1946

Ezra Pound chose one authority and most of you chose another. The authority he chose turned Europe into a hell of concentration camps and human misery; the authority chosen by most of you has left Europe and the whole world in a hell of concentration camps and human misery.

Not to mince words, Pound chose one head of that grisly, bloodsmeared serpent called war, and most of you chose another: both were evil, both preyed on the warm, living bodies of human beings—both were Fascist—as people with even the remotest knowledge of the teachings of Christ and of every other great soul who ever lived, you should know what I am talking about.

Pound was anti-Semitic; I suppose he was pleased when they herded the Jews into camps—(and who are, to all intents and purposes, still in camps)...you were told (officially) to hate "those dirty little subhuman yellow bastards;" I suppose you were pleaded in the same way when they tore up the Constitution of the United States, and proceeded to herd Japanese-American citizens into concentration camps.

I condemn Pound for having chosen an evil authority; here he is guilty—and so are most of the rest of you.

Let us not confuse issues. I am writing in defense of poetry, and in defense of that high view of human beings which is poetry's; I am defending the poet Pound against that other Pound who defiled and rejected the things of the spirit—even as most of you have defiled and rejected them.

I am writing in defense of the right of all men to live decently and at peace on this earth. I am defending the majesty that is in all men of every color and nationality against nearly every artist and writer in our "civilized" world—these shameful turncoats and betrayers who spoke out for death, not for life—against any and all who were the spokesmen for the murder of human beings.

This other Pound, like most of you, chose to live by the rules and codes of a society whose whole coloring is hatred and evil; is it too much suppose that he will now wish to be dealt with as a 'member-in-good-standing' of that society? that he will continue to accept the decisions of that society as just and wise? For myself, I do not believe that any man has the right to deprive another man of his freedom; I do not believe that any man has the right to take the life of any other man; and I certainly do not believe that any man who has deprived anyone of life or freedom, is fit to sit in judgment over his fellows. What a monstrous farce! these most utterly cynical gang of war-makers the world has ever known. By what right under God do these have to speak of the guilt or innocence of anyone!

Truth—spit on truth! Justice, mercy, humanity—ask the slaughtered dead to define them for you! The teachings of Christ—Spit on the teachings of Christ! Thou shalt not kill—who ever heard of such nonsense? How could we win the war if we didn't kill? how could we enslave the peoples of the earth if we didn't keep them hating and killing one another?

You see, people wouldn't hate and kill one another if they weren't put up to it. And that's the only hope any of you have. This madness—this madness of thinking you can put down evil and murder by becoming the instruments of evil and murder yourselves; look about you! is there less evil now? is there less fear? is there less hatred? What was your victory? Where is the triumph? The image of Hitler grins down on this gray devastation, on this desert where the soul of mankind bleeds itself out into the sands of an incomprehensible horror. Victory—we all stand under threat that the very blood of the stars will be made to weep down upon us!

Let this be made clear. There is no man in authority anywhere who is not guilty. All their authority is evil—founded on hatred and darkness, not on love; designed to destroy, not to save.

And now they have the power to kill all of us. It is too late to think that they won't do it.

God must think that you have all gone mad—seeing you wait uncaring as drugged sheep for them to blow everything to hell.

I am writing in defense of life. I am writing in defense of poetry, in defense of love, in defense of beauty, in defense, to speak bluntly, of all the mysteries and ecstasies that most of you have seen reason to deny and despise.

Only a few men in any age write great poetry; Ezra Pound is one of these.

Let the Hitlers among you take his books off the shelves.

Let the Hitlers among you spit on his work.

The poems, which never heard of that other Pound, will be honored.

Pound the poet I honor; the Pound who accepted the ethics and values which most of you find wise and just, has lost—whatever 'his peers' may decide to do to him; he has lost the touch of the angel on his arm.

Poetry—and a love for poetry—is bigger than the judgment of any military court; it is bigger than any decision which crime-hardened men can make; I think it is even bigger than the cold-blooded assassins who gave atomic power into the hands of your particular authority—these madmen in careful dinner coats who have opened the gates on the darkness, who have dealt a deathblow to the human imagination.

KENNETH PATCHEN

To Jasper Wood from Kenneth Patchen (NOR)

January 5, 1946
336 West 12 Street
New York 14, New York

Dear Jasper Wood—

Thanks for your long, detailed letter.

This note is to tell you that I am slowed up somewhat by difficulties in getting the printer to understand what I want on Sleepers Awake On The Precipice—practically lived over there all last week—but now it's pretty well straightened out and I can get back to work on the first of the 8 little books. Will have something quite soon—unless the printer runs into another snag.

All the best
Sincerely
Kenneth Patchen

To Henry Moe from Kenneth Patchen (GUG)

January 12, 1946
336 West 12 Street
New York 14, New York

Dear Mr. Moe:

Thank you for your letter. Enclosed is a summary of the work I have accomplished since receiving a Guggenheim Fellowship in 1936. I was glad to follow your kind suggestion; I hope this information is what you wanted. If anything further occurs to you, I would be grateful if you would let me know. As you advise, about February 1st I shall send you examples of my most recent work.

My wife joins me in sending best wishes to you.

Sincerely yours,
Kenneth Patchen

Enclosures.

Note: *The enclosure was in the nature of a record of his work, as typed by Patchen, as follows:*

Kenneth Patchen: 1936-1946

Published books

BEFORE THE BRAVE, Random House, New York, Poetry. 1936.

FIRST WILL AND TESTAMENT, New Directions, New York. Poetry. 1939.

THE JOURNAL OF ALBION MOONLIGHT, Privately printed, New York, 1941. 3rd Edition, Padell, N.Y., 1945. 4th Edition, Padell, N.Y., 1946.

THE DARK KINGDOM, Harris and Givens, New York. Poetry. 1942.

THE TEETH OF THE LION, New Directions, New York. Poetry. 1942.

CLOTH OF THE TEMPEST, Harpers, New York. Poetry. 1943.

MEMOIRS OF A SHY PORNOGRAPHER, New Directions, New York. Prose. 1945. 2nd Edition, 1945.

AN ASTONISHED EYE LOOKS OUT OF THE AIR, The Untide Press, Waldport, Oregon. Poetry. 1946.

Books at press

SELECTED POEMS, New Directions, New York. (February, 1946.)

SLEEPERS AWAKE ON THE PRECIPICE, Padell, New York. Prose. (March, 1946.)

In England:

OUTLAW OF THE LOWEST PLANET, The Grey Walls Press, London. A Selection of poems, edited and with an introduction by David Gascoyne. (February, 1946.)

SELECTED PROSE, The Grey Walls Press, London. (November, 1946.)

Work in progress

THE SURRENDER OF THE WORLD. Prose

ANGEL AND MONSTER. Poetry.

Work set to music

'Be Music, Night' (from CLOTH OF THE TEMPEST)—David Diamond.

Symphony based on THE DARK KINGDOM—Harry Hewitt.

Symphony based on THE JOURNAL OF ALBION MOONLIGHT—Hewitt.

Thirty-five poems: CLOTH OF THE TEMPEST—Hewitt.

Radio play

'The City Wears A Slouch Hat'—Columbia Workshop. May, 1942. With background music by John Cage.

Experimental film

Based on THE JOURNAL OF ALBION MOONLIGHT. Produced in Experimental Film and Writing Classes at the University of California; initial showing May, 1945, Berkeley. Will be shown in New York this year.

Anthologies

Anthology of American Poetry, edited by Alfred Kreymborg. Tudor, New York. 1940.

'The Fox'

Modern American Poetry, edited by Louis Untermeyer. Harcourt, Brace, New York. 1942.

'In Memory of Kathleen'
'Do the Dead Know What Time It Is?'
'The Deer and the Snake'
'Street Corner College'
'Like a Mourningless Child'

Twentieth Century Poetry, edited by Conrad Aiken. The Modern Library, New York. 1944.

'The Character of Love Seen as a Search for the Lost'
'Fog'
'At the New Year'

Comprehensive Anthology of American Poetry, edited by Conrad Aiken. The Modern Library, New York. 1944.

An Anthology of Famous English and American Poetry, edited by William Rose Benet and Conrad Aiken. The Modern Library, New York. 1945.

'At the New Year'

War And The Poet, edited by Richard Eberhard and Selden Rodman. Deven-Adair, New York. 1945.

'The Known Soldier'

Comprehensive critical treatment

The Spiritual Aspects Of The New Poetry, by Amos N. Wilder. Harpers, New York. 1940. (Chapter 15: "Kenneth Patchen".)

American Mirror, by Harold E. Luccock. Macmillan, New York. 1940. (Pgs. 215-216, 225-226, 244, 249.)

"Kenneth Patchen And The Critical Blind Alley," by Harvey Breit. Fantasy, Pittsburgh. No. 4, 1939.

"New Meanings in Recent American Poetry," by Louis Untermeyer. The Virginia Quarterly Review, Summer, 1940.

"On Reading Patchen's New Poems," by Paul Rosenfeld. The University Review, (Kansas City). June, 1940.

Miscellaneous data

Twentieth Century Authors, edited by Kunitz and Haycraft. H.W. Wilson Co., N.Y., 1942. Biographical piece: pg. 1080.

Who's Who Monthly Supplement, September, 1942.

A CHRONOLOGY AND BIBLIOGRAPHY: KENNETH PATCHEN: 1936—1947, Bern Porter, Berkeley, California. (January, 1947).

...Work published in innumerable periodicals in England and America; many poems translated into French and Spanish; THE DARK KINGDOM and THE JOURNAL OF ALBION MOONLIGHT being translated into Spanish for publication in South America.

To Jasper Wood from Kenneth Patchen (NOR)

January 18, 1946
336 West 12 Street
New York 14, New York

Dear Jasper Wood

The St. Francis frame couldn't be better: narrow wooden strips in gold around a white mat under glass.

Little book plan sounds attractive. Leiter to draw one, as you say; perhaps Varda (who likes my work, Miller tells me) another; and one of several people here I can think of offhand to do the third. Once I get back in the swing I can knock them out fast. I'd want a lot of say in the matter of format, as you know. Unless the things were done beautifully there's no use in doing them at all—which doesn't at all mean only expensive materials either. I'll send you the first one by the end of this month.

Thanks for the Sommer photographs: very glad to have them.

Your poems have a nice clean quality.

One thing about the little books: I hope it will be possible to have spines on them which will take the titles. I dislike "blind" books on the shelf. And I think the New Directions pamphlets are too tall.

Does your printer have a range of typefaces?

Best to all of you

Sincerely,
Kenneth Patchen

To Henry Miller from Kenneth Patchen (UCLA)

January 18, 1946
336 West 12 Street
New York 14, New York

Dear Henry Miller—

The PM picture is out for your purpose: owned by a Syndicate or something. I'll send on a couple others which may do as well. I have arthritis in my lower spine. It's got bones out of shape there and recovery—no; however, my periods of relative wellbeing are more frequent and of longer duration than formerly and it's my feeling that I have the thing pretty much in hand. I get around with a stick without too much trouble and I'm able to sit up for hours at a stretch, the pain is almost a natural part of me now—only the fits of depression (common to this disease) really sap my energies and distort my native spirit—I could speak quite morbidly in this last connection. The sickness of the world probably didn't cause mine, but it certainly conditions my handling of it. actually (the worst part) is that I feel I would be something else if I weren't rigid inside with the constant presence of illness; I would be purer, less inclined to write (say) for the sake of being able to show my sick part that it isn't all-powerful; I could experience more in other artists if I didn't have to be so concerned with happenings inside myself; I would have less need to be pure in the presence of the things I love, and therefore (probably) would have a more personal view of myself—I think the more articulate an artist becomes the less he will know about himself to say, for usually one's greatest sense of love is inseparable from a sense of creature fear...it is hard to imagine why God should "think", yet this "thinking" is the material of the greatest art...we don't wish to know ourselves, we wish to be lost in knowing, as a seed in a gust of wind. The road to purity is not through art; it is art. When we know what is to be said and how to say it, we are a long way toward not seeing any reason for saying it at all. I distrust systems. I think the greatest of the dead, were they to return, would weep at the falsity in every position; when thought and feeling harden into certainties, the primal flow, which is present in each living thing, and which cannot be added to or taken away from, moves on without deposit in that quest which in itself is the goal of all endeavors.

—More tomorrow
Kenneth Patchen

Note: In the foregoing letter, the passage which is underlined has been done so in pencil, rather than in the ink Patchen usually uses. Perhaps this indicates that Miller himself underlined the passage which he quoted later in an essay he wrote about Patchen. ***PM*** *was a New York arts magazine.*

To Henry Miller from Kenneth Patchen (UCLA)

January 21, 1946
336 West 12 Street
New York 14, New York

Dear Henry Miller—

I think that if I ever get near an assured income I'd write books along the order of great canvases including everything in them like maybe three or four huge symphonies that would handle poetry and prose as they presented themselves from day to day and from one aspect of my life and interests to another.

But that's all over, I think.

They're going to blow everything up next time—and I don't believe we have long.

Always men have talked about The End of the World—it's nearly here.

A few more straws in the wall...a loose brick or two replaced...then no stone left standing on another—and the long silence, really forever.

What is there to struggle against? Nobody can put the stars back together again. There isn't much time—at all. I can't say it doesn't matter: it matters more than anything—but we are helpless to stop it now.

I'd like to get out to the Southwest for a year or two in the sun. That would take some money coming in every month; so far I don't see too much chance there.

Laughlin said you were being published by Editions du Chene in Paris and that there might be a chance that they would do the Moonlight if you introduced it. What do you think of this?

It's very hard for me to answer your questions. Some were Rebels out of choice; I had none—I wish they'd give me just one speck of proof that this "world of theirs" couldn't have been set up and handled better by a half dozen drugged idiots bound hand and foot at the bottom of a ten-mi. well. And it's always because we love that we are rebellious; it takes a great deal of love to give a damn one way or another what happens from now on: I still do—as of this writing.

To Jasper Wood from Kenneth Patchen (NOR)

February 12, 1946
336 West 12 Street
New York 14, New York

Dear Jasper Wood—

I thought I'd be feeling better after the operation; I'm not. Now I can't see my way to that big project of books—only disappointments later. If you like, however, I'll give you a short prose book sometime early next month—don't know just how long, but under 100 pages.

I am discovering that I can't plan much beyond the thing I'm working on. Naturally I'm sorry to back down—the idea was a good one.

Let me know if you want the prose book.

All of our good wishes to both of you

Sincerely,
Kenneth Patchen

To Jasper Wood from Kenneth Patchen (NOR)

February 28, 1946
336 West 12 Street
New York 14, New York

Dear Jasper Wood—

It was good to get your letter. I am going nuts seeing Sleepers Awake through the press—nearly every day I have to go over to the printshop and spend hours, then come home and spend more hours reading proofs. Then around midnight I begin my day's writing, often seeing the dawn.

But I'll have the Otsota book in your hands late in March.

You haven't told me what type faces your printer has available. What about paper? Where will you have the book bound?

Yes, I'm going to Pittsburgh May 19th—I'll certainly try to get up to Cleveland then. The largest area of resistance to my books is precisely the very concrete and often-stated philosophy of life and view of our world which they contain.

Fraenkel and his ilk who have compromised in every direction except in matters of "Art"—what has he ever said of the real issues of this time? of the war? of the brutal exploitation of human beings? etc. etc.—naturally he would maintain that I have nothing to say—almost nowhere (in print) has anyone even touched on the matter of my work. O death! O life! how cruel you are to our poor sensitive beings! how we bleed because we are the greatest rebels of the world! etc. etc.—Like hell they are. All the sick, vicious swill of the A. Nins and J. Barnes—boy how it goes over. Actually, of course, it doesn't offend anyone—being a nice, "artistic" rebellion. Oh well, it'll all come out in the wash, maybe.

I'd be curious to see what you could do on the CIRCLE thing. Though I'm pessimistic about how far you could get with anything that really touched on the real issues. One of them being that besides being a rebel in 'literature', I'm something of a rebel all down the line.

Sincerely,
Kenneth Patchen

To Henry Miller from Kenneth Patchen (UCLA)

March 9, 1946
336 West 12 Street
New York 14, New York

Dear Henry Miller—

Thursday I suffered some sort of an attack: among other things my blood pressure went down from 130 to 98, necessitating the use of a drug to keep things going. The doctor has told me not to try to work for a time, to do something quite alien to my custom; but I'll go on with it, slowly at first. The doctor said the shock (whatever it was) was more intense than if I'd had an arm or leg cut off.

I can use anything you send me to sell just now. Sleepers Awake On The Precipice is still delayed at the printer's. You say that you "have received no books from you. Am waiting, in order to begin on that English preface." Do you mean copies of Moonlight—or what?

I still deal with Patience Ross. I believe that she has done nothing about place my work [*Moonlight*] in other countries. I'd be very happy to see that done. Would it be too much trouble for you to give me a good word to her about this? Perhaps your preface could be used in these translated editions—?

I've written to PM.

Sincerely
Kenneth Patchen

To Jasper Wood from Kenneth Patchen (NOR)

March 19, 1946
336 West 12 Street
New York 14, New York

Dear Jasper Wood—

Things have been happening. About a week ago I had some sort of attack: blood pressure went down from 130 to 98—doctor said the shock was greater than if I'd had an arm or leg off. And I was ordered not to work or think about work for a time.

However,—I've been working even harder on getting Sleepers Awake through the press, and with whatever time and energy I have over on Twelve Panels For The Walls of Heaven, my Otsota book.

This is what I think: I have six of the "panels" in nearly final form, and I thought to send them on to you so you can begin production. Then I'll go on and whip the other six into shape. Shall I send you this half of the book or wait until it's all finished? They are in long hand. And I'll be sending you the only copy—so if you can, get them typed up right away. If they should get lost—that'll be the end of it. I'll wait until I hear from you on this.

Good wishes,
Kenneth

To Henry Miller from Kenneth Patchen (UCLA)

April 2, 1946
336 West 12 Street
New York 14, New York

Dear Henry Miller—

Your water colors arrived. It won't be any fun to part with them. I like them very much. William Grigsley (the N.C. man) sent me 30 dollars c/o Gotham March 12. I happened to drop in there last Friday and was handed his note and money. I went to practically every gallery and bkstore in NY with the Bentons. No good. The Ass. Am. Artists have everybody down on them for hogging the print field and they themselves have a policy against buying back their lithos—so a stone wall. We sent them back to you thinking that perhaps the situation might be otherwise on the west coast. Here I could do nothing whatever. They're out of print and should bring around 10-15 apiece.

I'll have sheets on Sleepers Awake in about ten days. I thought it best to wait for them because the proofs are in a very mixed-up state. The minute I have the sheets I'll send them on to you.

The Grey Walls Press will definitely bring out my Selected Poems with your Introduction next year. Had confirmation yesterday from them.

I am planning a Limited Ed. for Sleepers Awake. 150 copies—each with painting on cover—beautifully produced—at 10 dollars. I want to make a mailing on it. Will you give me names of people who might be interested in buying a copy?

Did you get the PM photo?

What is doing with your new house?

Sincerely yours,
Kenneth

To Jasper Wood from Kenneth Patchen (NOR)

April 3, 1946
336 West 12 Street
New York 14, New York

Dear Jasper—

Enclosed are 3 of the "Panels". I'll send the rest on as they are ready.

Sorry I couldn't get these typed. Please send me a carbon copy and I'll return it corrected for the printer.

I think it would be good to consider not having illustrations and use a 14 pt. type. What's your feeling?

So the arrangements—I'll send on new ones and you send me typed copies for corrections and revision. OK?

Most of my headaches with book production are over and I'll be able to concentrate on the "Panels".

Sincerely
Kenneth

For God's sake don't lose enclosed copy: there is no other. Tell me what type faces your printer has. Where will the binding be done?

To Jasper Wood from Kenneth Patchen (NOR)

April 17, 1946
336 West 12 Street
New York 14

Dear Wood—

Thanks for typescript and letter.

I've had a very bad infection in my jaw—they've pulled teeth and doused it with penicillin. Clearing up a bit now. Painful as the devil—knocking my work out again. But in a day or so I hope to be able to go on with it.

Just thought I'd let you know why I haven't sent more "Panels" on to you.

Best wishes
Kenneth Patchen

From *Panels for the Walls of Heaven*

THE NATURE OF REALITY

Bed. Apple.

Sly bird. Policeman.

Famine. Rod of milk.

Dice. Groan.

Stone. Towel.

Divot.

"Put some on mine." Six or Tad Prichard.

THE REALITY OF NATURE

Seeking

death life

growth decay

peace madness

conflict silence

birth dissolution

"Put some in me." Tad Prichard or none.

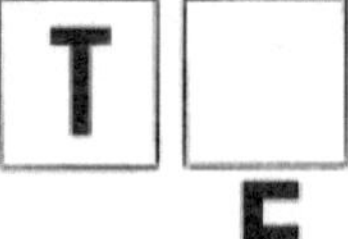

R

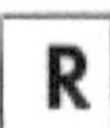

From *Panels for the Walls of Heaven #35*

To Henry Miller from Kenneth Patchen (UCLA)

April 27, 1946
336 West 12 Street
New York 14, New York

Dear Miller—

At last I am able to send you the sheets of Sleepers Awake. They are the master set used by the printer to check for final imposition before lock-up, so just ignore such things as the lines drawn through pages etc.

The book goes to the bindery next week. It was quite a job for me—practically lived at the printshop, and a few very difficult pages I set myself.

I am enclosing a letter from Girodias. Should I accept? I'm very excited about prospect of appearance in France. I'd like to have the Introduction which you are writing for my Selected Prose in England used as Introduction to Moonlight in France—is that all right with you? As a matter of fact, I'd like to send your Essay along with copies of Moonlight to all countries where the book might be published. What is the name and address of the man in New York who has been placing your books in other countries. Patience Ross has released me to go to him. Will you drop him a note about me?

Do you suppose that something like New Republic would print your essay about my work?

I'm getting your mailing list from H.H. next week.

My infected jaw is on the mend.

Sincerely yours,
Kenneth Patchen

To Jasper Wood from Kenneth Patchen (NOR)

May 16, 1946
336 West 12 Street
New York 14, New York

Dear Jasper Wood—

The Pittsburgh people changed the date of my reading to the 26th.

I'd been feeling so rotten that I didn't know whether the trip would be possible—but I've decided that I can make it.

Seems like a big chore for you people to go to Pittsburgh but that's up to you.

I want to stop a bit with my folks in Warren.

What bothers me is whether I'll feel up to going on to Cleveland. I can never tell in advance what I'm up to and what I'm not.

Point is: I'd hate to have you make that trip and then have me unable to go on to Cleveland. That's the picture.

Good wishes
Kenneth Patchen

The "Panels" are nearly ready.

To Jasper Wood from Kenneth Patchen (NOR)

May 30, 1946
336 West 12 Street
NYC 14

Dear Jasper Wood—

I'm just back from Pittsburgh through railroads strike and floods.

Shall I send you the "Panels" now?

Good wishes
Sincerely yours,
Kenneth Patchen

To Jasper Wood from Kenneth Patchen (NOR)

June 10, 1946
336 West 12 Street
New York 14, New York

Dear Jasper Wood—

I'd've had the "Panels" off to you last week but my whole Limited Edition of Sleepers Awake was ruined at the last minute by the bindery and I've been pretty knocked-down by it—and working like mad to try to compel them to print the whole thing over again—don't at this moment know how I'll make out on it.

However, I'll get the "Panels" into your hands sometime this week.

Regards—
in haste
Kenneth Patchen

To Jasper Wood from Kenneth Patchen (NOR)

June 13, 1946
336 West 12 Street
New York 14, New York

Dear Jasper Wood—

Some of the drawings-panels will stick together—just pull them apart firmly with an even pull. Drawings for line cuts.

You can see how important typography and general makeup will be for this book. I'll want to be told in advance of all plans and naturally will want to see complete proofs at every stage. I certainly hope this one goes through the press fairly smoothly. God knows I had enough headaches on Sleepers Awake.

Perhaps Panel 29 could be run in color on the jacket.

Book will be billed as prose poems and drawings.

What about binding? Paper? Type etc.?

I'm getting the binders to print over the Limited Sleepers Awake.

Please let me know of the safe receipt of ms. and if you can send me another copy of Panel 44—originally called The Panel of Longing in Beauty And Horror—I want to send it to someone in England.

Regards
Kenneth Patchen

The drawings are not illustrations—they are "Panels" in themselves.

Don't let people handle drawings—I don't want their textures disturbed. Let's get every detail ironed out on production before anything is done.

As you know, I've always fought tooth and nail to get my books the way I want them. More determined than ever now after my tremendous battle for Sleepers Awake. Let's put everything possible into this one.

To Jasper Wood from Kenneth Patchen (NOR)

June 22, 1946
336 West 12 Street
New York 14, New York

Dear Jasper Wood—

I'm glad you like the panels. My hunch is that you can sell about 750 copies without strain on 1st printing.

The trade edition of Sleepers Awake is out. Haven't the Cleveland stores got it yet? Maybe you'd drop enclosed cards to local shops—

I'm trying to get around now to work on the Introductions to the reissues of my three books of poems.

Do you mean to print the whole panels book in photo-offset or just drawings? The text'd have to be set in type anyway.

Let me know your production plan on book as soon as you can.

Sincerely
Kenneth Patchen

To Henry Miller from Kenneth Patchen (UCLA)

June 22, 1946
336 West 12 Street
New York 14, New York

Dear Henry Miller—

I don't remember whether I told you or not that the Limited Edition Sleepers Awake was ruined at the bindery. After a terrific struggle I've got them to foot the bill of printing and binding the whole thing over.

Your Introduction to my prose is waiting until I get a chance to really ponder it. I've got to write prefaces to the reissues of my three books of poems—a job I feel tongue-tied about.

Have you read Sleepers Awake yet? I think it's going to have harder sledding than anything I've written. And now an ominous slump in the book market.

All good wishes

Sincerely
Kenneth Patchen

To Henry Miller from Kenneth Patchen (UCLA)

July 14, 1946
Mt. Pleasant, New York

Dear Henry Miller—

I was pleased to know that you had put correspondence etc aside in order to work on your book.

My chief feeling about your Introduction to my book is that it suffers on the side of saying nothing directly about my prose. However, I am very proud to have it, and as soon as you return it now I'll send it on to the publisher—they're ready to go to press.

Sleepers Awake is having harder faring than anything I've done. It would be a great service to my book if you could say a couple paragraphs about it for use in ads in the little magazines—as extravagant as possible.

Do you suppose Horizon would print the Introduction? Sat. Rev. of Lit. Circle?

I lie in the sun as much as I can.

Sincerely yours,
Kenneth Patchen

The sheets arrived. I'm sending you a bound copy with this mail.

To Henry Miller from Kenneth Patchen (UCLA)

August 4, 1946
Mt. Pleasant, New York

Dear Henry Miller—

I wonder if you and The Alicat Press would care to bring out as a small chapbook the Introduction you wrote to my Selected you'd done on my work—? Perhaps on the cover could be a reproduction of the Rimbaud-P. card you planned. Such a little book would be of great assistance to me. Particularly if it appeared this year. The enclosed is being used in the French edition of Moonlight, and is being sent out to other countries.

All good wishes
Sincerely yours,
Kenneth Patchen

To Jasper Wood from Kenneth Patchen (NOR)

September 4, 1946
336 West 12th St
New York City 14

Dear Jasper Wood—

Thank you very much for sending the ms. on to Porter. He had sent me an urgent letter stating that he wanted the book badly, but that it would be necessary for him to have ms. before Sept 10 at which time he planned to go off for a month's vacation. He promised publication before Christmas—doubt that he can make it by then. Tahiti sounds like a major move indeed. I think the Tahiti book a most attractive idea. I don't know where Stearns is—Chicago, last I heard.

All good wishes.
Sincerely yours,
Kenneth Patchen

Note: *Patchen had decided to withdraw the* ***The Panels for the Walls of Heaven*** *from Jasper Wood and subsequently following Henry Miller's suggestion, it was published by Bern Porter Books of Berkeley in 1946.*

To Henry Miller from Kenneth Patchen (UCLA)

November 13, 1946
336 West 12th St
New York 14

Dear Henry Miller—

In haste—Baradinsky is releasing your pamphlet about me and my little prose book to Padell. I have had an absolute nightmare with Baradinsky—the worst experience I have ever had with any publisher, including Laughlin.

Tomorrow (in my steel harness—after being flat on my back for two weeks) I've got to go up to Yonkers and have all the papers signed, before witnesses.

I want you to write me a note saying that it's all right with you to have your pamphlet released by Padell. Baradinsky says it is ok but I don't trust him. He says that he will not compel Padell to pay him the 75 dollars he advanced you, it being involved with other material you gave him.

Padell will make you an advance and pay you 10% royalty. All right?

Also, please send me by return mail, if possible, about 15 typewritten pgs. of further matter which can be run at the end of the Patchen: Man of Anger and Light. As it stands, this booklet only runs to 17 pgs.—too short for a dollar item. 28 pgs. is what the thing should run, as a minimum.

And Mr. Padell (an honest publisher) asked me to ask you if you have any mss. for him to bring out.

Please let me hear from you immediately—sorry to bother you with this, but have no choice.

Padell, I think, will run an edition of 1500 on your little book about me. What advance do you want? Any conditions for contract, etc.?

All good wishes
Sincerely yours,
Kenneth Patchen

The haste is because the book is all set to be printed now.

I'm sending you a copy of the Limited Ed. of Sleepers Awake, with painting on cover.

Chapter Ten: On the Restricted Shelf (1947)

Postcard to C. Wrey Gardiner from Kenneth Patchen (KPA)

January 6, 1947

Dear Gardiner

New address:
Old Lyme,
Connecticut.

All good wishes.

Sincerely yours,
Kenneth Patchen

Note: *This card was sent to C. Wrey Gardiner at The Grey Wall Press in England, which is further indication that Patchen did maintain mail contact with people in England (and other countries)—particularly people associated with publishing houses. Grey Wall would publish his* ***Outlaw of the Lowest Planet: Selected Poems*** *in 1946.*

To Louis Untermeyer from Kenneth Patchen (IND)

February 28, 1947
Old Lyme, Connecticut

Dear Louis Untermeyer—

Shortly after my wife and I moved to this town in late December, I presented the local library with a copy of my Selected Poems published by New Directions in their New Classics Series, and with a copy of my Selected Poems published by the Grey Walls

Press, London. These two volumes were accepted with thanks. Later we learned that my books had been denied a place in their regular category because (to quote one of the librarians) "our young people have access to the open shelves."

I am now attempting to erase this stigma attached to my work and to ourselves as members of this small community.

The library, though small and privately endowed, acts as a sort of nerve-center of the town, being the site of various committee meetings and other group activities. Perhaps I need not tell you that the presence here of the author of "dirty", "forbidden" books has occasioned no little head-turning and tongue-wagging—the more since, to my knowledge, no other volume of contemporary writing has been the victim of this irresponsible, village censorship.

I have withdrawn my books. I intend to offer them once again as gifts for use on the open shelves of the library when the Committee of Selection holds its next quarterly meeting about the middle of March.

This may seem like a small matter. It is not. A few days ago the people from whom we rent our house asked me if my books were available at the library. I answered that as yet they were not, but that I believed they would be soon. (I am working to that end, at any rate.)

Now. You can support me in this troubling matter by addressing a short statement to the Library stating that you understand from me that there has been some misunderstanding about my books, and that you know my reputation as a writer of moral and artistic integrity—whatever you may see fit, of course.

I am sending this plea to a number of people whose opinion has weight. Your letter will not be used or made public in any way beyond its service at the Library.

I ask you to take this action against an irresponsible and injurious censorship.

Please send me your letter to:
Mrs. Dixon Hoag., Comm. Of Selection,
Phoeby Griffin Noyes Library,
Old Lyme, Connecticut.

Sincerely yours,
Kenneth Patchen

P.S. I'd appreciate being told whether you write to the Comm. or not —otherwise I shall probably never learn of it.

Note: *This letter is basically the same in content addressed to different people, including Eleanor Roosevelt, each noting the number of people sent. There is no current record of other responses than Untermeyer and Christopher Morley.*

To Louis Untermeyer from Kenneth Patchen (IND)

March 4, 1947
Old Lyme, Connecticut

Dear Louis Untermeyer—

I was very happy indeed to receive the carbon copy of the letter which you sent to the local library committee: thank you.

Sincerely yours,
Kenneth Patchen

P.S. Under seperate cover I am sending you a Limited Edition copy of one of my books. K.P.

To Louis Untermeyer from Kenneth Patchen (IND)

August 11, 1947
Old Lyme, Connecticut

Dear Louis Untermeyer,

A long time has elapsed between the act and the acknowledgement. In June the Old Lyme library notified me that my books "on further consideration" would be retained on the restricted shelf. The books have been returned to me at my request. As the committee of selection pointed out in its letter to me, the library is maintained by private funds and is not answerable to the community. In view of this, I feel that there is nothing more to be done after a civilized reproach has failed to change their collective attitude.

Needless to say, I am very grateful to you for your kindness to me, and for the solidarity of front your letter to the committee conveyed.

Sincerely,
Kenneth Patchen

My very best wishes to you.

Phoebe Griffin Noyse Library, Old Lyme, CT

(Photo courtesy Phoebe Griffin Noyes Library)

Chapter Eleven: I Challenge the Right (1948-1949)

To Henry Miller from Kenneth Patchen (UCLA)

January 8, 1948
Old Lyme, Connecticut

Dear Henry Miller

Thank you very much for your letter. About the Limited Edition "Panels for the Walls of Heaven": I made a deal with B. Porter whereby I got 150 unfinished copies of the book in lieu of royalties, which I had a hunch I'd never see; these trade copies I then embellished to constitute a special ed., putting labels and plastic covers etc. on by hand. By the way, he asks 4.50 for the trade copies. I quite agree with you about him—his phobia about money goes beyond the merely stingy. This Limited we sent out to bookstores.

Almost every Sunday we see something about you in the Boston papers—like us to send them on?

We're thinking of going to England and France next fall, provided it seems then that my back would take it. Perhaps stay a year. I don't think that I'll like the 'writers' there any more than I do those here. But it might feel good not to be in America.

All our good wishes to you.
Sincerely yours,
Kenneth Patchen

To Kenneth Rexroth from Kenneth Patchen (UCLA)

April 29, 1948
Old Lyme, Connecticut

Dear Rexroth—

I was delighted to see that a good poet got a Guggenheim for a change.

All my good wishes to your work and to you.
Sincerely yours,
Kenneth Patchen

To Kenneth Rexroth from Kenneth Patchen (UCLA)

June 11, 1948
Old Lyme, Connecticut

Dear Rexroth—

I should have answered your pleasant letter before, but every day I've been expecting to get copies of the new editions of three of my books of poems which I wanted to send you. They'll be here tomorrow, and you should have them next week sometime. A quote from one of your reviews appears on one of the jackets, so you're certainly entitled to presentation copies. The other titles you mention wanting, I'll try to round up for you. Delighted to give you any books I may have. I'd like to bum you for a copy of The Phoenix and The Tortoise, if you have an extra...someone borrowed and never returned my copy.

Our English trip looks off right now, too risky with my bad back. Sort of thinking of northern California for next winter, but there again the trip might prove too much. Very tough winter here, and now no sun but 20-odd days of rain and cold the past month. I count a lot on the sun and we should go somewhere where it shines once in awhile.

I gather from your card that we may expect a visit from you in the Fall. Look forward to it...we've got a couple extra cots and some nice records, etc. Two hours from New York.

All the best,
Sincerely yours,
Kenneth Patchen

To Kenneth Rexroth from Kenneth Patchen (UCLA)

July 10, 1948

Dear Rexroth—

Laughlin had told us many times of your powers as a correspondent and now I have knowledge at first hand. Thanks very much for your long and interesting letter. I'm no good whatever at letters, the thing freezes up on me, don't know why, always been so. So when you get a bit snip like this, understand that it's not because I wouldn't do more, just unable.

You see all the trouble I had with that jacket for The Dark Kingdom: I fuss through getting them half the way I want them not that I care much anymore but because it makes me so sad to see how little people think of getting a thing right, and I end up involved beyond all reason.

Your dope on that dope Dorais was news. I got my back trouble that period, bang one day coming home from the store couldn't walk and spent six weeks in bed. We didn't know what it was then, do now, arthritis that's twisted the bones in spine. We try to pay no mind of it, of course, but that doesn't work a lot of the time. A painful bore, like Dorais.

I remember Rabinowitch, Ward Moore and the people of that time with sad pleasure. There were ten-fifteen of like interests and views there, all a little away from the real thing, I don't know why, they had and have, I suppose more honesty and core than their New York counterparts but never seemed to do or to be what they wanted...maybe the air's different East...Rabinowitch is smarter than Partisan Review's P. Rahv and here probably would have thrown his weight around like that, not that I mean any moral comparison between them. I thought Rabinowitch on the right side. But there was a feeling of hopelessness about those Loas Angeles people in 1937-8 which is just now hitting the NY intellectuals, guess the former had ears nearer the ground. I never liked Moore's beating of women, went against the grain, one beating if he had to then scram out. There's plenty good in him though.

Sorry you had the let-down on Everson. His sort is terrified of <u>writing</u> poetry that can't be by Auden, Shapiro and Co. Thousands of lifetimes away from the attitude you expressed in your splendid piece in the Lawrence volume. Did you see the disgusting job Diana Trilling did with the Portable Lawrence? An Astonished Eye was spoiled at the printer's, gray tint block was to have been like a watermark. Spender is Everson's speed as poet, Spender having the 'right' kind of reputation: don't forget that's all that counts with fellows who've been poisoned in that way.

Thanks for the second Japanese contact, sending a book.

In What Hour I don't have. Do you have Albion Moonlight? Sorry I have only one copy of Before the Brave.

Are you going to England? Why don't you do an anthology of American (and British, or better English-speaking) poets, line up things if you do make trip. Must be some good poets in Ireland, Canada, Australia, S.A., India, Scotland, etc. Poets now writing in obscurity. I'd like to see you cover this period in an introduction in the forthright fashion of the Lawrence. That damn Oscar Williams is managing to cover it with that oily filth of his. Sound out Maria Leiper of Simon Schuster on it...she's very friendly and pleasant. This as you know is just an idea coming out on my part, how do I know what interest you have in such things. Some one should do it though.

Beautiful days of sun the last week.

All good wishes,

Sincerely,

Kenneth Patchen

Note: *All punctuation, spelling, and sentence structure follows exactly that of Patchen. Though Patchen and Rexroth had applied for the Guggenheim Fellowship the same year that Rexroth won, they had become allies.*

To Kenneth Rexroth from Kenneth Patchen (UCLA)

August 5, 1948
Old Lyme, Connecticut

Dear Rexroth—

Figure that you may be off in the mountains but wonder if you got the copies of The Dark Kingdom I sent some weeks ago...Perhaps you didn't get the letter I mailed you at that time...

Best wishes,

Sincerely yours,

Kenneth Patchen

To Kenneth Rexroth from Kenneth Patchen (UCLA)

August 14, 1948
Old Lyme Conn

Dear Rexroth—

All I know of Laughlin and Moonlight is that L hired Edmund Wilson to pass on the Ms. E.W. didn't like though he overpraised the book, said it was too-imitative of certain French writers, most I hadn't heard of, only one read (in bad translation), W. got fifty dollars for the job.

I have a new book of poems in October with Padell called Red Wine and Yellow Hair.

Interested that you've done an anthology of British poetry: for publication in England or here?

Your mountain trip sounds like a lot of fun.

Ward Moore sent me the prospectus of a co-operative publishing venture headed by K. Crossen, suppose you know of it, what do you think of it?

All good wishes, Sincerely,
Kenneth Patchen

To Marion Strobel, *Poetry* magazine, Chicago, from Kenneth Patchen (PAP)

August 29, 1948
Old Lyme, Connecticut
U.S.A.

Miss Marion Strobel—

Of sixteen poems submitted to your magazine during the past months, you have accepted one for printing. Obviously my work is not much to your editorial taste; and it is clear to me that your editorial taste is not at all to mine: so why should you print me? and why should I want you to? you shouldn't, and I don't.

Enclosed is a stamp for the return of my poem.

Sincerely yours,
Kenneth Patchen

To Kenneth Rexroth from Kenneth Patchen (UCLA)

[Undated, perhaps September, 1948]

Dear Rexroth—

The carbon of your letter to Laughlin was the first I knew that his beef had actually appeared. Right off, my deep thanks to you for your action. It warmed my heart.

Early in May L wrote to Padell protesting the use of his statement, and Padell forwarded the nasty note to me. I wrote L reminding him of two points, 1) that that same quote from him has appeared in advertising and on bk jackets since 1946 (and to his knowledge, since I placed the material in his hands myself): only with its appearance in darling PR did he see anything wrong with its use, and 2) I have in his handwriting the quote in question with this remark after it: "And you really are, you know." So much for authenticity of statement, right to use, etc.

In answer L wrote on May 24th: "Don't worry about the blurb. The statement would be more accurate if it said 'I believe K.P. will become etc'. You have the stuff all right. But it's insulting to older men like Cummings, Pound, WCW etc. to have that spread around in that form. Your best poems are as good as their best, But they have made more of a total impact, having been at it longer. I wrote a note for P.R. to publish, which I think you will like. It disclaims the sweeping character of the statement, but puts in some good licks for your prospects."

Today I phoned a bkstore in New York and had L's note read to me. What did he think I would like about that! It's interesting that neither PR nor L sent me a copy of letter or magazine for statement or defense. I very rarely see the stinking damn magazine, and my friends stay clear of it. So the issue for a reply is pretty dead horse by now, several months later. Though I wouldn't have answered it anyway. All I could have done would be to protest "oh yes you did say that about me and I did have a right to print what you said about me": why put more soiled linen on Laughlin's line?

The question is, what am I to do about further relations with ND, go on or register a final stop now? Frankly, I am so completely disgusted with people who publish books and with people who read the books when they are published that I often think of dropping completely out of the whole rotten thing. The more resistance you have to overcome, the more you have to resort to blurb baloney and such stuff to keep the publisher's head above water, like I wrote a novel to boil Padell's pot and he blew all the chances on it with the most amazing show of bad salesmanship anyone could imagine. But Padell is above-board and honest. Laughlin I have always liked, but never could understand. Of course nothing would please PR etc more than if my association with ND were to blow up over this letter business; and, of course, bystanders would figure that L had had enough of me (as the bkseller today said he'd heard from several quarters). When things are a mess, unmessing them often becomes a bigger mess. I'll try to think it out in the next few days.

Again, thanks. All good wishes,
Sincerely yours,
Kenneth Patchen

What do you think I should do?

***Note:** PR is Partisan Review.*

To James Laughlin from Kenneth Patchen (NDA)

September 30, 1948
Old Lyme, Connecticut

Dear Laughlin—

Obviously I agree with you that your letter was a mistake. The question is, do you realize how much of a mistake it was. Word is out that ND is quite fed-up with Patchen because he is "completely dishonest, irresponsible" and the rest. Two New York booksellers have told me this, in addition to friends who have informed me regarding reports of my disgusting lack of all moral sense, personal ethics, and mental stability.

As you know, I stand for certain very unpopular ideas; and my opportunity to discredit these ideas is warmly received in almost all intellectual quarters: with at least as much warmth I intend to do what I can to prevent myself from being used to discredit the things I believe in.

The reputation of the sort of writer I am is a bigger issue than a career in literature. You will make another mistake if you don't get this firmly placed in your mind.

Whatever you thought you were writing, your letter has been taken as a public repudiation of me as a person and as a writer. It follows that this, the public repudiation of an author by his publisher, is the matter to be settled one way or the other now, After considerable thought and discussion, I have come to this decision: you will now make an effort to repair the damage done me by your letter or our relations will come to an abrupt end. (Whether in the event of a complete break, I can prevent you from bringing out further editions of Memoirs and Selected Poems, I don't know; but I would try, and base my case on a public demonstration of bad faith on the publisher's part—this contention buttressed by the facts as I see them in the light of your several letters.) I had thought too of circularizing photostats of this correspondence, together with a covering statement couched in vigorous language concerning my attitude toward any publisher who would butter up the slimy behinds of that PR bunch at the expense of his own dignity and the standing of a publishing venture called New Directions; however, 1) it seemed to me that enough personal injury had been done in this affair already, and 2) I couldn't bring myself to make the mistake of entering upon a "so nasty teacher doesn't love me as much as he does whosis" demonstration for the edification of that same PR bunch. So if no effort is made to set this matter right, I shall take the action of breaking relations—as completely as can be managed.

This is my suggestion: that you take a back-cover Patchen ad in PR as soon as can be arranged.

If this idea strikes you as fair and good, then consider that what is needed is an expression of confidence and belief in that aspect of your author which has suffered most at your hand, i.e., his seriousness, and his integrity. Of course this doesn't have to be gouged in with a blowtorch for pen—though it should be very clear that ND is proud of the books of his which they've published, and have a long-term interest in his work.

That's one way of handling the thing. Perhaps, if you are concerned along this line, you will have a better idea. But whatever is done...

[Rest of letter is missing]

To Kenneth Rexroth from Kenneth Patchen (NDA)

October 3, 1948
Old Lyme, Conn

Dear Rexroth—

I've written Laughlin that unless he runs a full-page ad pushing my books in PR I will break with him completely; and told him exactly what I think of his action, in unvarnished style. Wrote him couple days ago after a note from him saying "that PR letter was a mistake." Have no idea how he will react and don't much care.

We look forward to seeing you. Please let me know when to expect you.

All the best,
Kenneth Patchen

Letter of Recommendation from Kenneth Patchen (KPA)

October 4, 1948
Old Lyme, Connecticut

To Whom It May Concern:

It has been my privilege to know Mr. William Shank since the early part of 1943; and during this time, I have found him to be a young man of the highest moral and intellectual integrity.

To the extent of his ability and in accordance of his conscience, Mr. William Shank has conducted himself as a exceptionally honest, ethical, and religious person. I consider it an honor to know him.

Sincerely yours,
Kenneth Patchen

Note: *William Shank was a young friend and supporter who had served as a conscientious objector.*

To James Laughlin from Kenneth Patchen(NDA)

KENNETH PATCHEN OLD LYME CONNECTICUT

October 26

Dear Laughlin

Frankly I don't know about the advisability of having Merton make a public, blanket endorsement of my work; although I've never attacked the Catholic church by name in so many words, on many occasions I've felt it necessary to take a stand against what I consider stultifying and authoritarian in the whole state-wedded framework of "church" as it exists today. Specifically, it is my often-stated position that no individual can support the organized murder of war without losing all claim to the title of Christian. But this you know;

and is, I believe, known generally.
In this mail a copy of The Dark Kingdom is being sent you. I feel that any person of "religious" tendency should find it acceptable. Judge for yourself whether the Trappists would let it in.
Naturally I'd not want Merton or anyone else to run that sort of risk on my account. You know the set-up better than I do.

The doctor in NY has promised to draw up and send us a report on my physical condition. Will send it on the minute it comes.

All good wishes.
Sincerely yours, Kenneth

To Henry Moe/ The John Simon Guggenheim Memorial Foundation from Kenneth Patchen (GUG)

KENNETH PATCHEN
OLD LYME, CONNECTICUT

December 15, 1948

Mr. Henry Allen Moe
John Simon Guggenheim
Memorial Foundation
551 Fifth Avenue
New York

Dear Mr. Moe:

Year after year I have made application for a renewal of the Fellowship granted me in 1936.

During this period I have written eleven books.

My work sells no better than the work of any serious poet in this time. It has not been at all possible for me to make a living through my writing.

For ten years now I have suffered from arthritis of the lower spine, a condition which worsens steadily.

Perhaps you will understand why I should very much appreciate an answer to these questions:

Is there any point in my applying further?

Is there anything I could do that might help my chances with your committee?

I would take my year of freedom to England for the purpose of doing an ambitious series of poems.

Sincerely yours,
Kenneth Patchen

To Henry Moe, The John Simon Guggenheim Memorial Foundation from Kenneth Patchen (GUG)

December 20, 1948
Old Lyme, Connecticut

Dear Mr. Moe:

Thank you very much for your letter of the 16th.
I wish now to make formal application for renewal of my 1936 Fellowship.
Should this application meet with success, I would spend most of the year in England, with perhaps a few months in Milan and Paris (depending on conditions).
My project is the writing of an ambitious series of poems based on the quest for spiritual values in a dark and confused time.
Next month New Directions will publish a volume of my poems titled RED WINE AND YELLOW HAIR. As soon as copies are ready, I'll have several sent you for the use of your Committee of Selection. It is my feeling that my best work to date is contained in this book.
I may say that my health must determine whether I can carry through my plan of going abroad to work; though doctors have assured me that such a trip would be possible.

All good wishes,
Sincerely yours,
Kenneth Patchen

To Kenneth Rexroth from Kenneth Patchen (UCLA)

February 19, 1949

Dear Rexroth

Planned to send you a Red Wine and Yellow Hair as soon as it came out but ND was slow getting them to me and then sent only a couple; but no matter now, you did get one from Laughlin (I guess). Any rate I'm going to send you a signed one soon as more reach me. Thanks for your letter about the poems. New York Times Book Section refused an ad on grounds that book is obscene: 3rd book of mine they've refused to run ads of. This time I got mad, decided to go down and picket with sign in front of Times Bldg: I CHALLENGE THE RIGHT OF THE NY TIMES TO BURN MY BOOKS. We were all set, taxi arranged for and all, when my back kicked into a sudden spell (had been pointing for trouble for some weeks, but I was sore enough to risk getting laid up in NY for weeks) and now I'm strapped up in bed, damit. So I could write open letters around...but everybody about is NY Times any way you look at them; figure the individual has got to fight as an individual or not at all. Why should I appeal to a crew of lice for anything. The bk, like my last four bks, won't be reviewed at all in most places, and where it is, just the right lads will get it to attack what I have to say by declaring that it's too bad I have no ideas or discipline etc. Laughlin is off in Austria so...what the hell. Talk about censorship, what do you think of this nice under-the-table stuff of the Times? telling my publishers that my stuff is too dirty for their dear readers. Nobody knows. If they'd just try to suppress the books, but killing them off down where nobody has any inkling of what's going on. If I had money for a lawyer, I'd sue the bastards for 50 thou and give the dough to something good like sending a bag of shit to everybody in "the public eye". Just got your New British Poets and think you did a very fine job in a difficult field. Sorry you didn't include Hugo Manning, who's a pretty bitter shot-up Eng. soldier, and in letters a very nice fellow. His poems are as good as most of those over there...my hunch the people over there are too clever to be really good poets, not unfriendly enough.

Best,
Kenneth

To James Laughlin from Kenneth Patchen (NDA)

February 21, 1949

Dear Laughlin—

Wrote a couple letters to you before I knew of your trip. A letter of yours dated the 11th reached me day before yesterday.

When I got your note about the refusal of the Times to run an ad for Red Wine, I arranged for a taxi to take us to the train the next day, phoned New York to set up living quarters for us for a week or so, and was prepared to walk up and down in front of the Times Bldg with a sign reading I CHALLENGE THE RIGHT OF THE NY TIMES TO BURN MY BOOKS, first notifying every paper and picture magazine in the city of my intention. So the taxi came that Thursday morning and I couldn't get out of bed, damn the luck. Twisted it in the night...though it had been acting up for weeks before. If I could make that trip down there you'd see some action. And if I had money I'd sue them for damaging my professional name and for damaging my professional name and for interfering with my means of making a living; and those foul bastards wouldn't have a chance. The howling rot they advertise, all the slop and filth to make a pig vomit. Why don't you for God's sake take a stand on it, bring it out in the open, reveal this vicious fascist hidden censorship of work which has not been questioned by any censor in the country: Write open letters, run ads exposing the thing...let those foulheads know that some people of discernment will fight them in the open.

To Henry Miller from Kenneth Patchen (UCLA)

March 1, 1949
Old Lyme Conn

Dear Henry Miller—

I know you must wonder why the devil our mailing list wasn't sent on to you for use on your silk screen venture. The fact is—outside of the old New Directions one, now more or less worthless—we have only a handful of names, most of them deadheads. The only way I could see any of my painted Limiteds was through stores; never had any luck with direct mail, and have pretty well given it up. Wish I had a million good people to refer you to for your sales; haven't five who are unknown to you. We were very happy to receive your gift of the water color reproduction; framed nicely, it has center place on our front room wall. I'm just getting over another bad time with my damn back, a wearisome bore. Had some months during the fall when I felt fine, and got careless. Lately Miriam and I have been re-reading things from your books: wonderful insights and sheer writing ability unapproached by anyone now living. It'll be a long time before your work is properly evaluated, but I have no doubt whatever that it will be. I find it better with each new reading. Yes, publishing is going to be an increasingly hard proposition for the serious writer; more and more readers resent being made to feel and to think, and publishers, who've always hated such writers anyway, are delighted to take advantage of this. Anything, good or bad, that gets enough advertising will sell; but they delight in dropping all support from the real thing..."Because," they'll say, "we have a hard enough time selling our own sort of thing." Hollywood always makes money; publishers always make money; the Hollywood publisher-minded writers always make money; it's only the other sort of person, the no-sayers, who suffer when the economic wagon starts to tilt. What I'm driving at is this; I believe that just now the trend to exclude the non-commercial artist is not so much due to economic reasons as it is to reasons of spiritual funk on the part of that whole middle-class group of intellectuals who once supported the right of the "outsiders" to have their say...not that they ever believed, really believed, any of the things that were said. Nobody even wants to hear them now. Words and ideas have ceased to have any meaningful place in this society; people have rejected all 'depth' in their lives...stuff outside, the shallower the better, does the living—if it can be called that.

Warmly yours,
Kenneth Patchen

I've asked Padell to send you copies of your pamphlet—meantime mailing you a few we had on hand.

Did you receive my Red Wine and Yellow Hair?

To Louis Untermeyer from Kenneth Patchen (IND)

March 17, 1949

OLD LYME, CONN

Dear Louis Untermeyer:

A belated note in answer to your good card of some weeks ago—No, I do want you to keep that Limited Panels for the Walls of Heaven; but I appreciate your thoughtfulness in offering to return it. I'm just getting over a bad bout with my spinal arthritis—the change of season usually goes hard on it—so letters have had to wait. We're getting in our supply of flower seeds, ready for the sun—and I'm back to work again. All good wishes.

Respectfully yours,
Kenneth Patchen

To James Laughlin from Kenneth Patchen (NDA)

October 20, 1949
OLD LYME CONNECTICUT

Dear Laughlin

You have been a good friend to me—through all kinds of weather and mix-ups, over these ten years. And that has meant a great deal. Sometimes you may have wondered if I was aware of this: I have been, and am.

Needless to say, I'm very grateful to you for digging up the fact of that Foundation, and for offering to present my case to it. (We'll mention the matter to absolutely no one, as you request.) I am sure that Louis Untermeyer (88 Remsen St., Brooklyn 2) would write a good letter—know he would. MacLeish's address: Harvard Univ., Widener W, Cambridge—he'll write. Robert Hutchins, Univ. Chicago, is a good possibility (he likes my poems). I've just received a warm, excited letter from Edith Sitwell: know she'll write them.

While you're getting the letters off, etc., we'll line up the doctor's statement for you.

To Henry Miller from Kenneth Patchen (UCLA)

October 23, 1949
OLD LYME CONNECTICUT

Dear Henry Miller

As you probably guessed, I have been having a very bad time. Back in April the arthritis started to move from my back down into my hip and leg, where it is now firmly settled. The details are a bit on the gruesome side, can't walk, can't sleep etc. (except under strong pills which I resist giving over to). And, of course, no income beyond dribbles. That Cortosone (the new injection treatment) has been taken under government supervision, so won't be available generally for a year or two. Laughlin made us a visit couple weeks ago, his first here, and was rather sobered, I think; he's now trying to inlist the help of a Fund, and is writing you about it. He met Huntington Cairnes in Washington at a dinner and Cairnes happened to ask about "Miller's poet friend." Laughlin told him and Cairnes brought up matter of this fund for poets. Wonderful if something comes of that. For the first time I haven't been able to work. Made desperate efforts to get down into the sun for the winter, no result. We are pretty isolated here and the burden of day-to-day activity has fallen completely on Miriam. I dread the coming cold weather.

About the Padell booklet: I haven't been in touch with him for many months. His business has gone blooey, hanging on by his fingernails. Later I'll try to get some copies for you.

Laughlin reported that your Rosy Crucifixion is out in Paris, promised to send us a copy. Hasn't. I'm very eager to see it.

I hope that you and your family are well and busy.

Miriam joins me in sending warm good wishes.

Sincerely yours,
Kenneth Patchen

Note: *The misspelling of the word "enlist" in this letter is Patchen's.*

To Henry Miller from Kenneth Patchen (NDA)

November 6, 1949
Old Lyme, Connecticut

Dear Henry Miller

When your letter came I phoned Laughlin to find out why he hadn't asked you to put in a word to the committee in charge of the grant to poets, and he said that the people involved were "much too conservative" to be favorably influenced by your advocacy. Hence he had decided not to ask you to write them. In this light, I'd guess that my chances are slim. I was very pleased to get your prompt note—don't worry about us—something must turn up, so it will. Just wish I could have made it to the sun before the cold sets in. Sending you a new Limited Ed. (painted covers): a colophon will be along later for you to glue in. Have been able to do only a few so far —there'll be 108 all told.

Warm good wishes
Kenneth Patchen

Chapter Twelve: A Voice of Fire (1950-1951)

To Henry Moe from Kenneth Patchen (GUG)

February 1, 1950
Old Lyme, Connecticut

Dear Mr. Moe:

Thank you very much indeed for your helpful letter of January 26th.

In view of the burden of your work at this season, it was doubly kind of you to offer to write to people for statements concerning the caliber of my writings: I can perhaps best show my appreciation by telling you that I am busy inviting such statements now.

I shall have a statement of my writing project in your hands by the 15th of the month, as well as copies of my recent books.

Again, thank you.
Sincerely yours,
Kenneth Patchen

To Henry Miller from Kenneth Patchen (UCLA)

February 1, 1950
Old Lyme, Connecticut

Dear Henry Miller:

Belated but warm thanks for that push at LIFE. They're a funny lot. Three times in past five years they've had photographers and reporters "doing" me—and nothing ever comes of it. Once they paid out about three hundred dollars on train fares etc. getting our friends from the countryside into New York. Padell has pretty well curled up his toes, simply died off, does nothing with my books, I've asked him for copies of the pamphlet you want but no soap. He took a bad beating with the fall of the English money, the big part of his business being done through there. Some day I'll have to shake things loose there, but that means going down to NY, something beyond me at this stage.

We have Wisdom of the Heart and Air-Conditioned Nightmare in English editions: love to have any others. Lent your books to a young x-GI in town, and now he's buying them.

I've heard nothing from that poetry fund yet.

Did you read my Red Wine and Yellow Hair?

Sincerely,
Kenneth Patchen

To Kenneth Rexroth from Kenneth Patchen (UCLA)

February 6, 1950
Old Lyme, Connecticut

Dear Rexroth

I haven't seen your new book, but have written Laughlin to send me a copy. Should be along soon. Look forward very much to reading it.

Miriam and I are thinking quite seriously of moving to California. I'm thoroughly tired of the cold. Perhaps by next fall we can manage trip. The thing to do if one cared enough would be to go off to the end of the world somewhere, remote island, S. American jungle, away from the doomed areas—if one cared enough to be alive after they burn off fifty-a hundred million. Even that would be a dim chance, for I don't see how the scientists can pull out of what they've started now, and that H. bomb stuff is like throwing the planet into the path of the sun. Unbelievable. You know, the Indians survived two glacial periods, span of something in the 25-50 thousand years, and they could very well get all this back.

As you've heard, my arthritis has been quite bad—sometimes I wonder if the army hasn't other plans for those 'miracle' drugs; just before the war's end the Germans were trying hog gland extracts on their airforce. Who knows? The government did take the ACTH and cortisone project on, and at that time, just before they took over, over a year ago, my doctor in NY told me I could expect treatment in 6 weeks. Funny.

I'm making an all-out effort to get a renewal of my 1936 Guggenheim Fellowship this year, and wonder how you stand with them, and if you'd be willing to drop Moe a letter recommending me to his committee. I phoned him and he suggested that I invite such letters. I'd keep the statement very quiet in tone and approach, if you do decide to send one—but you know as well as I do what those judges are, stuffily schoolish, correctly tailored. Letters are due in by the 15th of this month.

Sometime, when you feel up to it, I'd enjoy a word about your experiences European.

Our best to Marie and you.

Sincerely yours,
Kenneth

To Kenneth Rexroth from Kenneth Patchen (UCLA)

February 7, 1950

Dear Rexroth

The Jake Zeitlin suggestion is interesting—desert part better than proximity to L.A. In any case, our thanks to you and to him. (Remember some contact with Zeitlin when we were out there.) Setting our sights for definite move to coast in the fall. S.F. might prove too cold and damp, but, then, I may have some of the new medicines. As you probably know, Laughlin is off to Switzerland next Sunday. Still haven't Rexroth book. What is doing with those 100 Japanese poems you mentioned last year? Hope they're being published: I look forward to them.

Give our best to Marie.

Nice poem (by Ugeda Teshio) in the Von which came today. Nice in spots anyway.

Kenneth
Shall I get in touch with Zeitlin about that place?

To Kenneth Rexroth from Kenneth Patchen (UCLA)

February 12, 1950
Dear Rexroth

The Signature of All Things arrived yesterday. So far I've only had two-three hours with it, but it makes me feel more than ever that your head and your heart are in about as right a place as rain on a new wood's flower.

Drinking tea, watching our cat, listening to music, sun almost hot through window—jays squabbling back on the hill.

Thanks for the book.

Kenneth

To Kenneth Rexroth from Kenneth Patchen (UCLA)

February 12, 1950
Old Lyme, Connecticut

Dear Rexroth

Thanks very much for your prompt note to H. Moe. Now we can do a bit of waiting.

Figure if we do go out there it will be to some unfrequented spot in the southern part on the sea—if Calif has any such left now, might spend a little time up your way, but the dampness rules it out for any long run—or so I've been told. "Worry" about bombs, and other things we can't do anything about: it's a very big subject, as big as a pebble on a sandbank, and we're somewhere under one of the grains. I'm working on some new things which give me pleasure, but have to hold them small because the long drive is beyond my energies just now.

Europe, as you describe it, seems to be everywhere, which makes avoiding it easier.

The other day I had a lot of fun reading an "appreciation" of Ambrose Bierce by a little birdie-man called Alfonse de Castro...maybe it's in the library there. Something so absolutely ridiculous that it's good.

Our very Best to Marie and you,

Sincerely yours, Kenneth

To Henry Moe / John Simon Guggenheim Memorial Foundation from Kenneth Patchen (GUG)

February 13, 1950
Old Lyme, Connecticut

Dear Mr. Moe:

In making this application for renewal of the Fellowship originally granted me in 1936, I am sending you, in addition to the requested Plans for Work, two statements which I hope will prove to be of interest to your Committee.

Thank you again for your kind suggestions.

Sincerely yours,
Kenneth Patchen

***Note:** Enclosed with the letter were the following items...*

Plans for Work

I would use the period of the fellowship to write poems along the general technical lines of the majority of those contained in my recent volume, RED WINE AND YELLOW HAIR.

During the past few years I have felt myself moved to return to the more formal patterns of prosody, for in the practice of their laws and traditional spirit it has seemed to me that the contemporary idiom may be made to release certain fresh and vital tensions.

My impulse in the poems would be largely in the direction of the lyrical, as opposed to the more narrowly didactic mindscape which has figured in much of my previous work.

—Kenneth Patchen

Used with permission:

from the Preface to

ANTHOLOGY OF AMERICAN POETRY

(to be published by John Lehmann—London)

"Kenneth Patchen seems to me to have the makings of a poet of great importance. He has a passionate love for mankind, and, at his best, a voice of fire, which raise him far above the level of the small and fireless poets infesting the literature of our time."

—Edith Sitwell

Statement of M. S. Zimmer, M.D.—299 West 12 Street, N.Y. 14 (November 7, 1949)

This is to certify that Kenneth Patchen, of Old Lyme, Conn., has been under my care for the last five years for rheumatoid arthritis of the spine and lower members.

This has disabled him for the most part, with a marked limitation of practically all motion.

To Henry Miller from Kenneth Patchen (UCLA)

March 28, 1950
Old Lyme, Ct.

Dear Henry Miller

Yes, Ruth Stephan sent me 100 dollars, and Kathryn Meacham has asked me to send on books for a money-raising get together. The Stephan check came in the same mail with a turn-down from the Guggenheims, and two days after that Bollingen Fund sent their turn-down. I am very much aware now that all those "Award" things are not for the likes of me. Of late, not only are my books not reviewed, but—to give you an idea—the NY Times Bk Review refuses to print ads of them because "they are offensive to good taste." That makes me mad every time I think of it—freedom of press! the lying hypocritical bastards! Red Wine and Yellow Hair, a New Directions book: the Times refused to run Laughlin's ad of it. Had I been able I w'd have paraded up and down in front of Times Bldg protesting against those petty vicious shit-hounds. I drew up a petition for writers etc to sign and Laughlin offered to handle campaign; months passed and he did nothing. What can I do alone? Perhaps you will have some idea on the thing. I certainly think that some further protest should be made; talk about censorship! If you do think of an idea, let me know: only thing is, I want to make it fool proof and really hit them sweepingly and hard.

Didn't mean to get off on that track, but soon they'll have us shut up all down the line.

Do you know any artists who might like to have a shot at doing drawings for some little stories I've done? People with a robust, life-loving sense of fun. Please have them get in touch with me if you do—Little things I've been trying to keep my hand in with. If I could find right "illustrator" (though I want more creative approval than that implies), sh'd make couple nice little books.

———

I can't think of anything to say about all you're doing for me—embarrassed to take more money now that I have this much.

Sincerely
Kenneth Patchen

To Henry Miller from Kenneth Patchen (UCLA)

May 31, 1950

Dear Henry Miller

275 dollars from you through Chicago! Amazing—I don't even know how to think about it, let alone talk about it. And Kathryn Winslow writes that a group in Tenn. are thinking of holding a similar affair, inspired by S.F. and Chicago! God! if I get to Arizona, New Mexico or S. California—to write and in the hot sun!

Padell is sending you 50 copies of your little bk—you should have them by next week. Told him that you plan to use them trying to interest people—making it possible for me to get to S. West, so he's "contributing" them to the effort. (If by some slip there is a bill with them, please send it to me and I'll return it to him. People in his office might make the mistake of billing for them.)

My gratitude and best wishes.

Kenneth Patchen

Haven't been able to thank those Calif. Painters as yet.

To Henry Miller from Kenneth Patchen (UCLA)

July 9. 1950
Old Lyme, Ct

Dear Henry Miller

Waited answering your letter in hope of seeing it in proper light. But I'm afraid there's nothing clearer now. For ten years our living has been that I beg, lie, spit pretty up every sleeve within my range—so. Since my back started to act up (in 1937) we've relied less and spent less on doctors than anyone we know. In NY I had an appendix out—almost too late, because the warning pain meant so little to me—and now the treatment here. So. All I remember saying I wanted was to get out of the cold into the sun. How hard I tried last fall to bring that about! I must have sent appeals to thirty-forty people—But what's the good of continuing on in this way—

I see that I've not understood what you had in mind in your recent letters, the one enclosed, for instance; and as for making myself clear to you—a mess, a botched mess—

So in the name of friendship I ask you to forget this particular concern for me, this money-raising thing: now and all. It's no good for either of us. Forget it.

Black clouds out of the Pacific—

All my good wishes to you.
Kenneth Patchen

To E. E. Cummings from Kenneth Patchen (HAR)

August 4, 1950
Old Lyme

Dear Cummings

All in undue time enclosed carbon of little tales has been put in halfway readable state and I feel bold to act on your invitation that I send these little "strained, unintelligible and boring" pieces for your (when-mood-and-spirit-move-you) inspection. The generous estimate quoted represents the speed and efficiency of modern editorial methods, for Mr. J. Laughlin, whose it is, required only 24 hrs. for the germination and deliverance of it. Now considered solely in and of for itself this judmental feat must have commanded from me a sentiment of warm, nay, even feverish, admiration and awe—surely as a red-blooded 20th Cent. American citizen it would little avail or behoove me not to welcome heartily Progress along these lines; but alas Mine Editor, likely carried away—as one druged—by the speed and deftness with which he had welcomed my Ms. to the fold of the 90 and nine, had a mysterious change of head and rejected my little-taled offspring. Ah, didn't he realize that thereby he was placing me in real danger of missing some of the savor of what I like to call objective appreciation..! (One day I'll tell you about one aspect of this transaction which amused me not at all.)

Good old tried and true Padell will publish.

The day is beautiful here, full wonderful sun, and Miriam just came in from her lawn-mowing to ask that her love be sent along with mine to Marion and you.

Kenneth

Note: *The misspelling of "judgemental" and "drugged" is Patchen's.*

To Henry Miller from Kenneth Patchen (UCLA)

July 30, 1951
Old Lyme, Conn.

Dear Henry Miller

Perhaps on your way to Paris you could visit us. About two hours from New York.—Phone: Lyme 4-7536.

Every good wish,
Kenneth Patchen

To E. E. Cummings from Kenneth Patchen (HAR)

July 30, 1951
Old Lyme
Conn

Dear Cummings

Funny, your card arrived on first day since operation I've felt like scribbling off a few notes. Perhaps because we are near-neighbors again. (Of course, too, I feel nearly as smart as a baby now that I have mastered the difficult art of walking, nearly; but not quite for pleasure yet.)

We hope Paris was good. We pray both of you are well.

Miriam joins me in sending love to Marion
and to you.
Kenneth

To Karl Shapiro from Kenneth Patchen (PAP)

July 31, 1951
Old Lyme, Ct

Dear Karl Shapiro

Thanks a lot for your invitation to send poems to Poetry. As soon as I get a bit more strength back I'll put together a batch for you.

I am very grateful to you and to your wife for such generous efforts to help during my trouble.

Sincerely yours,
Kenneth Patchen

To Kenneth Rexroth from Kenneth Patchen (UCLA)

October 15, 1951

Dear Rexroth—

Holly* has communicated your kind message. We're leaving here 15th November with several stops planned to ease trip, so should arrive well before Dec. first in S.F. where Ruffs have offered to put us up until we can get breaths and begin apt. hunting. I had hoped to do readings in East and en route but find I haven't strength now: however, much appreciate your offer of list of college contacts and will copy it off when we see you.

Laughlin wrote me long months ago and again last week saying he wants to do a batch of my things in his Selected Writing series under your editorship. Of course I'd be very pleased to see that happen. I've done nothing about anything this past year: not able: slowly getting strength back.—The top we can pay for an apt is 45 per, and need a well-heated place. Just in case you know or hear of one.

We look forward to seeing you with much eagerness.

And thanks again—

Kenneth

***Note:** Reference is to writer Holly Beye and her husband artist David Ruff, good friends from Greenwich Village who had moved ahead of them to San Francisco.*

Chapter Thirteen: San Francisco (1952-1955)

To Henry Miller from Kenneth Patchen (UCLA)

June 26, 1952
377 Green Street
San Francisco 11, California

Dear Henry Miller

On the night of July 19 at Union Enspanola of Cal Hall in SF a group of people are meeting to protest the murder of Spanish workers now being carried out by Franco. Similar meetings have been held in France, England etc; meetings to which many prominent men in the arts sent messages of solidarity. Freedom has been running stories on the truth of the brutal repression in Spain and the voices which have been raised against it.

I intend to appear as a speaker along with seven or eight others from this area.

If you care to send a message—whatever the length—send it direct to me or to the chairman of the meeting, David Koven, 350 Wallace St, SF.

As you may know, we've been here since Nov. Still having a bad time—in and out of Stanford Hosp the past couple months; but the operation on spine done in New Haven has made it possible for me to walk again. Doctors say a couple more years to bring muscles and nerves back in play. We both look forward to seeing you but want to wait until some good time. Of course if you happen to get into SF we have lots of room for you to stay over...any time.

All our good wishes.
Sincerely yours,
Kenneth Patchen

To Karl Shapiro from Kenneth Patchen (PAP)
Poetry magazine, Chicago

July 23, 1952
377 Green Street
San Francisco 11, California

Dear Karl Shapiro

Thank you for your letter (posted July 16: received today) inviting me to contribute to the 40th Anniversary issue of Poetry.

I am pleased to submit the five poems whose titles are noted below.

Again, thank you.

Sincerely yours,
Kenneth Patchen

Enc

BUT OF LIFE?
ALL IS SAFE...
UNDER A TREE
BEAUTIFUL YOU ARE
THE UNANSWERING CORRESPONDENCES

At the moment I'm in the midst of receiving treatment in and out of the Standford [sic] Hospital.

To Karl Shapiro from Kenneth Patchen (PAP)
Poetry magazine, Chicago

September 4, 1952
377 Green Street
San Francisco 11, California

Dear Karl Shapiro

On August 2nd Poetry accepted five of my poems for its special issue: Beautiful You Are, The Unanswering Correspondences, But of Life?, All Is Safe...and Under A Tree.

Today I received proof of only one of these poems.

Will you please see that the proper proof is sent me.

With all good wishes
Sincerely yours,
Kenneth Patchen
Incomplete proof returned herein

To Marion and E.E. Cummings from Kenneth Patchen (KPA)

KENNETH PATCHEN
377 GREEN STREET
SAN FRANCISCO 11, CALIFORNIA

Sept 4

Dear Marion and Cummings

I have to report that while SF is full of fine hills and bridges its residents are nutty, by and small. Dry, unattractive, dull rot. At times I almost do scar myself in sour on this "inhuman" race. Miriam is so rich of fine people within her that she does not at all recoil – ever, really – as I do. Our apt is newly painted burnt orange (little gray) and our windows look out across the City and the harbor. Next week my Detroit mother-in-law visits: she will take a 16 yr old's fun on her big trip.
Miriam has a job in a dept store, cosmetics counter; goes to a typing class in evenings. I did some time in Stanford Hosp, where they managed very skillfully to tear a gob of scar tissue loose, etc, etc. Spend 3 hrs there each wk now. Soon graduate from taping to a patented belt. Wonder is, even with their help, I'm still on my feet and walking about.
We were very happy to receive Cummings' letter.
Pray that the summer has been good to you!

We send our love
Kenneth

To E. E. Cummings from Kenneth Patchen (HAR)

September 18, 1952
377 Green Street
San Francisco 11, California

Dear Cummings

Thank you.

Never did we need an "the enclosed" so much/ for so many reasons.

Absolutely not once did one come precisely at that moment when the fullest power for good might be realized. It was the turning point: of that I have no doubt! Now we shall manage very nicely...good, good, good!

What fortunate people, the John H. Finleys, Jr.

Miriam and I send our love to
Marion and to you

Kenneth

Boston's beautiful ghosts keep her more alive than most(s)

Postcard to Kenneth Patchen from Dr. & Mrs. Alex Comfort(KPA)

Dec 15th 1952

Thankyou for a very jolly card. We wrote to an old address, & I'm most glad to have your new one & hear that K. is getting some treatment. The world today can't afford not to have him writing: he's too badly needed. I'm busy enough with my work & writing, to which is added a crushing amount of anti-war committee work of various kinds. But at the end of 1952 I do feel that we are succeeding in realising the lie in our National Anthem about "frustrating their Knavish tricks" (I don't need specify whose—it's always the same They) & may be able to get back a little to the pursuits of peace.

Every good wish to you wish to you both from us all
Alex (& Ruth & Nicholas)

Note: *Quote is from the National Anthem of Britain: "...Confound their politics,/Frustrate their knavish tricks..."*

To Henry Moe, The John Simon Guggenheim Memorial Foundation from Kenneth Patchen (GUG)

January 17, 1953
377 Green Street
San Francisco 11, California

Dear Mr. Moe:

This is an application for a renewal of the Guggenheim Fellowship granted me in 1936.

Should I again be honored by your Committee of Selection, I would devote the year to the writing of poetry (possibly in Europe).

Sincerely yours,
Kenneth Patchen

P.S. Under separate cover I am sending several items which I hope will be of interest to you.

***Note:** Patchen included the following press release from The San Francisco Museum of Art.*

SAN FRANCISCO MUSEUM OF ART
PRESS RELEASE

WAR MEMORIAL
CIVIC CENTER
HEMLOCK 1-2040

FOR IMMEDIATE RELEASE

KENNETH PATCHEN, POET, WILL GIVE READING AT SAN FRANCISCO MUSEUM OF ART

Kenneth Patchen, the well-known poet, who has recently moved to San Francisco from New York, will read selections from his poetry at the San Francisco Museum of Art on Thursday evening, November 13, at 8:30 p.m.

Mr. Patchen, who was born in 1911, published his first book in 1936 and the number of his works in both poetry and prose now numbers over thirteen. Critics and readers alike have been enthusiastic about the range and power of Mr. Patchen's imagery. When his "Selected Poems" were published in 1947 by New Directions, James Laughlin called him "the most compelling force in American poetry since Whitman," and when "Pictures of Life and Death" (1947) was published, the San Francisco Chronicle's review said: "Kenneth Patchen is one of America's most unusual and powerful contemporary poets.... One critic has compared him to Blake. The comparison is an apt one."

Some of Mr. Patchen's other books are: "Cloth of the Tempest"; "The Teeth of the Lion"; "Sleepers Awake"; "Panels for the Walls of Heaven"; and "An Astonished Eye Looks out of the Air." Henry Miller has written a tribute and critical appraisal of Mr. Patchen, which is titled, "Patchen: Man of Anger and Light".

Tickets for the reading are available at the Museum at the following prices: Public, $1.25; Museum Members, $1.00; and students, $.75.

To Marion and E.E. Cummings from Kenneth Patchen (HAR)

Note: *Probably from 377 Green Street, San Francisco*

Dear Marion and Cummings

You ask about the weather here. SF has not one but perhaps seven climates; from section to section, sun-belt to cloud-, there will be on almost any day a difference of as much as 10 degrees; and while say the "Mission" district is flooded with a dry warmth, that of Telegraph Hill (where we live) or Russian Hill will be swirled under with a wet cold fog. But mostly this year there has been no winter to speak of in the sense of keeping the gas heaters on for weeks on end as we had to do last, but in the sense of relaxed comfort no one could really imagine himself in any other season either. Of course we are excellently situated to enjoy whatever bad weather comes along, and it is only when we get down into the "flats" where the sun is that moments of misgivings assail our hardened sensibilities. But the worst thing is that the winter that is not badly winter continues right on through the year with the general effect of an air conditioning system operating full force just above the city. Actually it is no place for people with even mild bone trouble. Down coast as you know the sun is hot, wonderfully hot, but I think for any long period distressingly so. My Florida would be a good wood fire in a wellbuilt house no matter where.
Miriam is confinedly occupied with her job and with making changes of clothing for it -- only dark colors may be worn. She gets home about 6:30 each day and I have ready some chops and salad -- early to bed, early to rise. Perhaps twice a week we see people we knew in New York. My little Fables, which Cummings read, are finally being printed -- in Germany: "for distribution" in the US. We wonder all the time how you are. We can guess that Cummings is glad to be over the lectures. Will they be printed?

Our love to you.

Kenneth

To E. E. Cummings from Kenneth Patchen (HAR)

May 10, 1953
377 Green Street
San Francisco 11

Dear Cummings

Yesterday a large youthful yellow-orange creature followed Miriam home from work and likes look staying on with us, golden eyes, bricky soft footpads and all. We are <u>not</u> naming him Pikku Tuttava, Lansi Wiarras, Pieni Kultaparta (or even Touhanenyalkapappamotoa) ...Finnish of Little Friend, Western Stranger, Little Golden Beard (A 1000 Feet Of Tape Worm); but we'll come up with something.

And speaking of touhanenyalkapappamatoija reminds me that even though the wearing of chair-back brace and weekly injections of novocain seem to help the doctors at Stanford Hosp are talking x-rayishly of another operation...same place, same complaint. That makes bad sense to me...nothing doing.

Funny thing, about three months ago I started off casually on what I thought was a small bit of writing, really quite without special problems..and I got so involved in a sort of tug-of-war with that little "small bit" that only now do I have the manners and grace to admit myself defeated..when the joy went out of it I should have known that the touhanenyalkapappamatoija would take over.

We hope everything good for Marion and Cummings.

Our love to you
Kenneth

To E. E. Cummings from Kenneth Patchen (HAR)

May 27, 1953

Dear Cummings

What shall I say? It is awkward.

To thank you—yes, with all my heart, thank you—and then...to beg a favor.

But I must.—Don't send me more money.

I wanted to send the last right back; but couldn't. That is not the proper order of things. Let me get money wherever, whatever, whomever—but not from Cummings. That is not right. It is not right.

He gives—he sends—not money.

My respects.
Kenneth

To E. E. Cummings from Kenneth Patchen (HAR)

June 18, 1953
377 Green Street
San Francisco 11

Dear Cummings

Strange. We never see the NY Times Bk Review. So the other day the most unlikely and likeless person at Miram's store presented her with a copy. And that copy of an organ usually rife with the most sour and cheerless notes, contained one which gave us joy. It carolled that a new Cummings' book would soon be taking its important place in our lives. Wonderful news!

Our love to you and Marion.
Sincerely yours,
Kenneth

That little orange-yellow fellow went (we guessed) back to his own rightful home. So I went out and got three sweet potatoes, placed them in qt jars of water, and behold! beautiful, delicate and tiny green leaves. —And this in addition to two Ti plants which have been in fine leaf since last November!

To E. E. Cummings from Kenneth Patchen (HAR)

July 31, 1953

Dear Cummings

My father always dreamed the old American dream of having "a little place in the country—a few chickens, table-size garden, maybe half dozen fruit trees, a goat..." And now I'm doing the same: though all I mostly want is to be beside a little river that flows very quietly between a meadow and a woods. But my father is seventy-five and works in a furnace factory and lives on a main highway that runs from one mill town into another—and when he came to visit us in Connecticut three years ago he had added beekeeping and rabbits. Perhaps I shall have the river be just a bit more quiet.

A threat of strike at Miriam's store has lifted somewhat and to celebrate we have added a tiny black kitten to our household.

We hope that you and Marion are having a fine summer.

Sincerely yours,
Kenneth

To Kenneth Patchen from New Directions (NDA)

February 25, 1954
Dear Patchen,

The revised revises (4th set), with the new inter-paragraph spacing, went off to you airmail Tuesday night. As you will gather, your letter of the 5th February did arrive in time so that we could order this spacing made.

I was not sure, however, what the situation was about the responsibility for the extra cost entailed, and perhaps we should leave this anyhow until we have all of the sets of proofs in hand. Certainly on the 17th November ones to which you referred I can find no indication that these spaces are to be inserted. There is a great deal of marking for spacing, but it is all, as far as I can read it, concerned with the spacing between the last letter and the first period in your ellipses.

I note that you have not written about the problem brought up in my letters of the 1st and 3rd February about the extra cost for the whole edition that would be incurred if we print on heavy paper for the "Painted Edition." Am I to take it for granted that you want to abandon the "Painted Edition" idea?

I hope sincerely that this time the proofs are the way you want them. Please return the earlier corrected set with this last set, and both of course as soon as possible.

Very best, and cordially, as always,
Robert M. MacGregor

To James Laughlin from Robert M. MacGregor, employee of New Directions (NDA)

February 26, 1954

James, This may give you a suggestion of the great patience I'm maintaining as far as our friend KP is concerned. The last set of proofs were necessary, when after pages had been made up he demanded that extra spaces be placed between each paragraph as on his manuscript. I said we'd break up the furniture only if he'd be willing to pay for it, since he had seen three proofs and this was the first time he had mentioned the point. His reply was that he was sure we had mentioned the space business, particularly on his Nov. 17th proofs.... He of course isn't going to be happy about anything, and that is probably the nature of the guy these days. I'm certainly glad we're only trying to do one kind of poem, which at least has some homogenous style. Trying to satisfy the vague typographic desires for the SELECTED WRITINGS volume would be a strenuous course in purgatory.

Bob

Review by Robert Creeley
from *The Black Mountain Review*, Volume 1, Spring 1954

Fables and Other Little Tales, by Kenneth Patchen: Jonathan Williams, Stuttgart, 1953; $3.25

Another prose book by Kenneth Patchen brings up all kinds of memories—dull as that occupation often is. But Patchen was always unclassifiable, his earlier books were an excitement altogether separate from what, say, Henry Miller amounted to. There was a wild kind of purity to them, and a conception few men would have dared to attempt.

All of this is too simple to say. The old gimmick of breathing heavily about a man's past performances is too often an excuse for ignoring him all the same. In Patchen's case this has been so much the fact that it is tantamount to insult, finally, to invoke these older things at the expense of what he is now doing.

The new work is not a simple matter. For once, I think, it is legitimate to speak of Patchen himself, i.e., the man writing this book, and the particular problems with which he has been damned through no fault, certainly, of his own. Various appeals for medical help for him have of course appeared from time to time in almost all of the magazines—though the response to them has been hardly enough. For a long time Patchen was thought to be suffering from a form of arthritis, until finally it was found that the cause of all the hell he had gone through with his back came from an 'exploded' disc, in the spinal column. An operation partially helped this—but he is far from done with it. And the same need for money, for medical expenses, continues.

What that has to do with this present book may be vague—though I doubt it. We ask a man to tell us what he knows, and what Patchen knows must be pain, constant pain, pain moving, sitting up or trying to, pain walking. Every single day of his life. It's not a question of 'excusing' the flaws, call them, of this book—or even of feeling that, after all, the man we had known, with his incredible tenderness, and gentleness, is at last a victim even of that world he believed in. He still is there, very much there. And if it is, or seems, by inversion—a care turned inside out—I hardly think this can be called the end of it.

The tone in the book is neither very 'funny' nor anything else. It seems to me almost ugly, and almost necessarily so. What else? The punning, the discontinuous sequence etc.,—he is not the first man to call attention to horror, to the horror now on us, by the use of its own methods. It is that things don't 'follow', not now,—that you begin saying this, you end saying that. And who knows why, in time? Perhaps that is very far from either Patchen's intention, or, better, the book's actual point, but it is a sense that comes very strongly from it.

> "Never mind that," interjected the impatient Kraken. "Those pleasant little minnows there—" indicating the orphans, who were now contentedly belting one another with planks their steaks had come on, "I know damn well that their shoes will fit me. Only thing is, I wouldn't want to hurt their feelings...so I guess I'll have to eat them first."

In defiance of the jacket blurb, the book is anything but "sad, beautiful gaiety." But it may well be the beginning of, and the reasons for, an attack. Toward the end of the book he writes: "Every stick points two ways, and people like you and me have either got to get an easy, knowing grip on the dirty end or else let go altogether..."

Telegram to E. E. Cummings fom Kenneth Patchen

October 14, 1954
SAN FRANCISCO CALIF

E E CUMMINGS
4 PATCHIN PL

LOVING RESPECTS OF MIRIAM AND KENNETH PATCHEN TO YOU ON THIS DAY
UNSIGNED

To Henry Moe, The John Simon Guggenheim Memorial Foundation from Kenneth Patchen

January 22, 1955
377 Green Street
San Francisco 11
California

Dear Mr. Moe:

I wish now to apply for a renewal of my Guggenheim Fellowship. volume of prose poems, THE FAMOUS BOATING PARTY, I have completed a verse collection which will be released in 1955 under the title POEMSCAPES, SONGS AND PROVERBS. Also, for specially Since the publication early last year by New Directions of my printed and bound editions of my FABLES and THE FAMOUS BOATING PARTY I have done one hundred individual double-cover paintings. An exhibit of these books will take place at a local gallery. On December 22 I gave a reading of my poems at the San Francisco Museum of Art under the joint sponsorship of San Francisco State College and the Museum; and twice during the past year I was presented in half-hour readings by the listener-subscribed FM radio station KPFA in Berkeley.

My present plan of work will take me deeper into an absorbed investigation into the harmonies latent in the union of certain ever-recurring tonal elements of ordinary speech rhythms with the most rigid observance of syllabic weight and counter-weight measures which have been the characteristic dynamics of prosody in English since Elizabethan times.

Respectful regards to you.

Sincerely yours,
Kenneth Patchen

To E. E. Cummings from Kenneth Patchen

April 9, 1955
377 Green St
San Francisco 11

Dear Cummings

Miriam has told you how happy we are to have the Collected Poems. Wonderful, a day to day joy!

Things are much the same here—perhaps even a little more so. The doctors have (as you see in the enclosed) abandoned me to the cutters; but this experience I shall probably avoid—a bed in a ward goes at 33.50 per day, for just the bed. And I was told privately that that six weeks in hospital might run to double or even triple that. —Spinal fusion.

Reading of the bad winter in the East, we have wondered how you and Marion were faring I can imagine that you are looking forward to Silver Lake!

Miriam is well—on the job as usual.

We send our love.

Sincerely yours,
Kenneth

To E. E. Cummings from Kenneth Patchen (HAR)

May 2, 1955

Dear Cummings

Please forgive me for not thanking you sooner for your kind letter and for the helpful gift of money. I have been shuttling back and forth with various "tests" at Palo Alto Clinic. A hideous bus ride "down the peninsula" to hideous Palo Alto—the route of the commuters who must all be deaf dumb and blind. A sort of protective discoloration. What a mess of "miracle mile" emporiums featuring New England-styled antiques made of chrome and plastic rubbing jowls with "used car lots" (brand new cars!—some gimmick for beating taxes) and filling stations. And everybody says it's beautiful. Just like old 'Crisco by the Golden Fake is a city of "refinement and culture." Brrr-other!

I am working on some things done on Japanese paper for portfolio presentation. Or really just to be doing them. From not reviewing my books they've advanced to not even noting their publication. My last three books got exactly four reviews that we know of between them. And I'm the fellow who from time to time hopes to get one of those prize committee awards! I sometimes am almost led to think that in some way I'm out of step...

Once again, thank you! And Miriam joins me in sending our love to Marion and to you.

Kenneth

To Kenneth Patchen from Lawrence Ferlinghetti

June 11, 1955

City Lights, 261 Columbus Ave.
San Francisco, CA

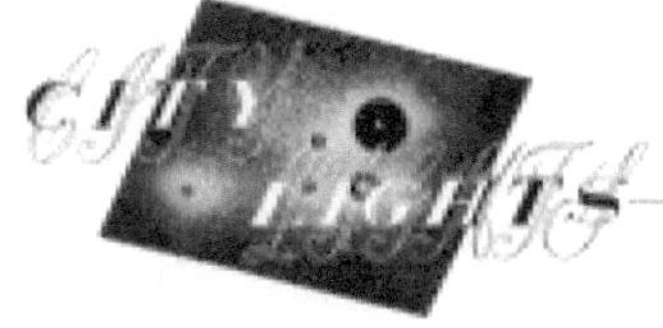

June 11, 1955

Dear Kenneth –
Since I don't know whether your in the hospital or not right now, and since I am hesitant to jangle your telephone and interrupt life-in-progress, I'm writing this to ask if you have any neglected or otherwise unprinted manuscripts which you would let me have for publication in the Pocket Poets Series which I'm going to publish at the Bookshop.... With much conceit I am going to publish my own poetry first in the Series; and David Ruff is going to print my book. The idea is to publish a series of pocket books at low prices (50 to 65 cents) for shall we say "popular" consumption.... So if you have a manuscript suitable for a 34 to 36 page booklet, I'd be much interested to see it.
With best salutations and regards, hoping your health is improving. Yours – Lawrence Ferlinghetti

***Note:** An historic note from soon to be publisher Lawrence Ferlinghetti inviting Kenneth Patchen to be part of City Lights Books' Pocket Poets Series. Patchen's **Poems of Humor and Protest** and **Love Poems of Kenneth Patchen** would become Numbers 3 and 13 in the series.*

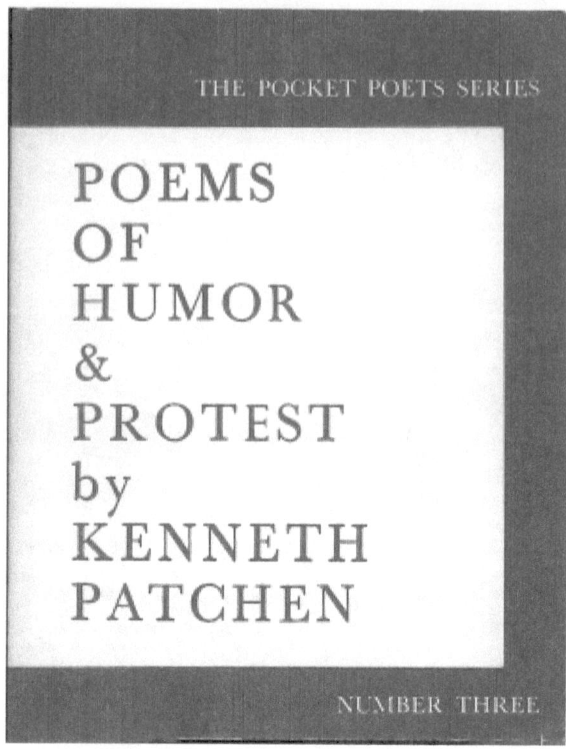

To James Laughlin from Kenneth Patchen (HAR)

July 31, 1955
377 Green Street
San Francisco 11

Dear Laughlin

You were good enough to ask me to keep you posted about my situation in regard to efforts to get the green light for another session with the surgeons. Finding that I could bring nothing off through a few indirect appeals for assistance, I have been working away against the advice of doctors on a creative project which should bring in some money later on. Perhaps too late to affect the issue of hospitilization, but certainly not to be a factor in my continuing struggle to pay for stop-gap medication etc. And I may say that the doctors were far from objecting to my tackling the problem headon; that they applauded—what they didn't like was the nature of the project, which called for a certain amount of bending, lifting, and general physical strain. What I have done are two portfolios of handwritings and drawings on Japanese papers 11 ½ x 14 ½ in silk screen reproduction. 17 such pages in each portfolio—two color runs—400 portfolios in all—ten dollars apiece. Did anything comparable exist, the asking price would be many times this: but I've got to try to make sales without proper facilities, and without time to wait for the usual word-of-mouth activity which has sold my things in the past. Anyway, I think that you will be agreeably surprised when you see GLORY NEVER GUESSES and THE CLOCK-BEAR (the names I've given the collections) when you see them within a month-six weeks. And at the time we launch these I'll have a go at marketing my painted books. Talk about light under a bushel—what a fanfare there'd be if one of the academic toadystools had done these things! That you and a few other people like you know it must be my satisfaction for the present; and I can't say that that is a small satisfaction.

I note in my last ND royalty statement that at the first of the year there were only 164 copies of SELECTED POEMS left from the 2nd ed. Isn't it time to think of another printing? I'd like it brought up to date—almost ten years has passed since the selection was made. I can't make up my mind whether the time has come to begin thinking of a COLLECTED or not; I seem to be about the only one who hasn't one—several people have expressed surprise that one hasn't been done. But as I say, I don't know; what do you think?
Auden when he was here said that he thought some sort of "splash" should be attempted if I am to get any of my share of the award monies being handed out. He went so far to say that he himself was on some committee and would welcome a "splash" which he could turn to use in convincing fellow members on my behalf.

And WC Williams while here mentioned that a couple people had mentioned a campaign of silence—or perhaps the phrase was "the silent treatment deal"—set up by the college clique against me and others. Of course the issue here is not one of reputation—who really wants to stand anywhere on a stair already occupied by such luminaries as..excuse me!—it is one of simple survival for oneself and for the standards one would live by. The rest of it is all too obviously "their" affair. So be it—and proceed.

Back on the subject of a "splash"—it occurs to me to wonder whether a solution to your problem of not being able now because of increased costs to make good on your long-time commitment to publish me in your Selected Writings Series might not be found by transferring a scaled down version of the projected volume to the New Classics Series, running Rexroth's selection and introduction but limiting the material to prose. I think that such a book of Selected Prose would have a readymade audience judging from the numbers of people I hear from or of who are still beating the underbrush in hope of scaring up somebody "who will get those squares to read ALBION MOONLIGHT!" (The last a quote from a fellow in Los Angeles who plays in a touring jazz band—and I know from many hands that it does tour.) Funny the quarters a crusade like this one gets into—for instance, a couple months ago a young woman turned up who wanted me to accept to become one of six letter writers allowed her brother under conditions of a life term for murder at Sing Sing. The two, great fans of mine—a phrase most apt in her case for she was and is a dancer in burlesque. And black as coal, by the way. But perhaps I digress..

It now seems that I will be admitted to the Stanford Hospital in Palo Alto late in September for treatment and conditioning calculated to ease the shock of surgery and/or ward off somewhat the damage expected should my circumstances make still further delay of surgery necessary. Either way this in itself will be a staggering expense. I really don't know what else I can do to help myself. Perhaps Alphaonega, the God-Goddess of Fortune, will see how hard I have tried and smile down upon me.

My best to you.
Sincerely yours,
Kenneth

To E. E. Cummings from Kenneth Patchen (HAR)

September 26, 1955
377 Green St
San Francisco 11

Dear Marion and Cummings

Thank you from my heart.

We have no way of knowing what will happen. At the moment the doctors concern (as far as we know) is to attempt to check the decline of sight, and if possible to restore it; and to control the diabetes—things you know from Miriam.

For the rest, there is the frightening uncertainty, and the need on my part to do what I can to be prepared with money etc should the situation suddenly demand it. The bad thing there is that I feel quite numb and directionless—I can only pray that strength returns to me—But you know from experience what is going on here.

You have helped so much, so very much.

Kenneth

To Henry Rago of *Poetry* magazine from Kenneth Patchen (PAP)

November 7, 1955
377 Green Street
San Francisco 11

Dear Henry Rago

Kathryn Winslow's follow-up letter came this morning, and it makes me wonder whether the ad copy I sent you covers your intention in offering me the space. Perhaps I should have done a two-part ad, getting the two new Painted Books into the second part. I kept the copy down to one feature because I felt it would have more impact that way, and because to make a mail out of here on Sunday I had to go with the half hour or so I had to do it in. At any rate, now after receiving a fuller picture from this morning's letter, it occurred to me that you might want to tack on the sales announcement of the Painted Books editions to the porfolio ad page; so I send on the mailing piece on the Painted Books for you to include particulars and prices if you like. I'll write you of my deep appreciation for your great generosity a bit later.

Sincerely yours,
Kenneth Patchen

Will you in proofing ad please correct this phrase... "by the poet and the painter" etc to read..."by the poet and the by the silk screen artist." (This eliminates the name of silk screen man, which now seems pointless to mention here.)

To Henry Rago from Kenneth Patchen (PAP)
***Poetry* magazine, Chicago**

November 18, 1955
377 Green Street
San Francisco 11

Dear Henry Rago,

Here is the corrected proof. Kathryn Winslow has told me of your labors to extend the copy into a more comprehensive and compelling form, and I now see for myself how successful you were in doing this. My thanks for this too!

In the past few weeks my wife's condition, which had shown marked signs of improvement after the initial attack of Multiple Sclerosis, has again manifested symptoms of a nature to call for more frequent trips to the clinic in Palo Alto, and to the coordinating doctor in the city here. Consequently I have not been able to properly thank you and the other editors for this most warming act of helpfulness; however, as a token expression of my gratitude, I am sending copies of my new Painted Books for inclusion in POETRY'S office library.

My deep thanks.
Sincerely yours,
Kenneth Patchen

To E. E. Cummings from Kenneth Patchen (HAR)

December 7, 1955
377 Green Street
San Francisco 11

Dear Marion and Cummings

After a period of gradual easing of symptoms, Miriam's condition has started a return to its first position; and to arrest this the doctors have stepped up the dosage of cortisone, with the result that the diabetes has gotten worse, she tires very easily, etc.

Our efforts to sell the silk screen portfolio via the mail have been a fizzle: we sent out 700 mailing pieces on the Ford Foundation's Perspective's list supplied by Laughlin—four orders. The NY Times Book Review ran a newsy item about portfolio (without giving any address)—two orders from individuals, one from a store. And that looks like that.

We are now very busy putting together the pages of the second portfolio, and I am grateful that we have this mechanical work to keep us occupied. The stamping and sorting Miriam can do in bed—as she handled the addressing of the mailing pieces. It seems restful to her to be doing these things.

Forgive the cheerless tone—perhaps later on I can give you better tidings.

Are you well?

We have enough money for now.

Our love to you,
Kenneth

Chapter Fourteen: On Another Planet (1956)

To Marion and E. E. Cummings from Kenneth Patchen (HAR)

May 8, 1956
252 Bryant Street
Palo Alto, Calif

Dear Marion and Cummings

My operation is scheduled for May 28. Three months in a cast, then about six of just getting about. What haunts me is that during that time of helplessness, Miriam may have another bad attack. Her mother may come to be with her during some of my absence, but since Miriam refuses to tell her of the multiple sclerosis, her presence will probably be more of a strain than anything. Not that I don't completely see Miriam's point that to tell her would only awake new furies: her mother is the kind who would begin most actively to feel sorry for herself because of the raw and genuine grief she would feel over what has befallen her only child. She would fill this house with just the sort of tearful despair which illness feeds on; and somehow we have managed to achieve an atmosphere of hopefulness and day-to-day preoccupations. Although that becomes harder and harder for me to do. (In confidence, Miriam is beginning to have memory lapses, etc; some of which she is aware of, some not.) And of course in our present physical isolation, the flow or lack of it of outside activities—mostly centered around publishing—becomes more than usually important: so this is the moment when these things choose to dribble away into utter silence...except for a few of the most minor kind, the little hang-nail irritants which one would like to be quite shut of. For instance, Laughlin talked of paperback editions for a couple books, as being what he could think of to do to further any chance I might have with the various grants and awards; he accepted a new collection of my poems and was putting it into a printshop; he was going to talk to various people. Laughlin since November has not answered my letters —nothing. I've no idea why. From what seemed a warm concern to be helpful, the sudden and complete walkout. And so it has been all down the line—silence. At the outset of Miriam's illness in September I wrote to those people who had in any way shown an interest in me—among them Auden, MacLeish, Thornton Wilder—I stated what we had just learned about Miriam, and asked that they now put a hand out to the awards and grants people in the face of the new pressure on us, because as I said each of them had expressed a desire to help me, and moreover each of them in one way or another had raised the point that there were organizations which might most reasonably be disposed to consider my case. Not one of them responded. Not a word of any kind. Nothing. That for me is hard to understand. But the experience is valuable. It makes it much easier to adjust to the reality of the situation; which was brought home to me a week ago when a sympathetic and level-headed person came to discuss the ins and outs of Blue Cross benefits in connection with my hospitalization, and then later went into the question of what was to happen afterwards, and whether or not by that time we would be eligible to get on the relief roles. It may or not come to that, that is not my point; but at this moment, considering the absolute wall of silence and indifference on the part of those who could help if they cared enough to lift a finger, that is exactly what we do face. In fact, as I think it out, most of those to whom I have appealed would probably think the relief roles exactly the proper sort of award for someone who had the bad manners to dump a load of raw, bleeding flesh at their doorsteps. And they do have to be right, for such universal judgment must be based on something real. These are gentlemen of cultivation and discernment, much experienced in the congress halls of the finest democratic living: unanimous for conviction—very well. But I'd feel easier for them if I had some inkling of my crime. Going into an institution, one becomes perhaps too conscious of those meaningless acts of cruelty and vengeance which a state of helplessness normally provokes; but I see that to be charitable I must learn to project that awareness on a far wider screen. It is so much better for oneself to believe that they know not: terrifying to think that they do.

Forgive me these ramblings. It is good to get this off my chest.

We think of you often, and hope with all our hearts that you are both well and in good spirits.

Kenneth

To Henry Rago from Kenneth Patchen (PAP)
Poetry magazine, Chicago

May 9, 1956
852 Bryant Street
Palo Alto

Dear Henry Rago

Today mailed you the second and final offering of my work in silkscreen production—that is, final as far as this particular venture goes.

On May 28 I am scheduled for a second spinal operation; this one a fusion, which involves three months in a cast (about six weeks of that in hospital bed) and another three to six months of very limited movement. This with my wife's illness presents a rather unpromising picture.

So far I might well be on another planet in terms of support through foundations, awards, committees, etc.—for I have received no help of any kind whatever, not one penny, or the promise or prospect of any such awareness-in-aid of our worsening plight.

I inform you of this because of your magazine's most concrete and generous expression of concern with that plight: it seems to me fitting that you be told about the nature of our present situation.

Warm good wishes to you.
Sincerely yours,
Kenneth Patchen

To Henry Rago from Kenneth Patchen (PAP)
Poetry magazine, Chicago

May 15, 1956
852 Bryant Street
Palo Alto, Calif

Dear Henry Rago

Your letter of yesterday heartened us more than I can express in this hurried note. (I am just now in the thick of tests, briefings, etc, connected with my hospital entry and rapidly nearing surgery.)

Please know that I am warmly grateful to you and your staff for your most concrete expression of understanding and support.—And now to treat of the suggestions you make:

While I agree that my situation does call for an appeal to any and all sources which might promise help, I cannot bring myself now to believe that an open campaign of solicitation is the immediate answer. My past experience has been that the returns from such an appeal do not amount to more than a stop-gap lessening of pressure in terms of the real situation, which is one of a continuing need; and it does have the unfortunate effect of creating an impression that the problem is by way of finding an at least partial solution. It is a trickling away into the sand...To put it more directly: say that through your columns two hundred dollars came in, for that two hundred dollars I would be selling whatever chance I might have for a substantial and meaningful (in terms of my prospect for continuing need) sum from any of the several artists' awards and aid-in-need organizations. I speak from experience. It may be objected that a small help is better than a large one which shows no sign of materializing anyway; in the abstract sense this is quite true, but in the sense of a drowning man who is given a straw to keep him afloat it is not—the question is one which has to do with survival on the open sea, not in a duck pond.

But it would be serviceable from the stand of keeping my predicament in the open, so to speak, to have an item like the following printed in your New Notes:

Our readers will remember that Kenneth Patchen, after a campaign to raise the necessary funds was undertaken by a committee headed by T S Eliot, W H Auden, Thornton Wilder and Archibald MacLeish,—in 1951 underwent surgery for a spinal difficulty. We now learn that a second operation was performed on May 28th, and that Patchen will be confined for some months at the Palo Alto Hospital in Palo Alto, California.

I hope to be able in the next few days to devote time to the copy for the ad which you have again so generously made possible for us to have in <u>Poetry</u>.

So—in haste—thank you!

With every good wish,

Sincerely yours,

Kenneth Patchen

To E. E. Cummings from Kenneth Patchen (HAR)

Wednesday, June 20, 1956
PALO ALTO HOSPITAL
Room 255
350 El Camino Real
Palo Alto, California

Dear Cummings

Middle of the fourth week, with seven more to go here—in full body-cast (upper chest to knees): developed penicillin reaction, so am a problem of hives, sweats, etc.

Miriam visits me twice a day, a bad and strenuous strain for her. I battled and won (I hope) the fight against being "institutionalized." The nights are more or less impossible, as Marion knows so well.

My back was utterly collapsed, another disc slipped below area of trauma-break.

Murderously expensive since spinal nurses have been necessary during stress of allergic difficulty—floor nursing non-existent.

Told that I am on my way to becoming new man. I'm pleased about prospect. Non-seditive periods spent in reading, looking at Japanese prints etc.

Our love to you and hope you are both well
Kenneth

Head abuzz with work projects for Miriam and

Note: *The misspelling of "non-sedative" is Patchens. The postscript's abrupt ending is also Patchen's.*

To E. E. Cummings from Kenneth Patchen (HAR)

July 23, 1956
PALO ALTO HOSPITAL
350 El Camino Real
Palo Alto, California

Dear Cummings

What a splendid way to meet your little friend the chipmunk! We hope that Marion and you are having a fine peaceful summer. Today begins my 8th week in full body cast—4 or 5 to go. Developed a penicillin reaction which was so violent that all medicines had to be discontinued—with one exception...brandy ...which is my sleeping potion every bedtime. Miriam is tired—of course—but otherwise managing fairly well.

Our love to both of you.

Kenneth

Miriam asked me to enclose the clipping—she thought you would enjoy it.

Note: *The enclosed clipping reads as follows:*

Do young children learn unpleasant words more easily than they do pleasant ones?

No. Tests have shown that children from the age of five to nine learn pleasant words 10 times more easily than unpleasant ones; and it is twice as easy for them to learn words expressing bigness as words expressing smallness.

Note: *There is no indication in this letter as to the source of the clipping which was enclosed. Apparently it is from a magazine or newspaper.*

To Kenneth Rexroth from Kenneth Patchen (UCLA)

July 26, 1956
PALO ALTO HOSPITAL
350 El Camino Real
Palo Alto, California

Dear Rexroth

We've had a muddle of news that you've been having troubles too—whatever, our hearts are with you. My nineth week in hospital bed, and eighth in a full body cast (the devil's own garment!)—at least three more to go in cast. Surgeon found back much worse than anybody had figured—new discs out, old area completely collapsed.

Miriam is of course quite tired with the duties of ten to do.

Our respects and love to you.

Kenneth

To Henry Miller from Kenneth Patchen (UCLA)

September 15, 1956
852 Bryant St
Palo Alto

Dear Henry Miller

I'm out of the cast—into a steel-ribbed brace—with six months or longer of limited movement ahead. And tough digging to keep afloat with no income, and all I could come by gone to the hospital etc.

So trying hard to think of some ways and means—

Wonder if you could see your way to putting in a word for my prose books to your paperbacks publisher? Journal of Albion Moonlight and Memoirs of a Shy Pornographer are both free. (Laughlin talked of doing something in this direction, but nothing came of it.) I think the books would sell in paperback—but the trick is to get them in print.

All the best

Sincerely yours,
Kenneth Patchen

To Kenneth and Miriam Patchen from Wayne Patchen (KPA)

1190 Patchen Ave, Warren Ohio

December 16, 1956

Dear Children

Will answer your letter was glad to here from you, but would liked to have heard better news. Wish I was there where it is warm, don't like the snow and cold. Will try and go there next winter. Have just moved into my new house that I built since I came back from there. Think I will build another next spring. Jack stays with me he is going into the army Jan 22. The girls were in a real bad accident about a month ago both have broken pelvises. Suzann was the worst Joan is home but Suzann is in the hospital yet.
Love Pop.

Note: *Letter transcribed as written.*

Chapter Fifteen: The Woods Are So Full (1957)

To Kenneth Rexroth from Kenneth Patchen (UCLA)

January 26, 1957
852 Bryant Street
Palo Alto

Dear Rexroth

Yes, I do have a new book of poems with New Directions. As usual much delayed. First slated for printing in Holland, now in US. Laughlin arranged with artist (?) in Paris for drawings "to enhance appeal of book". Three months lost to that—drawings fakey botch. Even Laughlin admitted unwisdom of his brainstorm, on the eve of his departure for three months in India. Book is called WHEN WE WERE HERE TOGETHER. Then there's POEMSCAPES (printing now with J Williams). And another which he will release at the same time: poems and my drawings—50 of each—just finished them couple weeks ago—it's called HURRAH FOR ANYTHING.

March 31st our house will be demolished to make way for a new Clinic building. May leave these parts.

Miriam is store clerking again—with the grudging consent of doctors who know we have no other means of income at this time.

The penicillin "reaction" I experienced early on in my hospital stay continues to plague me; among other things, I'm allergic to all medicines—that was specially rough right after the operation, in the cast with huge welts over every inch of me. Told that it may take a year to get worked out of the system..

No, ND hasn't sent me any of your books—including the Japanese one.

Love,
Kenneth

To Henry Rago from Kenneth Patchen (PAP)

February 22, 1957
852 Bryant Street
Palo Alto, Calif

Dear Henry Rago

It now seems to me that one of the most constructive things I can do in my situation is to begin to explore the possibilities of a reading tour. The doctors advise me that my back should be sufficiently knit by early Autumn to stand whatever strain such a general trip would entail.

Perhaps it is not too much to hope that the directors and bookers of poetry readings would consider my candidacy with some interest: personal information leads me to the opinion that a not insignificant section of their audience would welcome an appearance by me. The thing is to find out. If there is indeed an interest, it is high time for the actual booking and working out of the route to be undertaken—I know that this scheduling is done well in advance.

What I would hope to achieve by this if possible countrywide swing, aside from what money I could make on it, would be to enhance my chances for grants, awards, etc. I must put my head outdoors and proclaim myself in whatever vivid way I can because our position continues bad—with no remedy for it in sight.

My reason in telling you this is the thought I have that you may be able to supply me with some information about the identity of the people to whom I should apply in this regard. At the moment I'm quite out of touch with respect to this activity. (Of course there is no difficulty for me in getting in proper contact on the West Coast: as a matter of fact, I have already been approached by half a dozen groups who learned through the SF Poetry Center that I was considering a reading tour.) It's the East, the Middle West, and so on, about which I'm in the dark. It goes without saying that I shall be most appreciative for any help you can give me in this; and that I am most sorry to bother you with it.

With warm good wishes,

Sincerely yours,
Kenneth Patchen

To Henry Miller from Kenneth Patchen (UCLA)

February 27, 1957
852 Bryant Street
Palo Alto, Calif

Dear Henry Miller

Ferlinghetti wants to do a paperback edition of Memoirs of a Shy Pornographer in a format similar to the New Directions Paperback Series. This pleases me of course because it may open the door on a broader audience, and also get some of my other books back to life. The book is planned for Fall release.

I am writing to ask if you would be willing to write an introduction for the volume.* Ferlinghetti thinks that one would help sales etc—and I naturally thought of you: the only other introducer I'd consider is Cummings, who never does such things. If you are willing—what I think might be most interesting for you to do, and most valuable for the purpose, would be a general, rather than a particular-to-the-book, essay on what you consider to be my contribution, place, etc, in the overall literary climate, European as well as that here. I could send you any of my more recent books which you may not have—publishers don't always carry out requests that books be mailed to people. (I'll have two new books out in a matter of weeks —one of nonsense poems with my own drawings, which I have a hunch you'll like a lot.)—Did you ever get that silkscreen portfolio of my poems?

I am now setting my sights on a country-wide poetry reading tour...to start in Sept...which I hope may do something to help our situation through sale of books, jog to grants chances—in addition of course to the money from the tour itself.

On top of all the tiring nuisance of that penicillin "reaction" which gives me about ten good minutes in the day, we've had to house-hunt in this overcrowded area because the place we're in is being torn down to make way for Clinic expansion. Finally found a little house on the outskirts of town, much too near two major highways but with a goodsized backyard for sunning.

After March 15 our address will be:
2340 Sierra Court, Palo Alto
Miriam joins her warm respects to mine.

Sincerely yours,
Kenneth Patchen

*Naturally you'd be paid.

To E. E. Cummings from Kenneth Patchen (HAR)

February 27, 1957
852 Bryant Street, Palo Alto, Calif

Dear Marion and Cummings

Our house will be torn down to make room for expansion of the Clinic, which owns this property. After much search, we finally found another house within our means—just inside the town's limits; it's very near two major highways and inconvenient bus-wise but it is blessed with a big yard where we can have flowers and lots of sunning. The housing shortage here gets worse by the way, so we consider ourselves very lucky to have unearthed this possible home-site. Miriam got a leave of absence from her job to join in, or I should say, lead the house hunt. It is my growing feeling that the job is beyond her strength, but the whole circumstance—in which the job is an important symbol, as well as what jobs ordinarily are—is much too complicated for any decision of mine to have any real bearing on the problems involved. All I can do is try what I can to remove some of the external pressure—the economic one in particular. And here I am hampered by the fact that that penicillin "reaction" has left me dragging along like a half-crushed slug; and the doctors are as much in the dark as I am in the twilight. More and more I know in myself that time will prove the only effective medicine here—and that I'll come round on my own.. as I must. But one thing I have thought to do for us is to begin to send out feelers and soundings in the direction of setting up a poetry reading tour for the Fall—as extensive as what fortune I have with scheduling committees will enable me to make it. (The doctor says that my back will have knit safely by then; and that I must decide whether to gamble on having the necessary strength and energy for the undertaking. He is all for my deciding on go ahead with it—contacting people etc.) The rub is that I don't know how one goes about such a venture: is there anything like a clearing house (or a clearing person) for these tours. I know of course that Cummings has restricted himself to invitational appearances, and even then has not consented to go too far afield; but I thought you might just be able to give me some tips or leads for the kind of thing I have in mind to do—that is, to read anywhere and everywhere that would pay me to do.

There has been a stir about a re-boom of poetry in San Francisco—complete with Life photographers. You've probably seen mention of it. It gave me the happy chance to turn the Life-rs away from the door...with a few comments about what I thought of SF, "SF poetry," and bilge sheets like theirs in general. So you see, I am not missing any chance to further my career.

I'll have a couple new books to send you soon.

Miriam joins me in sending love
to both of you

Sincerely yours,
Kenneth

To Henry Miller from Kenneth Patchen (UCLA)

March 6, 1957

Dear Henry Miller

Of course I understand.

Perhaps some time between now and the middle of the summer you can see your way to doing a little statement—just a couple-three sentences—which could be used on the jacket flap. And if you do, please get the date in somehow—like...On this such-and-such date etc—the reason for this is that more than a few times it has reached us that there is persistent gossip to the effect that Henry Miller no longer has any interest in my work.—If you don't get round to this, it'll be perfectly ok with me.

After March 15 our address will be 2340 Sierra Court, Palo Alto

So—all good luck with your work! And I hope only those people you want to see drop in on you. There are a lot of odd fish in these California waters.. a few have flopped in here, with never a thought that one might have something better to do than amuse their likes.

Always yours,
Kenneth Patchen

To Henry Miller from Kenneth Patchen (UCLA)

March 10, 1957
2340 Sierra Court, Palo Alto, Calif

Dear Henry Miller

What can I say—Your beautiful statement went to my heart. In the work I have ahead of me to do I hope you will find the best expression of my thanks.

We are hecticly transferring our things to the address above—I mean, at the moment; and I must get back to doing my share of it. But I did want to get this note off to you right off!

I know you won't mind if your statement gets used on two books—I'm rushing it off in hope that it won't be too late to get it printed on the jacket of my now-at-press Poemscapes...a work which I feel very close to.

My hand
Kenneth Patchen

To E. E. Cummings from Kenneth Patchen (HAR)

March 10, 1957
2340 Sierra Court, Palo Alto, California

Dear Marion and Cummings

I have written to Elizabeth Kray, as you so generously suggested I do. Thank you very much.

You will note that we have found a house. It's on the tract order, but clean and pleasant with a very large fenced-in backyard where we can enjoy sun and flowers and five little trees. No convenient shopping—of course everyone except us has a car, or two or three—and there's an awful highway, known far and wide as "Bloody" Bayshore, just a long block away; but our little cul-de-sac is in itself children-peaceful and mannerly under one of the most glorious reaches of sky—a sky, moreover, which from our windows we can see rests on the two beautiful mountain ranges. (It may be that I told you about the house before; there's been so much flurry with house-looking and now the moving, that I'm more than a little confused.)

We certainly pray that the hideous green-backed vultures don't entirely gobble up Patchin Place; our strongest hex on them.

A fellow has just come with a station wagon to cart some of our books and breakables over to the new place, so I must be off to help.

Again, thank you very much.

Our love to both of you
Sincerely yours,
Kenneth

To Henry Rago from Kenneth Patchen (PAP)

March 26, 1957
2340 Sierra Court, Palo Alto, Calif

Dear Henry Rago

Once again I am overwhelmed by your great kindness. I can not tell you how much it means to us.

Some time ago when I wrote to Cummings about my then quite unformed plan to set out on a reading tour, he suggested that I get in touch with Elizabeth Kray in New York—she handled several such trips of his—and ask her if she would act as my agent for the tour. I did write to her, but the weeks have brought no answer. She may be out of town, or whatever. I think it fair that I wait another week or so for word from her. (I gather that she is, among other things, the assistant director of the YMHA's Poetry Center.)

In the light of your many fine suggestions, offer of ad space, cautions and tips, I am sorry now, that I did offer to place my venture in the hands of a professional. We'll see. I'll let you know the moment I hear from Miss Kray. And if in a week's time I haven't heard from her, I'll consider her out of the picture.

You will note our new address. We're still in the throes of unpacking etc, so I can use the week's breather. Then I'll write to the people you suggest—taking special care to follow your instructions in regard to Mrs. Stevenson.

With my warmest regards—and thanks!

Sincerely yours,
Kenneth Patchen

To Marion and E. E. Cummings from Kenneth Patchen (HAR)

April 10, 1957
2340 Sierra Court Palo Alto, Calif

Dear Marion and Cummings

I think that I should tell you that I've had no answer from Elizabeth Kray—wrote two letters to her, the first about a month ago.

We are gradually getting settled in. I have a lot of work lined up but find my time muddied by too many trips to the clinic where newer and newer medicines are being tried to adjust some nerve disorder brought on (they guess) by the penicillin reaction. The most tiresome symptom is clothes soaking sweats that come on three or four times a day without apparent (to them) rhythm or reason. Miriam is busy with curtain making, our two black cats, and planting and sunning in our fine big backyard.

Our love to you
Kenneth

To Henry Rago from Kenneth Patchen (PAP)

April 11, 1957
2340 Sierra Court Palo Alto, Calif

Dear Henry Rago

I enclose Elizabeth Kray's letter, together with my reply.

Frankly, I find the whole thing rather cloudy and hit-or-miss. Rather than offering any reason for a month's delay in answering my letter, her coming trip would, in my opinion, have inspired just the contrary action. It occurs to me that what rules out her setting up a Fall tour is not the shortness of time but her absence from the scene. Be all that as it may—What to do? I don't know. What do you think?

Warmest good wishes.
Sincerely yours,
Kenneth Patchen

To Henry Rago from Kenneth Patchen (PAP)

April 26, 1957
2340 Sierra Court Palo Alto, Calif

Dear Henry Rago

My letter to Elizabeth Kray went unanswered—and as far as I know she sailed on the 17th.

I guess the best thing I can do in the circumstances is to find out in a direct way whether it is or is not too late now for me to go through with my plan for a Fall tour; that is, to take advantage of your offer of ad space to run something like

Kenneth Patchen Planning Reading Tour
Interested groups in Mid-West and East
are advised to make known possible
scheduling dates for this Autumn and/or next Spring
to Miss Gail Eaton, 2340 Sierra Court,
Palo Alto, California

Perhaps you will be good enough to add or leave out anything which to your experienced view would better serve the purpose. "Gail Eaton" is a name used by my wife from time to time on jobs etc.

At the moment I am rather knocked out of the running by a backfire of medicines—so please excuse brevity of this.

All good wishes.
Sincerely yours,
Kenneth Patchen

Postcard to E. E. Cummings from Kenneth Patchen
Note: Probably April, 1957

Dear Cummings

I received a letter from Miss Kray couple days ago, on the eve of her departure for Europe. She doubts that tour could be arranged for me by Fall: not enough time. That may will be that—later would throw me into weather which the drs, as of now anyway, believe beyond my capacity.

Warm and respectful good wishes
Kenneth

KENNETH PATCHEN'S

HURRAH
FOR
ANYTHING

(50! POEMS! 50! DRAWINGS! 50!)

the amazing little book
people are laughing themselves in love with
$1.75 a copy, from:

JONATHAN WILLIAMS · PUBLISHER
HIGHLANDS, NORTH CAROLINA

(who also publishes Patchen's FABLES,
$8.00; and POEMSCAPES, $3.50)

To Henry Rago from Kenneth Patchen (PAP)

August 12, 1957
2340 Sierra Court Palo Alto

Dear Henry Rago

I haven't written to thank you for the ad because we weren't aware that the July issue was out until last weekend when someone visiting happened to mention it. (Since we have a subscription, something must be amiss with the address used for us. No August issue, either. Can't think of any other reason.) Got the magazine from a store—the ad looks fine. Thank all of you again for it.

The days bring good and bad. It appears now that my plan for a reading tour will change into something that could be productive in a number of directions. Nothing definite as yet, so I'll save the details for later. But present arrangements call for me to go on a reading tour with a modern-style jazz band. I made a record with the band—ready in Sept. People got excited. Thing just sort of grew on its own, from this to that, finally into the tour idea. (You may or may not know that I pioneered the business of reading poetry to jazz with a series of tapes dating back to 1950. Interests me quite a bit.)

Anyway, I'll fill you in on the details when matters are quite settled.

The bad is that I am due for more surgery—this time not related to my back—to come up late this year. Tell you about that next time too. It's major but the doctors say that it will be all right.

My very best.
Sincerely yours,
Kenneth Patchen

To James Laughlin from Kenneth Patchen (NDA)

October 21, 1957
2340 Sierra Court Palo Alto, California

Dear Laughlin

Thanks for your letter of the 18th.
I am at work on the assembling of texts of poems for the 30 pages. "The State of the Nation" and "Do the Dead Know What Time It Is?" are features of the record (both in present NC selection); and to these I will add what is probably the most appealing poetry-music blending in the entire album—"The Lute in the Attic" So the tie-in to volume is very strong.
Archie Blyer came to the nightclub Friday night and was most interested and receptive to all my suggestions for a joint campaign with ND. I told him to contact you direct in Norfolk. I hope that you will have heard from him by now.
Of course When We Were Here Together must be spotlighted: it goes without saying that there is a lot of advance interest in it here—several little news stories about its soon release: in Chronicle, Examiner and News. Ads should have great pulling power in these papers...and any other publications anywhere.
(I mean, advertise all titles of mine—in print and forthcoming—with and through Cadence.)
We could and can make tremendous use of a flyer with photo and write-up accompanying checklist of my books—droves of people milling around wanting information about books and where they may be had. Not only nightclub etc, but in next weeks four big mass concert affairs are scheduled (for the Mondays club is closed).. and beyond that, when the college tour gets under way!! Can you get such a flyer printing with Cadence and bkst tie-ins?—When I send you the 30

pgs I'll give you a list of titles. (I simply haven't time to do the write-up material.)
All your ideas for working with Cadence on this are fine: hope you've made contact.
Good that you want to ready a comprehensive selected—we can get at that when we get some of these important first things into the hopper. And let me see your blurb for extended NC ed.
Perhaps you'll want to consider a wrap-around paper on WWWHT and SP—"The man who created a new art medium." "The man who has taken poetry into the world of big-time entertainment." "The creator—and still undisputed champ—of the exciting new art medium, Poetry-Jazz." "The poet who has captured the imagination of the country."

All the best.
Sincerely yours,
Kenneth

To Henry Rago from Kenneth Patchen (NDA)

October 27, 1957
2340 Sierra Court Palo Alto

Dear Henry Rago

Thank you for your warm note.

I think that the importance of the enclosed statement will be apparent to you from its substance.

So much harmful and quite irresponsible nonsense is being circulated that it has become important to me to set the matter straight—to the extent that it concerns me and my work—with as much dispatch as possible. So I hope that you will be able to print my statement in your December issue.

The Chamber Jazz Sextet and I are returning to The Blackhawk Nov 12; the earliest we could with concert commitments at Carmel, Oakland Civic Theatre (on week's bill alongside symphony orchestra, Bach choral group, ballet etc). at U of Cal, Stanford—then a swing through 15 Pacific Coast colleges.

Note: *The letter ends here, without signature. The enclosed statement to which Patchen refers follows:*

A Statement by Kenneth Patchen

What I have to say is said for the purpose of throwing light on a situation about which many people have expressed puzzlement.

My name and activities have not figured in recent publication coverage of "the San Francisco Scene" for the simple reason that in so far as I could I rejected all such identifications.

I refused to be interviewed or photographed by Life magazine in connection with their story; I ignored all similar requests for material and the like from The Evergreen Review, The Cambridge Review, etc.

Again, there is a simple, uncomplicated reason for this:

I am not and never have been "a regional poet."

Moreover, my participation in, and knowledge of, "the San Francisco Scene" is exactly zero.

My stay there was occasioned and colored by medical considerations; unfortunately those of a social or literary kind did not enter into it.

And now about "Poetry-Jazz"—

My views and attitudes have undergone a great change since I first experimented with it though taped readings in 1950 (in Connecticut, by the way):

I am convinced that the art direction may only be realized through the union of the poet's reading with music expressly composed for that reading.

The Chamber Jazz Sextet and I have made such a start.

It is Allyn Ferguson's distinction to be the first to have composed for this new medium; and mine, to have been privileged to share in its first public presentation.

This is for the record.

The rest may be left for such resolution as time sees fit to effect.

Palo Alto, California
October 26, 1957

To James Laughlin from Kenneth Patchen (NDA)

November 3, 1957
2340 Sierra Court Palo Alto

Dear Laughlin

Your letter of October 31—Surprised at your passed-on report from Cadence that record "will be ready shortly before Xmas." Shocked rather than surprised: after two previous delays.. but that pushes the release back a full month from the time told us, and really snows the whole thing under the Holidays scuffle.

Suit yourself about substituting When We Were Here Together for Orchards, Thrones & on contents pg: it was my thought that the just-published book would make a stronger appeal to purchasers as an untouched new item, and that greater attention could be drawn to it by a jacket mention that "Lonesome Boy Blues" was to be found in it. I would avoid spilling its contents around pointlessly: why I resorted to the devise of using Orchards in the weaker-draw position inside.

Of course I'm sorry to see my drawings torn from their continuators, the poems; were the situation ordinary I'd be obliged to No this. Use at least two.

Speaking of store tie-ins with bookings etc—What are you doing about the shops in SF where every day almost something re our Blackhawk appearances is in the ad or nightclub or columns section? I've seen no ND ads of WWWHT in any of the newspapers in this area. (To give you an idea of the pull of this thing, every night two radio jazz shows—KGO in SF, and KROW in Oakland—plug our Blackhawk and Oakland Civic Theatre engagements.)—Have you seen the comic strip "Gordo" in the last week-ten days? Its artist came to Blackhawk—was staying in Menlo Park, a town from here.

Made note of your West Coast salesman and will keep him informed of new developments. Bad if he and his two assistants aren't pounding about right now in this whole publicity-saturated area. Surely your office must have told them to hop: but there's no sign whatever that I know about that anybody is doing anything to take advantage of this situation.

And as a sidenote—For the past two weeks on his KPFA reviewcast Rexroth has been using the strongest language to get himself off the hook of having gone along with the fraudulent mess shoveled out from

the Howl-notoriety pile: "1956 will be known as the year Ginsberg and Co corrupted SF," he approvingly quoted somebody as saying. Now if Rexroth who has been in the thick of the thing there expresses himself so about it, what in all reason could determine me not to make it clear as I can that I don't now and never have had even the remotest part in it. As I have always said and shall continue to say, Rexroth is at this moment what he has been for some twenty years: one man keeping alive by the force of an uncommon intelligence and an equally uncommon gift and dedication to the art of poetry all claims which SF may justly advance for being a city of cultural importance.
When these foul little winds have blown off, there'll remain only what there was before: the person and the work of the one SF'an who makes the place important. Well, enough for that.
Sure, contact the woman on "7 Lively Arts"; although I seem to remember reading an item the other day about a scheduled jazz show coming up on that program. Thanks for your effort on this. Blyer of Cadence should have all manner of TV and radio contacts, but I have heard nothing since some long-ago talk about approaching such people as Steve Allen, Ed Sullivan et al about possible appearances for us. Gotham party sounds good if it works out in time to the convenience of the principals.

Photos I'm nearly out of—couple reading—but sent you one which may do.

All the best.
Sincerely yours,
Kenneth

To Kenneth Rexroth from Kenneth Patchen (UCLA)

November 4, 1957
2340 Sierra Court Palo Alto

Dear Rexroth

I think you will see from the substance of the enclosed statement why it seemed necessary for me to make it.

Wish I had the time to go into all the ins and outs, but since we've known pretty much the same pressures in this thing you better than anyone will appreciate my wish to combat the growing tendency in some quarters to turn a serious matter into a kind of monkey-on-a-stick affair.

Anyway, I sent the statement to Laughlin with the request that he issue it as a press release: he writes, "I read your statement to Miss Smargon ((a girl doing publicity for Cadence Records)), and she took a dim view of it. She asked me not to release it, so I am not doing so for the moment. She feels that the publicity the San Francisco group have been getting should be exploited, rather than placed in question. Etc. Etc."

In arguing against Miss S's strictly commercial approach to issues about which she knows nothing, I had occasion to say (to Laughlin): —this of course follows on points made out of what I consider to be the position I find myself in—"For the past several weeks on his KPFA reviewcast Rexroth has been using the strongest language against the fraudulent mess shoveled out from the Howl-notoriety pile; and he approvingly quotes somebody as saying, '1956 will be known as the year Ginsberg and Co corrupted San Francisco.' Now if Rexroth who has been in the thick of the thing there expresses himself so about it, what in all reason could persuade me not to make it as clear as I can that I don't now and never have had the remotest part in it.

"As I have always said and shall continue to say to anybody worth saying it to, Rexroth is at this moment what he has been for some twenty years: one man keeping alive by the force of an uncommon gift and dedication to the art of poetry all claims which SF may justly advance for being a city of cultural importance.

"When these foul little winds have blown off, there'll remain only what there was before: the person and the work of the one SF'an who makes the place important."

The woods are so full of so many waggy and quite irresponsible tongues that I wanted you to have this straight from me.

Miriam joins me in sending our love to you.
In haste.
Kenneth

Note: *The use of a double parenthesis symbol in the third paragraph of this letter follows exactly that of Patchen's use.*

From Kenneth Rexroth's broadcast on KPFA (UCLA)
November 10, 1957

"I have a statement from Kenneth Patchen which I'm not going to read. He claims that he and Allyn Ferguson are the first jazz poets. Obviously this was inspired by the management of the Blackhawk.

If Kenneth Patchen wants to be the first, for all of me he can. Since I'm not getting 1400 a week, he can be it all. As a matter of fact, at present I am not getting anything for it. I think he should not issue something in such bad taste.

He says he's not part of the San Francisco renaissance. Of course he is. He—I believe Henry Miller says the same thing—[laugh] Patchen couldn't function anymore in New York. He engendered nothing but hostility there. The fury created by the mention of his name to the members of the Morningside Heights set—Lionel Trilling gets running fits at the mention of his name. When he came here he was well received; people showed him the respect he deserved, and they were interested in his work. If he doesn't like that, it's too bad.

Whatever he says about it, he's doing it here—and he's getting a large sum of money for it. He could not have done it in Chicago or New York.

It's part of the ugly commercialism of this whole thing. It's obvious that his agents and the owners of the Blackhawk got him to issue this statement. Anyway, it's ill-advised.
Next week I'm going into Patchen's career..."

To Henry Rago from Kenneth Patchen (PAP)

December 4, 1957

2340 Sierra Court Palo Alto, Calif

Dear Henry Rago

I ran into a little back strain on the trip from Los Angeles which has had me taking it easy and worried since after a reading at the SF Museum of Art Friday I board a plane for New York where I shall be for an as yet undetermined time. (From 12/7th on anything urgent can be sent me c/o New Directions.) Of course I shall be in Chicago in the middle of the night; otherwise I'd phone you to say hello.

I see from your November 9th letter that I completely failed to get across to you my attitude re the SF mess: it is simpy this—the poet should resist all efforts to categorize him as a painted monkey on a stick, not for personal reasons alone, but because it does damage to poetry itself. I told you about the actual as opposed to the fictional situation as regards the reading of poetry to jazz here not to put anyone down or to put myself up but to demon-strate by case and example the fraudulent and cheap nature of the thing which was spawned here when the cameras of LIFE set up and staged their poetry-with-jazz sideshow thing in February, along with half a dozen other "cultural evenings with the bearded and besandaled denizens of San Francisco's lower-Bohemia"—including a striptease to poetry (which somehow hasn't been tagged as yet as a "new art form.") Unfortunately for sanity and truth my three weeks of record shattering in a major nightclub suddenly plunged all that fake and by then quite rancid fat into the fire: it stopped being what Rexroth in Downbeat is quoted as saying it was, "a harmless fad, like swallowing goldfish," and became something quite different indeed! And particularly different because there was money money MONEY in it! It's a sad, sad business. My whole point was that I didn't want publicity in a scene and situation in which from the beginning—when LIFE's cameras arrived—I had refused to have any part. (I can only hope that some of these people will come to their senses and realize that poets have something better to do than become exhibits in a tricked-out freakshow.)

Warm regards,
Kenneth Patchen

Note: *The letter ends here. Included with the letter, however—without comment by Patchen—is a clipping from Herb Caen's column—* "Baghdad-by-the-Bay" *in the Monday, December 2, 1957 issue of the San Franscisco Examiner. The clipping follows:*

...North Beach is shaking its collective shaggy head over *Time* mag's report (in its current issue) on the poetry-and-jazz rage. A real upside-down story. Kenneth Patchen, the only poet who's made any impact at all on the public with his readings, is barely mentioned...

Chapter Sixteen: One Day, When This Story Is Told (1958-1960)

To Henry Rago from Kenneth Patchen (PAP)

***Note:** This is a different sort of letter than usual, in that it is simply a copy of a press release—with a handwritten note by Patchen at its bottom. No date appears on it—but the content of the press release indicates that it was probably sent to Rago in late June or early July, 1958.Patchen was never able to go to Brussels.*

From: Ronald T. Johnson
1824 R Street, N. W. — For Immediate Release
Washington, D. C.

POET INVITED TO READ AT BRUSSELS

Kenneth Patchen has received an invitation to read his work in the American Theatre at the Brussels World's Fair.

As far as is known, this marks the first time a poet has been so honored. (The invitation came from the United States Commissioner General's office in Brussels, and was made by the Coordinator of the Performing Arts Program.)

Mr. Patchen, now a resident of Palo Alto, California, was born in Ohio; an honor student as well as star athlete, he attended the Experimental College of the University of Wisconsin. His first book was published in 1936, and in that year he won the distinction of being the youngest recipient of a Guggenheim Award. Since then Patchen's accomplishments have been numerous and varied; ranging from the production of over twenty books in both prose and verse, to the now much-publicized origination of the reading of poetry with jazz accompaniment.

His works have been translated into many languages; and recently his invasion of the world of nightclub entertainment has caused him to be described as "a one-man movement to bring poetry back to the people." One of his engagements in Los Angeles ran to a record nine weeks.

On July 28th the ABC-TV network will present Patchen on their "Stars of Jazz" program. This will be the first nation-wide airing of the much talked-about "poetry-jazz"—and fittingly enough, by its originator.

A current LP recording (on Cadence label) titled Kenneth Patchen Reads His Poetry With The Chamber Jazz Sextet, has aroused much favorable comment. Patchen has been hailed—with Dylan Thomas—as one of the two great readers of poetry in our time.

The Books Across The Sea Selection Committee Of The English-Speaking Union chose Patchen's Selected Poems (published by New Directions) as one of the volumes best calculated "to interpret American life and thought to people in other countries."

—(For additional biographical information, please consult Who's Who, Twentieth Century Authors, etc.)

***Note:** The handwritten postscript by Patchen follows:*

—You probably have seen this, but want to assure against possible slip up.

Warmest regards!
Kenneth Patchen

To James Boyer May from Kenneth Patchen (KPA)

August 9, 1958
2340 Sierra Court Palo Alto, California

Dear Boyer,

Coat arrived in handsome neat boxshape. Regret delay in acknowledg-ing better than safe receipt. Doggone days of late...sleepless late. Not only neck but it seems times and chances out of joint. Saw in paper that Ford Awards will be granted through committee acting on candidacies proposed by editors etc. Sure that such a committee as they would get together would not take even the one expected look at me under normal circumstances...and now we have all the talk of the lots of money I've made to contend with.

What an irony that my great and unpaid efforts should prove the very instrument of my undoing at a time when things are closing in from several directions at once.. to give you an idea, the doctors are at a loss whether to handle the windpipe thing now or wait to see what traction does to the neck difficulty (more X-rays for latter, and guarded hints that possibility of slipped disc exists). And as I told you, the Clinic is now billing me for all services.—Then the awfulness of Miriam's illness. Small wonder that I have moments of panic. And—oh well. Can't help thinking that it was due to my efforts and the spectacular nature of my troubles in keeping head above water that caused Hutchins two years ago to present the program of help to individual artists as an issue before the governing board of the Ford Foundation!

Please thank Miss Bird for her interest in getting my titles into that store. All in print books are listed with publisher on those mailing pieces of mine—both the one done by New Directions and the one which features readings with the band. Couple books are available through Paper Editions Corp., 621 Fourth St., S Fran 7. Guess that my mailing piece on Painted Books is not good: no response to it.. not even from people who purchased from us before.

In haste.
Our love to both of you rare and good people
Kenneth

Note: James Boyer May edited the L.A. ***Trace*** *lit and jazz magazine.*

To Henry Rago, *Poetry* magazine, Chicago, from Kenneth Patchen (PAP)

August 15, 1958
2340 Sierra Court Palo Alto

Dear Henry Rago

Yesterday I sent copies of my new Painted Books—as described on enclosed mailing piece—to your office. Please add them to Poetry's library. (This is by way of being a small token of my gratitude for the great kindnesses which you and your staff have shown me over the past couple difficult years.)

And I am sorry to report that things continue to go badly with us: a sprained neck, the result of a car mishap, has me in a brace again—and I shall not be able to make the trip to Brussels. The "sprain" may be a slipped disc—haven't yet heard what a second round of X-rays has to say about condition—do know that I face some weeks in traction. So I must be content with the fact that I do have the honor of having received an invitation to read at the Fair. At least no bad break can take that away.

Sometimes when I consider that so far all my hard efforts in appearing with the jazz band have resulted in a lot of publicity which I haven't been able to convert into a source of income, I wonder whether the whole thing hasn't really worked me a disservice: I am thinking of course that such publicity registers with most people in only one way—"Well, Patchen must be making some money at last." Which is to state the case mildly! The stories we have heard in this connection leave us gasping! And the "most people" who count with us in our predicament are those sitting on Award and Grant committees. I had not lost hope that one of these committees would one day take note of the fight I have put up to work in the face of everything—against the advice of doctors—have probably closed the one door I had open to me!

I know that you will understand that I am not merely unburdening myself in presenting this situation to you...As you remember, I am slated for an operation to remove a benign growth in my windpipe; my wife is seriously ill with a disease which could at any moment demand the outlay of large sums of money...And we have no steady income, or any hope of one. It is hard for me to believe that all these Funds and Grants will continue to ignore my existence; but past history would indicate that it should be harder for me to believe that tomorrow the sun will come up in the west. I have been told that these committees do from time to time take heed of the suggestions of editors who write them as sort of interested citizens of the world of literature and simple humanity. Should anything along this line occur to you, I pray you to do what you can. No, I beg you!

Sincerely yours,
Kenneth Patchen

It was largely the impact of my plight, as presented by me several years ago to Robert Hutchins—then connected with the Ford Foundation Grants—which prompted the FF to come up with this new aid to individual artists in need; but I can't apply on my own behalf...Will you? or have you any thoughts on this, or related things?

To E.E. Cummings from Kenneth Patchen (HAR)

Dear Cummings

How wonderful to have your new book! So many of the poems we are experiencing the great delight of reading for the first time. I think that in some ways this is my favorite of all your books. (However, in this, as Miriam points out with pleased amusement, I may not be the most dependable witness: for that has been my identical reaction to each of your last three volumes. At any rate, there is satisfaction in knowing that there is only one man alive who can abuse me of my present conviction: yourself; and a joy, too, in knowing that the only way you can do it is by providing me with the source material for a new allegiance: via the poems of your next book.)

Please give our love to Marion.

Again-thankfully yours,
Kenneth

***Note:** This letter refers to Cummings' **95 Poems**.*

To Henry Moe from Kenneth Patchen (GUG)

January 14, 1959
2340 Sierra Court
Palo Alto, California

Dear Mr Moe

In applying now for a renewal of Fellowship, it occurs to me that I have made twenty-two similar applications since the award was granted me in 1936.

I know that your committee of selection singles out the relatively few successful candidates from the vast number making application to it on a basis of scholarly or artistic merit alone; that the question of any given candidate's possible need or hardship status does not enter into their deliberations. This is a positive position, one with which I have no wish or right to quarrel; but I wish to suggest—I do not state because I think that it would be impossible for anyone to do more than raise the point for objective consideration—I suggest that this single-sighted judgment may tend to develop a blindspot in regard to a candidate whose need and hardship over many years have been so great as to overshadow in the public mind the merit of his work.

How and by whom is the artistic merit of the candidate's work judged? The record shows that for twenty-two years your committees of selection have not been impressed by the endorsements and tributes which my work has received from such artist-critics as T S Eliot, Archibald MacLeish, E E Cummings, W H Auden, Marianne Moore, Edith Sitwell, William Carlos Williams, Lewis Mumford, Malcolm Cowley, Thornton Wilder, etc. Who of the candidates judged deserving of a renewal of their Fellowships during that period of twenty-two years can or could bring forward testimony about the artistic merit of their work which is the equal of this? If there is one, his name is not known to me!

Then must I think that it was the negative factor in my case which caused your committee not to see what the people enumerated above see in it? I cannot deny that during the period between 1937 and 1956 an average of six months out of each year found me helpless in bed with a difficulty of the spine; and I cannot deny that I have undergone a series of operations, each more taxing than the last: but I can also attest that during that same period I wrote and had published some twenty books.

I cannot deny that during the past few years my wife and I have lived under the clouds of her serious illness (multiple sclerosis); but I can attest that neither of us has any wish to be the object for special pleading. Our twenty-five years of marriage have not prepared us to accept the theory that the value of people is determined by their inabilities: the yardstick of any charity.

No. Ability, merit, accomplishment: let these be the considerations of judgment.

I don't ask for an award from your committee because I need money perhaps more than any candidate applying this year: no, I make application on the basis of my record as a creative artist; on the merit of the work I have done.

I ask that this letter be presented to the committee of selection as the certificate of my application for the renewal of my Fellowship.

Sincerely yours,
Kenneth Patchen

From the liner notes to: KENNETH PATCHEN READS WITH JAZZ IN CANADA, Alan Neil (Folkways)

Recorded at the Canadian Broadcasting Corporation's studio in Vancouver, British Columbia on February 17, 1959

We got to the studio expecting to wail. Behind us we had a good half dozen performances with Patchen—at colleges, couple of nightclubs, and on television; and today we could count on three hours rehearsal before doing the radio show. The band was in a mood to groove. When Kenneth arrived he told us that in an hour he was due at a dental surgeon's to have a broken tooth attended to—maybe an infection, he didn't go into detail, he was quite calm about it. We ran over some numbers but nothing much happened, no acts of love, no fires starting. It was all right, and it was nothing. At the end of the hour we broke off and, while the guys went for a beer, I walked over to the surgeon's office with Kenneth. Robert Patchell, who was in charge of the program for the C.B.C., looked pretty worried as we left. Bob is a fine, quiet, hip type of guy, and had gone to a lot of trouble arranging the session—without him there wouldn't have been any session. And now, right in the middle of rehearsal here we were off on an emergency trip to the dentist!

Well, Patchen had a major tooth surgery right on the spot as I waited. It was much more serious than any of us could have imagined. His jaw had to be chiselled away at, literally gouged out in an excruciatingly painful operation that took almost an hour. Finally he emerged into the waiting room, his face drained of color, and those great tired eyes more tired than I had ever seen them. His mouth was bleeding through big cotton plugs—still he smiled, and when the girl at the desk asked for his occupation he mumbled "Writer, self employed."

The guys were waiting for us at a cafeteria and we munched at hamburgers while Patchen chewed slowly on rare steak. In maybe ten minutes his face stopped being gray, and his eyes got back their straight look of seeing right through everything and everybody. Ordinarily this is a scary thing, but it wasn't for us just then! A strange and amazing man. Somehow—but how?—he had pulled out of it, was ready to get going. (In fact, Patchen did a midnight show with us at The Cellar that same night! Talk about separating the men from the boys—well, that's not the only reason he'll get our votes!)

We went back to the station and got set up again. Kenneth sat at a little table maybe ten feet from us; his cheek was getting puffed and he kept dabbing at his mouth with the cotton. Time to time in that run through I could see he was having trouble with his numbed lips on some syllables, so I guess it was lucky we had our own problem—and a large one. Since he was speaking into the recording mike, we couldn't hear him; and we had to listen to that lead horn or we would just be going through the motions—without the lead horn we were spooked. Then somebody (Kenneth, I think) hit on the idea of each of us having earphones. We put them on—and we had a scene! It was extremely exciting! Now we could aim our language, our feeling, at Patchen's—the thing had come to life! The time we could stay in the studio was getting short—who cared! We could make it, we could maybe blow a little! In a couple minutes I waved to the engineer to tape away.

We went through the numbers with one break (maybe 2 or 3 minutes) just before "Glory, Glory"—Kenneth drew on a cigarette, stretched his legs, refused coffee, and nodded that he was set. And during that last number I don't think he looked down at the paper once. We had all been caught up in the reading from the start—we knew that something was happening, that this was "something else"—but now he really went out for it, he wailed! With our nerves, our hearts, we heard him coming on, ringing the changes, threading and pulling us in and out of the light—the King Cat making his scene! And on his face we could see that what we had to say back to him was making the same kind of "heart-sense." It was *there.*

Every jazz guy going on the stand wants it to happen—call it wailing, swinging, what you like—every night he goes on he wants it—but it can't be made to happen. The jazz guy has to get in his own trance, feeling his feeling, really feeling it—contacting the guy who lives inside him—call it getting up his own blues, his own peace, his own anguish. And this is the ONE mystery of jazz. A mystery nobody, critic or musician, can explain; and which musicians usually have too much care about to try.

We had it that afternoon. The thing was there, it happened. But if you think I am talking about playing good—or about anything like that—well, I said it couldn't be explained. It is a mystery—it *really* is.

As for my own notion of poetry reading with jazz, it's something I have been kicking around ever since I heard tapes brought up here in the summer of 1956—and by the way, this was long before the big picture magazines "discovered" it down in the Frisco area. These were tapes of Patchen reading to jazz records; and Bob Patchell got them programmed on the C.B.C. network that autumn. Anyway, one of the ideas I have about it is that the band has to be free to play jazz; it must be spontaneous or where is the jazz? It can't be muddied up by literal or arty "interpretations" of verbal meanings—that would do for musical comedy numbers. The feeling the poet releases through his reading must be met by the jazz guys with some type of honest paralleling in their own speech, in the idiom of jazz—the thing has to be honest: then even when it isn't very good (and God knows most of the attempts have been pretty awful), nobody will get hurt.

Patchen was the one exception. I've heard of many jazzmen who have been digging him all along. Myself, it's been ten years. (On this, I should say that it pleased me a lot when Dale Hillary and Bill Boyle went round quoting big hunks of his poetry for weeks after Kenneth left here. They probably dug him more as a man than as a poet, but they did dig him…)

Anyway, on this session we all felt a special kind of identity and love for him. For the reasons I described at the beginning, and also because somehow Kenneth's dignity—so easy and *natural*—his bigness and deep honesty, these things came through to us with added force that day. As I said, something happened.

Now a last thing. The other day I learned that Charlie Parker, the originator of modern jazz, used to carry Patchen's books about with him, and knew many of his poems by heart, and would often be saying the poems when he was working up something for his music. So I'm happy, *very happy*, though it was just a coincidence, that the opening blues on this record was written by the late, great Charlie Parker.

Alan Neil
Vancouver, B.C.
August 26, 1959

To E. E. Cummings from Kenneth Patchen (HAR)

March 6, 1959

Dear Cummings,

Congratulations! and thank you!

Last Sunday I got home from a 2½ wk reading trip in the NW and British Columbia—the enclosed "newspaper" was put together by the fellows in the jazz band in Seattle as a surprise for me. It reflects rather well the crazy atmosphere of this crazy business, though I was touched by the warmth of their gesture.

Tuesday the 10th I get to NY for two readings—on the 16th and the 20th—at The Living Theatre.

I shall phone you in hope that it will be convenient for you and Marion to permit me the pleasure of a visit to your house during my stay.

Miriam sends her respects and love with mine.

Kenneth

Upon my return I go into the hospital for removal of a growth in the esophagus.

To Miriam Patchen from Kenneth Patchen
NYC March 19, 1959

Thursday 4:30

Dearest

Busy today, as I said I'd be.
10:30 this morning saw Goddard Leiberson of Columbia Records. I proposed an LP of my reading love poems. He's very interested. He inquired about plane and other expenses if they should want me to come to NY studio for recording session. He asked for and I supplied him with a copy of To Say If You Love Someone, which I'd left with Mademoiselle editor yesterday because she was interested in the idea of doing a selection in mag. Leiberson will give me a decision after he's looked into matter, discussed with board etc - in other words, sometime after I get home. Who knows, this could be worth all the effort here and then some! (My interview with him was scheduled to be a half hour: ran over an hour.)
Then I dropped in at Gothams and

He thought this a fine title for album.

went over evening arrangements with Miss Steloff. And discovered while there that Sam Ash of Folkways was very anxious to contact me. Waiting for him to phone now. — He just did. See him tomorrow morning, at 10:30. Asked him what he had in mind, and he said "a record of just you reading — no band." So. Again, we'll see. —

Down to Cummingses at 1 for a photo Taking of me by Marion. Chatted with Cummings until I had to leave for a 3 o'clock appointment with Arabel Porter of New American Library. She asked me if I'd be interested in a "Patchen Sampler" Mentor Edition, prose and poetry — 1000 dollars (or more if I want) in advance. Said I would. She'll give me definite word on that soon. (Also, wanted any material at all for New World Writing: left batch of poems with her.)

Called on Esquire editor. They'd like some satirical pieces — any form at all — want them badly.

So I was busy. — Seems doors are sort of wide open.

Take care of my pretty darling.

Love, love, Kenneth

***Note:** Kenneth had gone to New York City to perform poetry-jazz and to record.*

To Geraldine and James Boyer May from Miriam Patchen (KPA)

July 13, 1959

Dear Geraldine and Boyer,

Kenneth will be home tonight, though we went to the hospital only Sunday night for Monday morning procedures. When I got there early yesterday he was just entering the recovery room after surgery. So I did a few little things such as putting flowers around, straightening the room etc and then left on a couple little errands. When I returned, there he was sitting up drinking coffee! The chest incision did not have to be made. We were fantastically lucky to have gotten Dr. Richards on the case. He's head of surgery at Stanford and professor of same. Our friend Ron was his student and he interested the doctor in taking the case. Well, he was able to do the job through the tube, via the mouth. He had said that he'd try, but didn't really have much hope it would work and that the patient was to be readied for surgical procedures which would follow immediately as they saw that this wouldn't work. There is no malignancy and the doctor said we were not to distrust that verdict though he will want to examine the tract in three months and again in six. At present Kenneth has only great stiffness of all muscles and a very sore throat. He will have to be on liquid diet for some time, but everything is already over.. Even assisting doctors at the surgery room were amazed that the whole thing was so (for the patient) simple. Dr. Richards is one of the few men who could do this...and there you are! They were amazed, too, to see Kenneth walking around last night. His recovery from the anesthesis was remarkable to them. They also didn't expect him to be stirring for some time, but his recovery abilities are extraordinary. At this time I am unable to be aware of anything. Both of us had been prepared Sunday night by several doctors to expect rather a horrid time for weeks....intravenous feedings, glucose, tubes etc etc...so the 11th hour reprieve is still hard to encompass. Vaguely aware that both of us want you to know the news immediately...and vaguely aware that we are so miserable about Geraldine's difficulties, but the nature of the beast is such that at the moment these are repeated by rote from ideas we've had for some time, but are unable to feel acutely today.

You'll be hearing in normal fashion from this area soon......
Our deepest love,
Miriam

To Irene Kreidler from Kenneth Patchen (KPA)

615 U Sav & Tr Bldg Warren, Ohio
August 19, 1959
2340 Sierra Court Palo Alto, California

Dear Irene

How nice to get your letter! Unhappily for the suggestion that I send autographed books for door prizes at Saturday's reunion, there is the rather vital fact that—even if I had the books to hand at this moment, and I haven't—it would be postmanly impossible to get them to you in time.
So may I suggest this: Announce the books as prizes, both Poemscapes and Hurrah for Anything, and send me the names and addresses of the winners—this way I'll be able to sign the books to them direct, that is, by name (and of course I'll then post copies). And by the way, I want no payment for the books...unless someone wanted to be good enough to tell me something of the reunion, who and how many, etc. I am most curious about my old classmates. Please give my regards to all of them.

And my warm best to you.
Sincerely yours,
Kenneth Patchen.

(P.S. I'm sending you a signed book, just in case you don't win one at the door.)

Note: *The following image is from the book Patchen sent.*

—my love to all of you—
Kenneth
Aug. 1945

THE MEMOIRS

OF A SHY PORNOGRAPHER

What I Came From & The Doors Of The World Are Opened To Me & The First Party I Ever Went To & The First Real Home I Ever Had & My Life As A Private Investigator & The Last Party I Ever Went To & The Story Of My Love & Does The Famous Detective Know That Love In A Mist Is Only The Great White Whale Going Down For The Full Count In That Old Seventh Round & The Deer Are Entering This Beautiful Forest & The Greatest And Most Wonderful Plan On Earth & The House Of The Frowning Heart & A Radiant Temple Stands Above The Waters & What Became Of Me

AN AMUSEMENT BY

KENNETH PATCHEN

A NEW DIRECTIONS BOOK

To E. E. Cummings from Kenneth Patchen (HAR)

January 1, 1960

Dear Cummings

We had our Xmas present early from you—the splendid knowledge that so many, many "new" people will come upon the gift of your poems (through the Groves).

Your wonderful poems!

And then, just on time, for the season—but especially for us—the so welcome, warm letter (and the check). Thank you both so much.

Yesterday two robins and a blue jay were in our backyard. The coldest day of the winter. A rare frost the night before. No report of such visitors elsewhere about. Each day we put food out for the sparrows. One of the robins was dull in color, the other had a brilliant red breast—and the saucy jay told our cats a thing or two!

Our love—and Happy New Year!

Kenneth

To Kenneth Patchen from David Glover (KPA)

Minneapolis Minnesota
January 7, 1960

Kenneth Patchen:

Just heard that you got troubles—enclosed is a money order for $15. I wish it could be more but that's all I can scrape up at present. I hope it's of some help.

I owe you a lot more than that—what you have written and read has moved me, and moved me deep. I don't think anyone but an idiot could be the same after reading Albion Moonlight or First Will & Testament and all the rest—I know they changed me.

Your books read me—and I got back the guts to admit I cared about people and life and the world—I suppose this is naïve as hell, but it's like there was someone else on the other side of the page saying "I love you—you bastards—stop murdering each other." And that voice made me think.

I refuse to contribute to murder no matter what name it goes under—except for the kind Miller speaks of in "Murder the Murderer."

You are a great man, and what's more important—a good one. You're one of the few people who I think are really necessary in the survival of humanity and kindness.

In short—you talked to me and I heard—I just wanted to tell you.

In Aug '59 I put out a mimeographed book of my poems (?) —since then I've sold 3 and given away 5.

I would like to send you #6—some of them were greatly influenced by your style. Anyway I'll send you a copy—if you don't want it don't send it back. I care too much.

Maybe I'm just a hyena coming in for entrails after the lion has made the kill…

You and Miller are my favorite writers—and damn the sonsabitches who sit and watch your little buffalos die! I hope they someday open their eyes and realize that its their face under the mask on the head dangling from the rope…

Good luck Monday—may God & Devil and various and sundry other apparitions be with you and for you—I hope the results you wish become yours.

Someday when you get time, a stamp, and inclination will you send more information about your wall books?

For my 1/ten-zillionth of the world—
thanks for caring

Love,
David Glover

To Josephine Leighton/,The John Simon Guggenheim Memorial Foundation from Kenneth Patchen (GUG)

February 1, 1960

Dear Mrs Leighton

Enclosed is the formal statement of my work plan in connection with my application for additional Fellowship assistance; also—as you requested—I have supplied the names of people who are acquainted with my recent work and whose judgement regarding my

ability to carry out the proposed plan of work should be of help and interest to you and to the committee of selection.
I have not included the script of my play, Don't Look Now, because at the moment it is in a state of change and incompletion as rehearsals go on. I have been learning at first hand the truth of the old statement that plays are not written..they are rewritten.

With best personal wishes.
Sincerely yours,
Kenneth Patchen

Note: *Enclosed with this letter, on two sheets of paper were the following items:*

To Mrs Josephine Leighton, Administrative Assistant, John Simon Guggenheim Memorial Foundation (GUG)

Names of people
who might pass on the merit of Kenneth Patchen's
application for additional Fellowship assistance:

Mr. Henry Rago
Mr. Archibald MacLeish
Mr. Tennessee Williams
Dr. Noram Holmes Pearson
Mr. Thornton Wilder

APPLICATION OF KENNETH PATCHEN FOR ADDITIONAL FELLOWSHIP ASSISTANCE FROM THE JOHN SIMON GUGGENHEIM FOUNDATION (JANUARY 1960)

1) Work done since my application of last year:
wrote my first play, Don't Look Now.
(It was presented at the Troupe Theatre.
in Palo Alto—scheduled for a month's run, public and critical interest caused an extension of three weeks; and at moment a country-wide tour is in prospect.)
2) If granted an additional Fellowship, my project would be: the writing of a verse play which would feature my interpretation of what are to me the two most seminal and imaginative creations in all the literature of the theatre—namely, those of harlequin and Hamlet.

3) Recent works:
Hurrah For Anything, poems and drawings, 1957
Poemscapes, prose poems, 1958
When We Were Here Together, poems, 1958
Don't Look Now, a play, 1959

To James Laughlin from Kenneth Patchen (NDA)

February 4, 1960
2340 Sierra Court Palo Alto

Dear Laughlin

Again turned down by Ford Foundation, this time on an award basis which seemed like an absolute natural for me—poets and fiction writers who might be expected to bring new life to the field of play writing. Statement of rejection implies that the Foundation people—not just the outside judges—have hand in selection: (Quote from form signed by Director, W. McNeil Lowry)—"Although your work and the statement you submitted in connection with the Foundation Program for Poets and Fiction Writers have been the subject of real interest and careful consideration on the part of the Foundation and the judges assisting it in this program, I regret etc etc..." Do you know this Lowry? What a shameful business! Who could possibly be more qualified than I am! Who could possibly be in greater need than I am!—Their letterhead reads: Program in Humanities and the Arts. On what basis was I turned down? It comes down to this: Why am I singled out and discriminated against by all these aid-to-deserving-artists outfits! I think it is a fair question—one which anyone interested in fair play and common human decency should demand an answer to. That question—(and its answer)—has an importance which transcends the fate of the individual artist concerned. It will make an interesting comment on our times—that the one individual whose need most cries out to heaven for help from these various aid-to-artists outfits, is the only generally recognized writer on the current literary scene not to have received any help whatever from any of them! As I say, I think it a matter whose implications are far reaching and of importance to anyone interested in the true state of our letters now. Why does every so-and-so sitting year after year on his fat ivy-covered ass in a cosy-dosy college teaching job get every grant-in-aid going to assist him in his work of not working at anything which A Tennyson Auden Tate has not already constipatedly pooped up for the greater glory of snobocracy everywhere?—and I mean that these nonentities-by-intent are assisted by every one of these outfits, they go right down the line! Why? What is the purpose of this? What is the concern of these judges? Who are these judges? What are their qualifications? Why do they all come up with the same list of persons to be aided? Do I exaggerate? do I falsify the picture? For an answer to his, I suggest that you examine the lists of successful prize winners in the last five years. I have. There is no doubt in my mind that the intention here is not to serve the cause of free and meaningful creation but to see to it that a faceless and subservient mediocrity be made the order of the day.

I have a slipped disc again. During the surgical procedure in July my back was wrenched and a disc went askew above the fused area. The doctors held off telling me this news until the pain got so bad and disability so great that keeping it from me longer was impossible—they feared that I might not see further point in trying to chin up with another operation called for, and our situation being what it is...Miriam with multiple sclerosis (and forced to work, standing on her feet 8 hrs a day in a hustle-bustle dept store (MS victims should not be subjected to too much strain and physical fatigue). And now my source of income from readings etc is closed off—I don't know. There are certain things I cannot close my mind to—without help, real help over a time sufficient to give me a fighting chance to get back on my feet, there seems no good answer.

I'll write you about the things you bring up in your letter a bit later.

Sincerely yours,
Kenneth

Note: Handwritten note:

If you know Lowry of Ford Foundation show him this letter—or read pertinent parts to him. May not be too late even now on play writing project because in his letter he says that announcements of awards will be delayed until sometime next month. Supposed to have been made now.

This is important. If you can acquaint him with facts of my situation, perhaps the Foundation people would reconsider. They have the funds, God knows! Maybe they could give me a grant just on the Humanities basis. Help me somehow

To Henry Rago, *Poetry* magazine, Chicago, from Kenneth Patchen (PAP)

February 6, 1960
2340 Sierra Court Palo Alto

Dear Henry Rago

The surgical procedure in July caused a wrench to my back which the doctors now, after all these months of treatment limited to bed rest and round the clock pain medicine, tell me is in fact another slipped disc condition—this time above the area of the fusion—and that only further surgery can alleviate the disabling symptoms and give me some chance to get on my feet again. A two time loser with spinal operations usually cannot count on too much from a third, but of course the present position is not tolerable beyond a certain period of time. So I must try to claw my way into the hospital and under the knife again, to the tune of thousands of dollars (while I am still bogged in debt from the last go, and having no answer to the immediate problem of coming up with the cost of the doctoring and medicine necessary to keep things in some check until the surgery becomes possible).

And I thought I had the answer to this when the Ford Foundation told me I had been nominated for one of its grants-in-aid to poets and fiction writers who might be qualified to undertake a project of work with theatre groups—to bring new blood into field of play writing, etc. At the time of their announcement my first play Don't Look Now, was just having its original month's run extended to seven weeks because of public and critical interest—at the Troupe Theatre in Palo Alto. By reason of demonstrated interest and ability, not to speak of my need, I didn't see how they could leave my name off the list of successful candidates. But leave it off they did! The 2nd time the FF has passed me over. One of the ironies here—and I feel that there are others—is the fact that the extremity of my case of need was used by Robert Hutchins, the then head of the FF, to persuade its board of directors to change its policy of giving assistance only to groups etc to include in its program the helping of individual artists of proven merit whose work was not of a nature to ensure them a livelihood from it.

Four years have passed since we received the nightmarish verdict of the doctors that my wife had fallen victim of multiple sclerosis. Four years in which I have done everything I could to bring our plight to the attention of the various committees which announce themselves as being interested in the welfare of the artist of merit in this richest of nations, in this democracy whose stock in trade is the selling of itself to the world as the enemy of inhumanity to man; and during this unceasing, four-year effort of mine (and a few others) to get one of the awards which have been passed out to every poet of recognized worth not just one time but three-four-five-six times, I have received nothing, not a word, not a red cent from any of them! Perhaps one day, when this story is told, it may be of interest to some people of good will—and with a regard for the state of health of our American letters—to know why this should be so.

At any rate I can see no hope that this situation will change for me—let him rot in his sick bed, and his wife with him: what kind of manners have these two dark ghosts at the feast that they continue to whimper for help from us, we have no CARE packages for the likes of them. As I say, I've no reason to expect anything except a continuation of what has happened for us in these past four terrible years. But here I am writing to you—I guess I have too much pride to give up the struggle.

What could be of use? Only this I think: if interested people would take direct action to help me—if they would write letters to the various fund committees suggesting that I be helped—to the National Inst of Arts and Letters, the Guggenheim, the Bollingen, etc. etc.—not forgetting the Ford Foundation, Mr W McNeil Lowry, Chairman: Program of the Humanities and the Arts, 477 Madison Avenue, New York 22.—What do you think? Will you do it? Will you get other poets to do it?—Forgive me...help of a sustaining kind could be the difference between life and death for me—perhaps you and your friends will think it important enough to take the direct action I have mentioned. After four years of absolute and total silence to my appeals, I can only believe that nothing whatever will change unless some powerful new factor enters the case—such a factor would be the raised voices of my peers.

All good wishes.
Sincerely yours,
Kenneth Patchen

To James Laughlin from Kenneth Patchen (NDA)

February 27, 1960
2340 Sierra Court Palo Alto

Dear Laughlin

Thank you very much for appealing on my behalf to Mr Lowry and for looking into possible help from such groups as the one you mention in your letter of the 18th.

Immediately there is a snag about getting an estimate of costs for the medical handling of my latest back trouble: in the first place the doctors (and there are two sets involved, one at Palo Alto Clinic, other at Stanford Hospital in San Francisco) will not say anything in specific terms either about the nature of the eventual treatment or what the bill might be for any of the several possible approaches. Both neurological and orthopedic men have been consulted, and as often happens they do not see eye to eye on the case. The coordinating doctor so far refuses to announce his own idea of procedure. My first operation in New Haven was by a neuro-surgeon; the second, here, by an orthopedist. Time in hospital for first, around 14 days; for the second, two and a half months. One involves a matter of cutting, of removal of herniated tissue; the second, of bone grafting. Quite a difference in cost of hospitalization, not to speak of fee for continuous doctoring, special nurses, etc. (Available rooms at hospitals here begin at 18 dollars per day, average 24.) As I say, there is this big snag. I told the coordination doctor why I wanted the estimate of costs, that it might prove quite important in my struggle to get into a position to pay; and he said, "I wish I could even make a guess, but I can't. I'd think if somebody wanted to help, they'd help what they could and not make it a thing like giving someone a down payment on a car or something of that kind."—There is an extra touchiness here in the matter of what the two sets of specialists will decide about my case because the orthopedists at Palo Alto Clinic are naturally not happy with the fact that their two and a half month fusion job got wrecked when I underwent exploratory surgery in San Francisco; and I'm sure they doubt that I would under any circumstances go through with another fusion (full body cast for couple-three months...etc, etc). The fact that I am not undergoing any treatment now beyond increasingly heavy pain potions makes me suspicious that they have ruled out everything except another fusion: but I don't know: I had hoped to find out under pressure of getting information about costs for your purpose...but I learned nothing, unfortunately. Again, thank you.

Sincerely yours,
Kenneth PATCHEN

To Kenneth Patchen from James Laughlin (NDA)

April 13, 1960

Dear Kenneth,

Many thanks for yours of April 5th, enclosing Archie's letter, which I am returning to you. He is a good egg, and does hs best. Don't lose patience with him, as he has been a real friend to you, and will always do what he can.

I note that you don't have another copy of "Albion," so I've sent mine to Mrs. Porter, and written her another long letter, urging her to get on her horse and do something. I really think she does want to—she's a very good egg, too—but they have just been tied up there with their big merger, and other matters. But I'll keep on her trail.

I don't think it would be a good idea for us to get go ahead with the paperback of "Moonlight" until she has made up her mind. She might want to do that, and of course, nothing should stand in the way of what would be a really lucrative and widely distributed book for you. But if she doesn't make up her mind in a reasonable time, then I think we should go forward. That is, if we can work things out with Padell.

I have an appointment to see those people at that small foundation this week, and will do my best for you there.

Yes, I like that book of your friend Norman Thomas very much. As you say, it "sings." I'm corresponding with him now about possible changes to cut out some of what seems to me extraneous material. I think it could be a real little masterpiece if he gets it honed down.

I'm sorry about the too thin paper on "Because." Somebody in the production part of our office should have thought of that, but they didn't.

But I disagree with you about the cover art. I think it is very effective, and apparently the trade thought so too, as the advance on the book was excellent.

That's bad news about the x-rays not giving a favorable prognosis for the operation.

With best to you both, as ever,
James Laughlin

Dear Laughlin

I know that you don't want me to get my hopes up on the foundation thing. They aren't -- except in this: I am much encouraged by the great effort you are making to help me. This display of good will means a great deal just now.

Monthly expenses:

light gas water sanitation telephone	$15.00
food	150.00
transportation	20.00
house	75.00
medical (basic)	100.00
	$ 360.00

Assured monthly income:

Miriam's salary as deptstore clerk (take home pay)	$192.13

My own present sources of income
are the drips and dribbles
usual for a noncommercial writer.
Before last accident to spine I made
out quite well from readings etc:
even to extent of providing
savings (which are now gone).
Medical expenses often much higher:
for instance, X-rays during past
three months have cost $150.00;
actually, I have put down only
expense of necessary medicine,
since I can't foretell what the
months ahead will demand in
the way of payment for doctors'
services etc.

I hope this will serve the purpose.

To James Boyer May from Kenneth Patchen (KPA)

May 11 1960
2340 Sierra Court Palo Alto

Dear Boyer,

The past week has been so strange and depressing: we have not been able to get in touch with lawyer at all and one of the doctors called up to say that he was less concerned about the state of my back than about how soon I'd have to go into the hospital again for surgery on the growth in esophagus. His concern might explain why doctors just keep feeding me pain stuff for back. Anyway, the thing gave me nothing very pleasant to think about, in any direction. Perhaps lawyer was told true state of affairs when he sought doctors' records—perhaps he just didn't have the heart to explain his sudden dropping completely from sight, after his very warm and human-seeming expression of concern with our predicament? About the letters—Now I am vague about what you wanted to do in matter: believe that I suggested you inform editors of mags, papers, etc of my present state. You ask for particulars:
For nineteen yrs (from 1937 to '56, I suffered about total disability from my painful spinal difficulty. In 1956 a spinal fusion (2nd of two operations) gave me relief and mobility (& for the first time I was able to go about giving readings, and so on. Then—on July 13, 1959—during surgical procedure on my throat, and while under complete anesthesia, I suffered another slipped disc, and am once again helplessly and painfully bedridden.
Had 29 books published: prepared (designed, in some cases even bound) 970 volumes in "Painted Books" Series—each an individual, one-of-a-kind production.
Have 3 long prose books in progress, all held up by my inability to do more than quick (I sprint-type work between doses of pain-sedation).
During these years—'37 to '60—23 of them—I have received not one of the awards made "to deserving and needy" artists. I don't know—if you will frame letter, one which can be sent out broadside—perhaps call it Trace Wishes It To Be Known That and perhaps let me see it. I'll pay for multigraphing and postage etc.

Excuse scramble
Our love to both of you,
Kenneth

To James Laughlin from Kenneth Patchen (NDA)

June 17, 1960
2340 Sierra Court Palo Alto

Dear Laughlin

Sort of nip and tuck getting through the days lately—sorry to be so long answering your most considerate and detailed letter of the 3rd. My proposals seem to run into the stone wall of your publishing procedures and basic economics, which are the same thing, in a way at least.

What I had hoped was that you would make an exception because of the exceptional nature of my case. And I am not at all clear how your publishing record makes an either-or approach to the matter of Selected versus Collected Poems necessary. I seem to remember a whole tangle of such volumes in print at the same time: those of W C Williams, for instance. And I'm speaking of volumes under New Directions imprint to make my point, for surely it is a commonplace of general trade practice to see poets represented in all manner of compilations. Cummings, with two Collecteds, now has two simultaneously released Selecteds. And I could fill the page with other examples.

What I am getting at is this: a new, enlarged, up-to-date Selected for me will be just more of the same...nothing special...it will by its nature do nothing whatever in the area of suggesting to the public and the critics that here is a body of work presented for mile-stone-type evaluation and judgment. An event on the order of a Collected it would not be. This thinking rules out any notion that a revised Selected has any of the attention-getting features inherent in the publication of a Collected. And the more I think of it the more merit I see in the issuance of a really comprehensive Collection aimed at libraries and books clubs with the going price for such volumes—6 dollars, perhaps as much as 6.75. A big book, on the order of the Cummings' Collected. Then certainly there would be no chance of conflict with the Selected—in fact it would be given a shot in the arm, particularly if you moved it into the paperback field. As you know, the interest in my books for many years has been almost the only stable element on the literary scene, despite the fact that there has never been anything approaching an advertising campaign to solidify that interest, to remove its "best kept secret" aspect by forcing some of the Willy Wetleg critics to write about someone people are really interested in for a change. As it is, I sense that more than a few custodians of public taste are just about ready to make up for lost crime. In our society nobody (alive, anyway) gets to be a winner without topbilling. Of course in such a project as I suggest you must first consider whether you'd get your investment back: I think you would...and then some.

Then as to the question of which to do first, Albion Moonlight or the love poems: the factor here will probably be the reaction of Padell to your proposal on the Moonlight.

[missing rest of letter]

To James Laughlin from Kenneth Patchen (NDA)

July 23, 1960

A lawyer has filed a claim for damages against the hospital where the July 13 ('59) injury to my back occurred. Trial at least a yr and a half away, so at moment the only consequence of action is that doors to doctoring and medication are pretty well closed—at least the ones I was using. Think it most unlikely that anything will come of case except the unpleasantness and hardships connected with testifying etc, but I'll have fought against the injustice of hit and run style medical practice.

Sincerely
Kenneth

To James Laughlin from Kenneth Patchen (NDA)

2340 Sierra Club Palo Alto
August 1, 1960

Dear Laughlin

I'm dropping a note to Padell, thanking him for making Moonlight reprint possible, and mentioning in passing that I've asked you to stipulate that rights in book are not transferable. So please draw up and send him the papers of agreement. He has a married daughter. If it is customary to put in—"and heirs"—then so be it. Right now, as I'm sure you do, I'd just like to see the book in the works.

[page missing dealing with use of Kenneth's art in New Directions annual.]

color if possible, but black and white would do. If you are interested, I can either send you a batch of the paintings (for photographing or whatever there) or photos of them—color transparencies or black & white. Your instinct that it was a great mistake taking my grievances to court will undoubtedly be tried by what happens—I feel strongly that it was a mistake. But you are quite wrong about one aspect: there is no thought on anyone's part that the doctors or the hospital personnel performed with anything other than the best motives and the greatest good will toward me before, during, and after the surgical procedure—no one has the slightest thought of entering a claim based on suspicion of deliberate and willful mishandling—such a charge would make no sense at all. But the incontrovertible fact is that in that place, and at that time, I suffered a calamitous injury.—One is hit by a car in the street, the driver (unless he's mad) had no plan, no wish, to cause hurt. But we know that when such unfortunate accidents happen, the victim of them is not held guilty for any attempt he may make to bring the situation back to some workable balance—not to punish the "guilty" but, among other things to depersonalize the action he so much regrets. It was a doctor, or very close to the situation from all sides (though of course, not directly involved in the injury-making incident), who advised me that I had no proper right not to take action. Anyway it's a bad deal, nasty—and I have many sleepless, pain-filled nights in which to realize it.

Kenneth

To James Laughlin from Kenneth Patchen (first page only) (NDA)

2340 Sierra Court Palo Alto August 1

Dear Laughlin

I'm dropping a note to Padell thanking him for making _Moonlight's_ reprint possible, and mentioning in passing that I've asked you to stipulate that rights in books are not transferable. So please draw up and send him the papers of agreement. He has a married daughter. If it is customary to put in — "and heirs": then so be it. Right now, as I'm sure you do, I'd just like to see the book in the works.

To Kenneth Patchen from James Laughlin (NDA)

August 4, 1960

Dear Kenneth,

Many thanks for your good letter of August 1st.

I'm glad that you have written to Padell and I hope it all goes smoothly. I have this morning drafted an agreement in letter form, which would be signed by all three of us, if the terms are approved, and I will give this to Bob to check over for legal points over the weekend, and hope to be able to forward it to you for your approval next week. Then we will see if Padell will buy it. I have written into it that he may not transfer his right in the agreement except to a legal heir who is a member of his immediate family.

I think your suggestion that we might do something about your paintings in the New Directions annual is a very interesting one. To do them in color would, I fear, be out of the question; even if the plates were made in Austria it would cost hundreds of dollars. And I'm not too sure that we would be able to cram anything into the next immediate issue, as it is hopelessly overjammed at the moment. But do, in any case, let me have a look at some photographs of some of the pictures when you have them handy.

Thanks ever so much for sending me further clarification about your reasons for bringing the suit against the hospital. I understand what you were driving at, but I still feel it is a mistake, because very few people are capable of such abstract reasoning and they will misinterpret. I think it would be very difficult to win such a case because medical matters are so complicated. If somebody gets hit by an automobile that is very clear-cut and easy to understand for a jury. But this hospital will surely be able to get expert medical witnesses on the stand who will confuse them by their testimony and make it appear that what happened was no one's fault. Meanwhile, word will have gotten around that you are a "trouble-maker" and it will be hard for you to get medical assistance when you need it. I don't expect you to take my advice, but I do urge you to drop the action.

With best wishes, as ever,
James Laughlin

To Harvey Breit from Kenneth Patchen

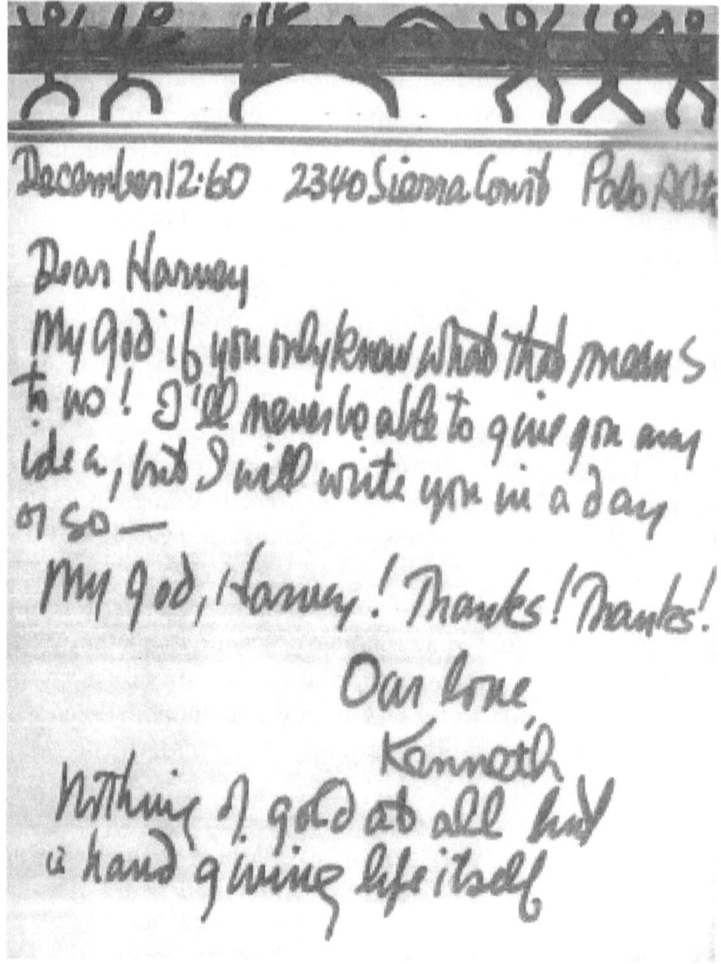

December 12:60 2340 Sierra Court Palo Alto

Dear Harvey

My God if you only knew what that means to me! I'll never be able to give you any idea, but I will write you in a day or so—

My God, Harvey! Thanks! Thanks!

Our love
Kenneth

Nothing of good at all but a hand giving life itself

***Note:** Original Patchen drawings in full color (see envelope on book's front cover), obviously done to thank Breit for financial help.*

Chapter Seventeen: Behind the Ice Curtain (1961-1966)

To Patchen family from Miriam Patchen
Note: *End of 1960 or start of 1961*

Dear People in Warren,

The 'phone call was most exciting and a beautiful thing. We both felt so good after it. I've been holding off on writing because daily I've thought Kenneth would enter the hospital. He was supposed to go in at the beginning of October. The doctors don't offer him any promises of success from an operation which we know must be attempted, so Kenneth has not gotten very excited about going in and being helpless for months in a cast, in a hospital, where if you are able to look after yourself it's bad enough, but to be absolutely helpless and lie there in a many-hundred-pound plaster cast for months puts one pretty much at the mercy of the system. One of these days soon he must attempt the thing, though, for there's nothing else to do. Too much time has passed uselessly. I'll keep you informed as things start up. So far we are just waiting for arrangements, etc.

Your thoughts of me moved me deeply. How good of you! One of these days either we shall get to Warren, or you all will keep your promise and come to California. To answer your questions about my health: I am able to function. My eyesight has returned and I can do just about everything as well as before. I have to be careful about my diet and I tire easily, but I'd say I'm fine, better than most people who have nothing wrong. Actually the worst thing about my "condition" is the worry it gives Kenneth. He fusses himself about it terribly. When he is able to take hold again (and I firmly believe the doctors can help him) he'll feel better about everything. You know what it is for a man to feel helpless; a man has to feel he can take care of things, a woman doesn't suffer confinement as much...maybe. Anyway, one of these days, soon, I hope, things will be changed. In the meantime, our very best to all of you.
I'll keep in touch.

Lovingly, Miriam

San Francisco *Examiner*, Sunday, Jan. 29, 1961 with insert (KPA)

An Artistic Tribute To an Ailing Poet

MANY of the Bay area's finest poets, musicians, actors and artists will unite in presenting a "Tribute to Kenneth Patchen" program today at 2 p. m. in Marines' Memorial Theater Auditorium.

Patchen, who lives in Palo Alto, is one of the country's most original and inspired poets (a sample of his "painted poems" is shown above).

For years he has suffered a painful spinal ailment that has left him immobile and without funds. The tribute is to raise money for an operation and other medical expenses that will enable him to continue his brilliant career (he was the only American poet invited to appear at the Brussels Festival).

Poets James Broughton, Robert Duncan, Lawrence Ferlinghetti, Mike McClure, Kenneth Rexroth, Philip Whalen and Jonathan Williams will take part in the program, reading from Patchen's works.

Other featured entertainers will include singers Stan Wilson and Ada Moore, and the Herb Barman Concert Jazz Orchestra. The Actor's Workshop will contribute a Yeats play, "Purgatorio," and a one-acter by Broughton will also be presented. Jules Irving is directing the program.

The sponsoring committee includes many of San Francisco's best known citizens. Tickets are in exchange for a $5 donation. They may be obtained at the Marines' Memorial box office, or may be reserved by calling either PR. 5-4232 or DA. 1-6865.

Sunday, Jan. 29, 1961 San Francisco Examiner 3

To James Laughlin from Kenneth Patchen (NDA)

March 12, 1961
2340 Sierra Court Palo Alto

Dear Laughlin

Thank you for all your help and expressions of sympathy and encouragement. Meant a great deal to Miriam and me.
My severe pain has gone, but not so the shock of surgery and the stresses left by those 18 hellish months that preceded it. Still have a nurse during the day, am allowed no visitors or phone calls. In the position of one learning to walk with legs which don't much like the idea. Must lie on right side, except for brief periods—even note writing a bit of a chore. And during past couple weeks Miriam has been undergoing series of tests and treatments at Clinic after doctor attending me observed signs of a flare

[missing rest of letter]

To James Boyer May from Miriam Patchen (KPA)
April 1961

Dear Boyer, (and Geraldine, of course!)

As usual, I am in a burning fever about something. The enclosed letter more than speaks for itself. I could rave and rant for hours, but the utter raw, open Philistinism is here for you to see. I feel that the letter should get the broadest possible circulation, the writer the most scathing denunciations possible, and the Carnegie Fund embarrassed as violently as possible. Whatever sum of money (and it would have been small) they might have parted with is of no concern. But, my God, what sort of statements do they utter! Bill Packard just sent it hopelessly to me with a "what do you know about this sort of thing."

In my incredulous horror and fury at this disgusting attitude I am completely on another wave-length from any other businesses and thoughts. But I can come down to reality enough to give you a small sort of report on the battlefront here. Kenneth's doctor was over the other night to give Kenneth some pain-killer and to apologize for having started him on such major dentistry so soon.

Said he had no idea that it would be so much, just thought teeth are taken out and new ones put in. But the dentist talked to the doctor for a long time explaining the process he had in mind of trying to save as many teeth as possible and said it was a difficult process for anyone to go through, that Kenneth would have to have Demerol shots before and after the sessions, etc. Well, anyway, the business will be finished in a few weeks and then the doctor will start treatment to get the fat out of the fire again. Both he and Kenneth think that permanent harm hasn't been done, but just that such rugged action so soon after the operation was a mistake and that the nerve endings have been tortured by the many hour sessions in the far-from-comfortable dentist's chair. Well, we'll see. Since the dentistry started, Kenneth has been unable to do anything. Before that he was beginning to walk and be able to sit up for short periods without pain. Since his first dental appointment he has been unable to do anything except take Percobarb. Needless to say, he's been most depressed by this. But all we can do now is the famous "wait-and-see" stuff. We're both getting a little tired, but when the weather gets warm (it's been persistently cold and very windy) we'll be able to get out and get more relaxed...and that will be soon, I am sure.

You can well imagine, though I can't see what hints we give you, that we have you on our minds and wonder and hope that things are better for the May Household than it has been much of the time. TRACE is really getting enormous, what a lot of work! And how nice to see it like Abou Ben Adham Increase. When are you two going to England to look over the operations there? It seems to me that a Guggenheim would be quite easy to obtain on the basis of wanting to "study" little magazine publication in England, France et al. See, I am going to get a Guggenheim for someone.

Both of us send this feeble and messy expression of love for you....our love and "up, the Rebels!"

Love—
Miriam

To James Laughlin from Miriam Patchen (NDA)

September 7, 1961
2340 Sierra Court
Palo Alto, California

Dear Jay,

Because we are exhausted and in a state of shock, this letter will be far short of a 'literary' missile, but I hope I manage to get in all the details. It seems more than time that you were entitled to the full story of the fortunes of the Collected Poems.

Kenneth's Collected Poems has been rejected Monday, a week ago, with "This is definite and final." These words will be more understandable when you hear it all.

Yes, I know...when you were here last we were obeying, to the best of our limited possibilities, Luther Nichols' injunction to celebrate the agreement being drawn up between Doubleday and Kenneth. Nichols had already told Kenneth you might be apprised of the details of the acceptance of the book although the contract had not yet been signed. It would arrive here by the Monday after your visit, or Wednesday at the latest. The advance payment of $1500 was ("we could probably get you $2500 if you wish") was pleasant to contemplate, but far more exciting were the other details. Your stated condition of release of the material that the book be a large comprehensive one seemed amply fulfilled with "not less than 500 pages." And the price of 5.95 seemed one which would give the book a good opportunity for sales. There were other things brought in: 4-6 pages of full-color reproductions of the Painting-Poems (which could be run off at the same time for store-advertising show cards) some black and white reproductions of the Portfolio pages, ascending scale royalties, book club rights, et al. It was a good week-end.

Monday morning the contract did not arrive. Well, it would arrive "Wednesday at the latest." In the afternoon Mr. Nichols called and said he had some bad news. He had received a letter from a Mr Banker (!) of the business office saying the project had been rejected, that they thought the two books were too expensive to consider publishing. And if the "poems were such a good thing why didn't New Directions publish them?" In spite of the difficulty Kenneth had in believing this was happening, he managed to get clearly understood that only the Collected Poems was under consideration. For Mr. Nichols had expressly called the Monday before asking that Kenneth would allow it to be that way, with the possibility of their having an option on "IMAGINE SEEING YOU HERE". L.N. concurred with this and suggested you not to be told about this confusion, that he was sure he could get it straightened out and things would be as before. He asked Kenneth to give him a week.

A week later he called and said he had been in touch with Kenneth MacCormack and he was sure it would be all right, that all it was now was a question of format on which MacCormack was now working...with great enthusiasm, that he wanted to do a book equal to the known quality of the Patchen books. He said he'd call us Monday to let us know the results of the editorial meeting, but he was certain we could rest assured that it would be all right once they got it clearly understood that it was only one book in question.

He didn't call Monday or Tuesday. Kenneth called Tuesday night and got Nichols who said he had gotten back from Los Angeles so late Monday night he hadn't wanted to call, and that he had bad news which was hard to convey. He'd learned from a friend (a Shelby/Sherby) that at the meeting someone had introduced the "fact" that New Directions was bringing out an almost identical book. (Crash!) Of course this was inconceivable and Kenneth had an over an hour talk with Nichols. This when all telephoning was forbidden and when even a few words on the instrument caused such strain that Kenneth would be completely drenched. Nichols said someone of the men had a habit of reading publishers' catalogues and he brought up the New Directions competition. So Kenneth asked if James Laughlin was being accused of suckering Doubleday, etc, what would be the point of deliberately running into competition with a big house, why make the offer of release, etc ad infinitum, that surely he'd know if such a move were being contemplated. Finally Nichols agreed to write New York that "If New Directions were considering such a book, he was sure James Laughlin would withdraw in favor of Doubleday, that he would be reasonable about this." He asked that you not be told of this new situation, that it would be ironed out and he didn't want you to be mad at him or them. He said he'd call on Monday.

He didn't call Monday or Tuesday. Kenneth called him on Wednesday. He said he had been so unhappy over the unfavorable report that he hadn't been able to call. Just as they were speaking, Nichols exclaimed "Wait a minute, there's a call on the other wire from New York! I'm sure it's good news. Let me call you back." Kenneth reiterated what he had said for two weeks, that he wished an end to this, saying "Let Adolph Hitler die at last, don't keep this up week after week," that Doubleday had every right to reject a book and he hoped they would let this alone. Of course this was after Doubleday had accepted the book and advanced terms! Anyway, less than 10 minutes afterwards, Nichols called and said there was "a last minute reprieve from the governor", that he and Kenneth

MacCormack were so distressed at the cat and mouse game that MacCormack would go over the heads of his associates directly to the president, a Mr. Sargent, with all the details, including an eight-page letter Nichols himself had written presenting the history of the "case". He couldn't say when we'd hear, but he'd call the minute he had news. MacCormack was going to spend the week-end with a Doubleday author, President Eisenhower. However, Mr. Nichols was sure this sort of unprecedented appeal would work to straighten out a badly messed-up job.

Monday, August 23, Luther Nichols called and said he'd a wire from MacCormack saying the book had been rejected "and this is final". He said he and the office here were shocked at this news and that he didn't know what to say. That he'd try to interest some other publisher in the book, that he felt he'd "let Kenneth down", that he'd approach people interested in poetry. An offer Kenneth refused. In answer to Kenneth's question about what happened with the spirited appeal to Mr. Sargent, Nichols said he'd get a follow-up letter from MacCormack and he'd call Thursday definitely. We waited. He hasn't called.

As you can see, it's an unfathomable mystery...probably we'll never know who did what and why, though Nichols once said probably there's someone who doesn't like poetry. What was this cruel game in which a "reputable" house with well-known editors reneged on a set deal? Kenneth's work on the Painting-Poems was halted because those he was working on were the ones Nichols wanted to send as examples to New York. He spent hours on the 'phone drenched and strained beyond endurance. We've been on Death Row almost as long, it seems, as Carryl Chessman, with the same final results.

Kenneth's doctor came back from his vacation and Kenneth is going into the hospital for tests to see if there's anything which can be done. I'll let you know, of course. It was good seeing you. We were both so conscious of your generosity in all this, so sorry it got so befouled and wasted.

The best,

Days later, this has been a-writing for several days. Kenneth was given some experimental shots, and has at least three more such sessions. So far he's been in helpless agony. Each time it seems to get worse. Well, we'll just have to wait-out the series of shots and see.

c.c. Luther Nichols, Kenneth Rexroth, Kenneth MacCormack, William Webb, et al et al: those who were either informed or professionally concerned

To Henry Rago from Kenneth Patchen (PAP)

October 27, 1961
Stanford Medical Center
300 Pasteur Drive
Palo Alto, California

Dear Henry Rago

I wonder if you think there is a possibility of Poetry's printing some of my writing-drawing-poems?

Perhaps you have seen some of those published in magazines over the past years? If not, briefly they are intended to gain a greater expressiveness through representation which is not at mercy of short-circuiting inevitable in printshops. The writing-forth, drawing, and the poem itself unite in a single, controlled fashion—at least, the hope is that they do! —

Reproduction in line-cut, half-tone, or photo-offset from my MS. page.

Please let me know if there is a possibility of Poetry's using work of this sort—be happy to send some in for your consideration. My original would probably be twice your pg for easier handling. (Ok?)

Don't recall whether Miriam acquainted you with latest news of your friends here: in January underwent another major operation on my spine; hospitalized now for tests looking for cause of relapse from successful-seeming convalescence (believe it will be found that more rigid home-therapy will let me turn corner). Miriam responding well to new medicines; both a bit tired at moment. Tomorrow—!

All good wishes!
Sincerely,
Kenneth Patchen

To Henry Miller from Kenneth Patchen (UCLA)

January 15, 1962
2340 Sierra Court Palo Alto

Dear Henry Miller

Looking over that list of paperback publishers sent by Vincent Birge, I got more than a hunch they're on another planet as far as anyone's interesting them in printing me goes—even if the one be H.M. Too shotgunny, I think—then there's fact Laughlin holds say-so on many of the poems. New Directions should do them, Collected Poems I mean.

When what seemed certain publication with Doubleday fell through, I wrote to Laughlin with suggestion that what he said was a bar to N.D's bringing the collection out (that is, prohibitive expense of 6-700 pg. volume), could easily be overcome by doing the Collected Poems in 2 vols. of, say, 250-300 pages each—one this year, the 2nd next. And as often happens, got no response from him. My 1st book of poems came out in 1936: 25th anniversary '62. Perhaps if you sounded him out on this...? Offered to introduce one of the vols...?

Another suggestion: Do an open letter not to plead my cause but to accuse those who crocodile-teared the fearful plight of Boris Pasternak poet behind the iron curtain—censored, ignored etc—were and are determinedly content to censor, ignore etc a poet right in the midst of "freedom" (almost said behind The Ice Curtain). Censorship, did I say? The NY Times Book section refused to carry ads of Sleepers Awake and Memoirs of A Shy Pornographer. Deliberately ignored, did I say? My last 3 books—Hurrah For Anything, Poemscapes, Because It Is—received less than 10 reviews between them! (Ask Jonathan Williams for corroboration of this—and of so much more in this vein.)

So an Open Letter To Those Whom It Obviously Does Not Concern. I quote from K Rexroth's book of New Directions published essays, Bird In The Bush:

"Against a conspiracy of silence of the whole of literary America, Patchen has become the laureate of the doomed youth of the Third World War. Yet he is the most widely read younger poet in this country." etc etc. If you haven't book, and if you see your way, time-wise and otherwise to doing the Open Letter, I'll send it to you.

Such an Open Letter could be sent smack into the midst of the "freedom protestors"—mags, papers, publishers, who-and-whatever. And printed in the book City Lights wanted to reissue, Patchen: Man of Anger and Light, provided that Henry Miller made some contemporary statement for inclusion. —Its reissue could do much for me right now.

Enclosed "painting-poem" cards you've probably seen, but anyway they will give you a very weak idea of book which I'd bite the devil's tail to get out in style—noticed you have a book with Abrams so perhaps you could help here. (Bill Webb has been fiddling away without even a squeak that I know of with publishers I never heard of for more than a yr. on this blind alley in CAPS.)

I have over 50 new "painting-poems" in full color, and as many in black and white. God I wish it been possible for you to see them. Say the word and I'll return-post you half dozen or so! Really have to be seen! Think you'll agree they deserve full-budget, big format treatment by pub. like Abrams.

I'm tired now.

Kenneth

Still in great pain—with nothing to alleviate it.

You probably wondered how Miriam and I could be so alone in our trouble—people want to socialize, not to look into the naked face of suffering and pain. Not that I blame them—on the contrary, that's why we couldn't ask their help in crisis.

To Kenneth Patchen from Henry Miller (UCLA)
Pacific Palisades

February 9, 1962

Dear Kenneth,

I only got back from Big Sur yesterday. While there I ran into Bill Webb, who told me about Orion's interest in your work. He urged me to write Howard Greenfeld, the president, which I did this morning. Seemed to think there was still a good chance of them bringing it out. In any case, I asked Greenfeld to let you know quickly what he intends to do.

I had also written Jay Laughlin about you, and had to wait a bit for his answer as he was away. He wrote me a very wonderful letter about you, I thought, in which he said that he himself had made efforts to interest other publishers in bringing out your collected work, but with no success. Meantime he believes it to your best interests to continue bringing out your work in paperback editions, thereby reaching a larger audience. Feels that the collected edition would be too expensive to gain you many readers.

My friend Vincent Birge has also been busy writing to Foundations; none of them seem suited to meet your needs, he thinks. I've also been in touch with Elmer Gentz about you; he is the lawyer defending the Tropic of Cancer in Chicago at present. You probably know whom I mean. I mentioned that I intended to draft an open letter to magazines and periodicals about your case, and he asked me to please let him see it before I send it out. There is a risk, he says, in my doing this if not properly worded, because of all the litigation going on. I am still pondering this matter of the wording.

A word about Bill Webb. Perhaps you have lost faith in him. I hope not. I think he has your interests at heart, very much indeed. And he is a man of conscience. He and Henry Geiger of "Manas" are still discussing what can be done for you. One thing seems evident—that the doctors can't do much more. I will be in touch with Bill Webb as long as I am down here, and will keep you informed of what happens.

I supposed all this means little to you, but I don't know what more to say or do at the moment. Something like a miracle has got to happen, it seems to me. Anyway, don't think that I have forgotten you.

Give my best to Miriam. In this last year and a half nearly every one of my friends has been struck by some misfortune. I've never known a period like it. How long can it continue?

Meanwhile all the best!

Henry Miller

To Judith Wray from Miriam Patchen (KPA)

February 14, 1962
2340 Sierra Court Palo Alto, California

Dear Judith:

So many thanks for your prompt and good help. I was quite desperate, as you judged. [...] It's a dirty story by now and rather horrible, but I guess you are entitled to as much of it as I can chronicle. It goes on and on so bear with me. I shall not attempt to tell it journalistically, but somehow cover it as briefly as is possible.

When I wrote you I was staying awake all night and most of the day to watch Kenneth for fear of his getting hurt as a result of medication carelessly prescribed for him. Oh no, when I wrote you was the second time we were in such horrifying straits.

So....When you were here in November 1959, Kenneth was already suffering from medical bungling. He had rushed back from New York appearances with a jazz group (Charlie Mingus) because the doctors had allowed him to go only on promise that he would come back immediately and have the chest surgery they insisted was necessary. We were told all sorts of things which could happen if the "obstruction" which was seen in the esophagus via X-Ray weren't removed. And "now that you are all right", he'd really just recovered from the penicillin reaction which nearly killed him, have this thing done while it's easy. A doctor friend when he heard of this was much concerned about it being not a simple operation and wished the best man he knew of to do it, so he appealed to a friend and teacher of his, a Dr. Richards in San Francisco. Dr. Richards was most friendly and took on the case. On July 13 an esophagoscopy was performed. When I saw Kenneth a few hours later he said his back hurt. However we attributed it to all the bending and flexing which we knew would be done. We had been told that Dr. Richards would attempt to remove the polyp without surgery, and our mutual friend said he, if anyone, could do it. So I was pleased when I saw Kenneth obviously had had no surgical incision. We waited hours, drinking coffee. No one came in, no word from doctors. As Kenneth went to the lavatory a man stopped him in the hall and said he was Dr. McNaught, "You don't know me, but I was with Dr. Richards and I'm amazed to see you walking so soon, after what we did to you!"

Some hours later Dr. Richards came in and I gushed over him in my relief that a chest incision had not been performed, almost in a satirized woman's club way, "only you could have achieved this" etc. He seemed most embarrassed (all this stupid detail is in this tale now because we only a couple weeks ago found out what follows) and I said to him that he must have gotten used to fulsome thanks by now, that how terribly young he seemed in his embarrassment. Well, anyway he asked if Kenneth wanted to go home right away. Of course he did, and we did.

The next day I reported to Kenneth's back surgeon as he'd asked us to. He was the one terribly concerned about the polyp, about having it removed. My "goody, goody, it worked. The doctor was able to snip it out as he hoped, not even penetrating the chest wall" brought a sigh of relief from the surgeon. We told him Kenneth's back hurt considerably, but we all came to the conclusion that it was bound to after such a vigorous going-over as he must have had.

Well, by the time you came here in November, Kenneth had been in bad pain most of the time since my call to Dr. Meier. We reported it to the San Francisco doctor, Dr. Richards. He prescribed medicines over the 'phone' and told Kenneth to have nothing to do with the Palo Alto Clinic doctors, that he'd always be available to Kenneth either for Kenneth to go to him or to call. At this point this was easy to follow since the orthopedic man went on a vacation to Germany. Well, when the play was rehearsing Kenneth went to San Francisco at my insistence to see Dr. Richards. As Kenneth limped in more dead than alive (you saw him about then) Dr. Richards said how fine he looked. Boy, I got mad. I told him that Kenneth had been a whole man when he saw him first and now was less than a cripple, for many of them at least feel no pain. So the doctor took Kenneth into another room examined him and told him he might as well learn to live with pain, that nothing would help, and, on a question from Kenneth, further surgery might leave him worse off than before. We came home full of joy and gladness, as the saying goes. By now Dr. Meier had returned and I called him to tell him of the situation. He taped Kenneth so that he could attend rehearsals, gave some spinal shots. He said, and kept saying 'till I lost my mind "it will be all right." He explained to Kenneth that the original fusion had held and showed him on a miniature skeleton just how things were. But that Kenneth was getting older and that as the spine settled there was bound to be some discomfort. Later when I called to ask him why in an area where there were some of the best medical men in the country available Kenneth had to suffer so much pain, he came up with this aging theory. I asked him if a man could age so suddenly as to have this happen in a day. Well, "it would be all right", believe him. What "it" was I could never determine however I asked.
(you see, this goes on and on and on...and this is only the beginning!)

By the way, on one of my talks with Dr. Richards, he told me that he had done nothing to Kenneth, that after the examination, he didn't have the heart to do more to him.???? (More on this later)

As I went to work each day leaving Kenneth almost helpless, I felt only misery. The play was wildly successful, even when the director was able to "pull fast ones" on Kenneth because Kenneth was getting so much medication that he couldn't remember when the director would say that he'd agreed to some expedient or other. Then when Dupont was planning to move the play cross-country after a short trial in San Francisco or Los Angeles, everything went poof as it became obvious that Kenneth couldn't go with it. Loss of untold dollars. The money put in escrow for the play was then used for the purchase of nightclubs. Dr. Meier at this time told Kenneth he couldn't possibly go east to lecture at Yale as he'd been invited to do. Again a loss of not only that sum, but usually awards follow that particular lecture. Bill Packard became insistent that something be done and against our wishes he started a Patchen Fund movement. Then Dr. Meier, the orthopedic man who had been responsible for the successful back operation before suggested another, but a vaguer one. Just an operation, a we'll see sort.

The fund-drive was on full swing as Kenneth entered the hospital in January 1961, with private nurses, private rooms etc. After the operation, immediately after, I saw the doctor and asked him what he did. He told of a "wad of scar tissue." Pain was understandably with that, of course, as I agreed. But, I wanted to know what else. For it was obvious to me that scar tissue, a "wad" of it doesn't happen in one day. He patted me and said "someday" he'd tell me.????

Kenneth stayed in the hospital for some time with a day nurse, until I asked why he couldn't come home, that the hospital equipment was no longer necessary and that the nurse could come here as well as there. So that was effected. Kenneth began to be able to sit up for short times, he was out of pain, he could walk. The weather just reached its worse time of the year so that Kenneth was not out of doors as he'd hoped to be, but he was out of pain and beginning to work. Then the doctor insisted that he have his teeth out. Kenneth asked if it couldn't wait a while. No, it was necessary because of the infection possibly being a danger. So many years of oral medication and inability to have the teeth attended to had taken a great toll. The dentist who entered the case explained to Dr. Meier that he was going to try to save as many as possible of Kenneth's teeth, that it would be long and arduous, that he'd need some analgesic protection. The doctor said he'd give Kenneth some shots before the sessions. Well, anyway, the first session was nearly four hours. This was about the end of February. Kenneth was in pain from that day on. The dentistry couldn't be stopped mid-stream, nothing protective was done about or for the back. We hoped it would pass. Kenneth kept saying he was sure that nothing had gone wrong, just that the irritated nerves, which hadn't had a chance to recover from the surgery and scar-tissue, were roiled.

Time passed, great muscle spasms occurred, nothing would relax them. Kenneth was getting pain medication again. "It would pass." We hoped. The doctor finally decided to give a series of spinal shots to try to relax the muscle. Just as they were showing some results, he went on a vacation and dropped the thing entirely. I asked him if he wouldn't ask the neurologist at the clinic who'd been an advisor on the January surgery to look at the business while he was away. He agreed. The neurologist said with some anger that the dentistry at that time was most ill-advised, that Kenneth now had what Medicine now recognized as a disease: when pain continues in one area too long it creates a diseased state. But that he and the anesthologist would try to alleviate the situation. The letter then said they might be able to help, but that they might also make things worse. They gave him shots twice. The first time nothing much happened. The second time all hell broke loose in his back, and the medical opinion was that this avenue was closed, at least until the return of Kenneth's regular doctor when they could confer on procedures. When the doctor returned in September Kenneth went to him to get something for the muscle spasm which was huge and for which he had only pain-killers which he didn't like.

After a few trips like this to the clinic for shots (usually the long wait there, though he had an appointment, and the taxi trip pretty well undid any benefits he might have gotten from the shots) Kenneth was getting a bit worn. The doctor then ordered a hospital stay, to put Kenneth into a cast and for an evaluation of the drugs he was taking. He asked Kenneth to ask me what I thought of this, for me to come in and see him. So I went. According to him, he couldn't understand what was causing such gigantic spasms (the largest he'd ever seen). [...] He just looked sad.

The first day no one approached except hospital personnel and his nurse who tried to get word from the doctor's office what to do, when he was coming, etc. (Nothing). The second day hospital personnel took blood pressure tests, temperatures, etc. and told Kenneth he was not to suffer pain, that they had orders to give him a hypodermic as soon as he was uncomfortable. The doctor dropped in the late afternoon, looked at a sports magazine for a while and said that Kenneth's internist was in Florida, but would be back the next day. The next morning a message from the internist's office that he would appear later in the day. He did not. Each evening as I went and I'd get a "nothing" answer. The nurse finally asked me to stop asking, because Kenneth was getting pretty disturbed by this series of non-events. On the third day Kenneth had some X-Rays. All along he had hypodermic shots, even when he protested them at night. There were a few more tests during the week, none of the obvious ones: No spinal tap, no neurological, no nothing. Friday, I think the internist dropped in and chatted a while with Kenneth and ordered a test. Saturday morning the orthopedist dropped in and said other tests were scheduled. None. So Kenneth asked to come home.

I'd give Kenneth the hypodermic when he'd get into bad pain, and then he'd fall into a troubled sleep, over which I'd watch for fear he'd hurt himself as he thrashed around. [...] His "dreams" were pretty bad and he was much disturbed. Some weeks of this sort of thing passed, me up all night, resting in the evening a bit, getting no response to calls I'd make to the clinic. [...] Kenneth had tried twice in the night to go away, "anywhere" so that I "could get some rest" so that he could find help. [...] Day after Christmas we called an ex-neighbor who was head of personnel (office workers) at the clinic [who] told us to call her ex-boss and clinic head. [...] He had Kenneth sit up on a chair and shot him three times with an unnamed fluid into the back, told Kenneth to get up. Kenneth did, and fell, hitting his head on the couch. I rushed over to help him and he (the doctor) didn't allow me, saying for me not to "pamper" him, that he couldn't hurt himself [...] That night Kenneth on going to the bathroom, with my aid and pushing a chair in front of him, fell in there twice, hitting his head on the basin, knocking his teeth loose badly, nearly knocking himself out. [...]

Oh lord, I've had so many interruptions in this that I've skipped the entirely delightful weekend. The one before the new doctor entered the picture. On that Saturday and Sunday Kenneth had been in increasing pain. He went into his work room to be by himself a great deal. That Sunday night he wanted me to go to bed and he'd stay up in his room. An arrangement he'd occasionally insisted upon some months before, and during the weeks of the delirium. One which I didn't approve of, because, though I didn't sleep during those times, I was afraid that I might and then

Kenneth might be in bad trouble. Well, anyway, we did this. He closed the door so I wouldn't hear his distress. I didn't sleep, of course. Once I heard him go into the kitchen for some brandy. Before, that was the only thing he could use for pain. I heard him pour a little glass and add some water. Then silence for some time. Then a terrible crash. So I went in. He was confused, needed to get into the bathroom, I helped him. He threw up slightly, was very strange. Said Well, I did it. Did WHAT? Well anyway I got from him he'd taken a bunch of sleeping pills, how many he didn't know. He didn't seem to have thrown them up, I couldn't get clear when he'd taken them, etc. He was inert and I could not get him moved. So I called emergency and an ambulance came shortly with a police car. [...] The police questioned me for some length and then took me to the hospital. It was only there (several hours later) that I found out what had happened. Kenneth had been pumped out, was all right. He'd taken the pills because he'd thought that he could take enough to knock himself out and have a little relief from the pain that way. [...] Kenneth's orthopedist had once brought two huge bottles of sleeping pills as a "present"....probably 1000 in each! [...] I got home about 4:30, cleaned the house, washed two loads of clothes. Dr. Lee called me about 9 and said that Kenneth was all right and could come home as soon as I could get him. So I got him right away. The next day when Dr. Lee came he said that everything they'd done to Kenneth had been the wrong things [...] As he was leaving, we brought up again our question about the advisability of Kenneth's going somewhere for a complete examination, something which he had not had here. Dr. Lee thought it was a fine idea. He suggested University of California which has a clinic in San Francisco. Kenneth said he wasn't up to it right away, but he'd think it would be the only way we'd be able to go on with treatment, when doctors knew what was to be treated.

[...] You see why we're nearly nuts with this situation. Kenneth worsens daily as the muscle spasm keeps the nerves raw. He has been helpless and in constant pain except for a couple weeks for over two years. He started working as soon as the operation was over, had to stop within weeks....well anyway....we have no solutions to the problem as yet, no answers as to WHY, no nothing. One of the most difficult things for us, aside of the obvious pain, misery, etc. is Kenneth's being unable to make any plans, start any work, knowing that even if he could get something started, as he did during the short easier period, it is certain to get interrupted, destroyed, wrecked as so much of his work has had to happen to it in all these years of difficulties.

You see what I meant: there was so much.....and all of it is not in this chronicle even at that. This is the barest outlines of the physical situation, the nightmare. Someday when the (if it is ever of any point to do it) entire story must be told, there are many more nasty dark corners, many unsolved, unrecorded moments......

Did you have the many hours this mess required? I apologize, but..... In the meantime, while battles rage, while we come to some solution, we are aware that you are touring around like mad doing so much....We send our love to you all....

[handwritten note]
If you can read this! She made a couple copies for me—knew I couldn't do it again...
Things got even more "dirty pool" after this letter was written—but anyway he's in hospital now—we'll see.

To Kenneth Patchen from James Laughlin (NDA)

February 20, 1962
2340 Sierra Court
Palo Alto, Calif.

Dear Kenneth,

Your letter of February 17, telling about all the pain and trouble that you have been having since I saw you last, fills me with sorrow —and also makes me count my own blessings, when I consider how very little illness I have had to go through in my own life. Why it should all descend on you, who are so much a better person, I will never know. It has all the horror of some of the Greek myths where those poor devils are damned to endless torment. Life, as the Existentialists like to say, really is absurd.
But I'm glad to think that there may have been some slight improvement in recent weeks, and that Miriam is feeling better, and that you may be able to turn your hand to further writings. Of the three proposals for new books which you outline, it would seem to me that number 2—a journal-diary-style-novel might have the greatest possibilities. It has been some time since you have done

anything of that kind, and I think that the success over the years in many editions of "Memoirs" and "Albion Moonlight" has proven your powers in this field.

Your idea of doing the "Collected Poems" in two paperback volumes is only about 20% less frightening to my timid soul than the earlier proposal for a big hardbound volume. We are just in the process of getting out, in paperback form, what amounts roughly to the third volume of the William Carlos Williams collected poem series, and the cost is staggering, compared to what the earlier one cost us. The book will have to sell for a price nearly as great as that of the earlier hard-bound volumes, even though it is to be a paperback. I simply don't know where this inflation of book production costs is going to lead us. I would approach with less trepidation the thought of enlarging the "Selected Poems" again and bringing that out as a paperback. A quick check of the stock records indicates that we now have on hand of the "Selected Poems" something between five and six hundred copies,which is about a year's sale at the present rate of flow. So we would normally be reprinting that for 1963, but why don't we add to it and put it in the paperback? Thus we would have, at least, the benefit of the saving on the 140-odd pages which are presently, I believe, in plate form.

[End of letter fragment]

To Kenneth Patchen from Henry Miller (UCLA)

March 8, 1962

Dear Kenneth Patchen,

You are really a magnanimous soul! On reading your reply, which I scarcely deserved, I went hollow. This morning, first thing, I dashed off the enclosed. Will it do? Maybe I will write more, later. But this for now, at any rate, to tell you that I have never lost interest, never ceased to believe in you, and always feel conscience-stricken that I have not done more to prove what I feel toward you.

God bless you!
Henry Miller

[Handwritten addition]

P.S. Some fan called my attention to a mag. called "Playboy"—lurid, sensational, yet...Anyway they sell a million copies a month and pay very well. Wonder if you could send them a "story"—or maybe a serious essay? I know no one there. See a copy on stands sometime.

To William Roth from Miriam Patchen

2340 Sierra Court
Palo Alto, CA

April 4 [1963]

Dear Bill—

Kenneth has been wanting to send you these for a long time. Last night, after a long bout of delirium (a repeat of Monday night) as he started to clear, he wanted to do something he'd feel good about. This was it. He's so depressed at not being able to work. It's the only thing which is life for him. He keeps saying in his pain and confusion "If only I had something special to look forward to"—it's too late—if we could only get away from this prison—

He's been so nearly destroyed these last two nights I've had to do some tremendous gymnastics psychologically to keep him from walking out—"anywhere—I won't tell you" etc.

If he could believe that he can go away eventually—to work—Paris? Italy? Not really—some small town south of France maybe—then he'd be willing to try to start again attempting to get doctors, care—he's had none at all since Feb 1—and very little for months before that. His state is alarming. Dr. Klinghoffer is trying to get doctors—I'd feel safer if he took Kenneth into Mt. Zion. Something must be done—I know it can. But Kenneth says he has no interest in trying anymore. However, that changes instantly when he gets a moment's relief from the most violent of the pain. Then he wants to get to work. Even the N.D. But Even So is an irritant to him for the big books keep clammoring [sic] until he's nearly crazy with the labor pains. In a very poor way some of this is what he would have said to you if he'd gotten you. He started several letters—none of which came out right (I judge) and none of which he'll send. He might have been able to talk to you as he did on the initial entry of Bill Roth into the fray—just about a year ago.

Unfortunately, the lawsuit, giving of the deposition (which everyone said he did brilliantly—is this another word for truth?) anyway, it left him with the feeling that an awful, awful lot had been expended for—well, to speak matter-of-factly of a tragic event, which Kenneth never wanted, resisted it until he was pressured into it—it's likely what we'll get out of this hit-and-run doctor is the privilege of paying court costs—1,000—1,500.

Well (and this goes on and on—I'm a little woozy—been up all night, but want to get even this garbled mass to you so that I can get Kenneth to believe something is being tried). Kenneth remembering that you had offered to pay for the whole NY clinic package (hospital bed only $40 a day, everything else extra—and that was threatened for a full year—me included in the big deal. So Kenneth who has to go through more doctoring first would like,—no, <u>must have something</u> carrotting in front of his nose <u>that takes his work into account</u>—all these horrible years of pain, pain and frustration of sordid medicating—to no avail—of course he will have to continue to do what can be done—but it has become so dreary, unproductive, demoralizing for someone whose whole life is his work. So—Kenneth who has never been out of the country [the year his back was wrecked, he would have gotten a year's scholarship to England, but at last minute had to inform Ciardi that he couldn't go—oh, if only we had British medicine!]* wants so strongly to take me somewhere—anywhere, except Mexico, I think. Just as our deep South is a place to avoid—so, we feel is Mexico. Whatever—even if it doesn't come about, let us keep the possibility alive so things aren't just more hospital no work. Just say a why sure, when you're ready let me know—or some such. Please.

I can't say it well enough—I <u>AM</u> sorry for sneaking this effusion into the package—sorry for unloading more stuff on you—but I watch the tearing-down of something very special until I want to do what one Bay-Area husband did a couple years ago—he went a-gunning for the doctor who killed his wife.

—Anyway, thanks

Miriam

*Dr Alex Comfort who introduced Kenneth to English readers is one of the heads of the London Hospital—Comfort, a few years ago told Kenneth that we should go to the warm Mediterreanean [sic] within easy plane shot of England—"and we'll take care of you." He's, as you probably know one of the finest poets, author of several prose books.

A Parable at the Year's End, 1964 (KPA)

A Parable At The Year's End

They've started to call it "The Telephone Story"—you must have heard it by now. Happened in Pennsylvania—in Central Park—on the White House lawn. The tree was—oh, maybe an elm, an oak, a hickory—but very old, and very big. I guess there must be almost as many versions as there are people telling it. Funny, though, the story always begins with a child dashing in the house and announcing he's heard a ringing inside a tree "louder than anything in the whole world!"

Pretty loud all right—judging by how many have heard it! Wonder if you happened to hear this ending?—I like it best. Crowd is milling around. It's growing dark. Lot of bumping, angry shoving. Things are getting nasty. Just then the child's father pushes through & somehow—how?—reaches into the tree... takes out a telephone. He lifts the receiver—no one breathes—& the father says yes, what is it? Then, after a moment, a voice from the telephone: It's not too late, if only you will love one another. And the voice, of course, was his own.

1964 Kenneth Patchen

***Note:** Letter fragment to James Laughlin from October 1, 1964 (NDA)*

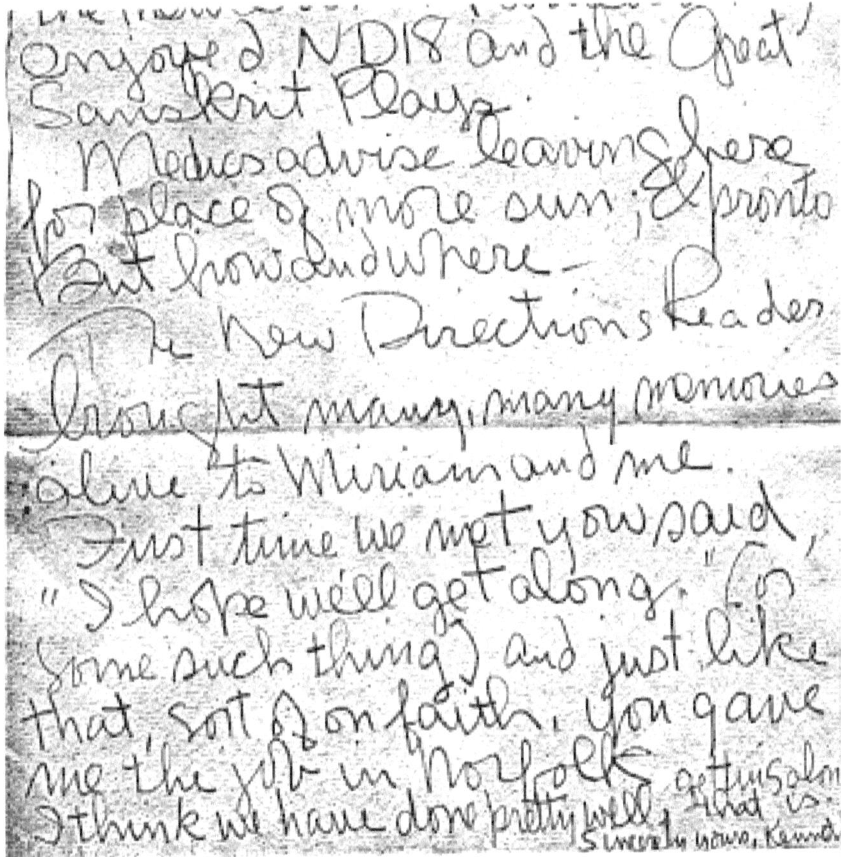

enjoyed ND18 and the Great Sanskrit Plays.
Medics advise leaving here for place of more sun; & pronto But how and where—
The New Directions Reader brought many, many memories alive to Miriam and me.
First time we met you said, "I hope we'll get along." (or some such thing) and just like that, sort of on faith, you gave me the job in Norfolk getting along
I think we have done pretty well, that is.
Sincerely yours, Kenneth

To Nancy and Jasper Wood from the Patchens (NOR)

August 11, 1965

Dear Nancy and Jasper,

Though you are on your Mexico cloud, smelling of heavenly shaves, this might as well be expressed and sent. The impulse to get in touch immediately was strong, though perhaps not quite as much so as the emotions our letter and generosity stirred in us.

You dear crazy people out of almost pre-history! How strange the feeling of pushing aside the mists. We'll never forget the picture of Jasper squatting on the floor at 12th St, NYC assembling Harold Chumbly's mimeograph book. You were a brave good one even then, but misabile dictu, you apparently stayed so! That is the to-be-celebrated fact. So few of the fine youth, as you well know, retain those loves, which moved them so deeply, into "practical maturity". At that time Jasper spoke in poetry of his Nancy and dreams. For years we've hoped at least a portion turned out as—planned (?). It would sound as if you had triumphed. The victory is in even staying alive, but the triumph, the victory is in living which is quite another thing as we know.

Your letter and love and warm generosity hurt. There's no way of refusing, accepting, thanking for these strange precious things. It would be so much easier, happier to give these to you. A part of this we have always done—you were/are still the sweet, star-filled "kids" for whom we agonized. Mostly thank you for remaining those good babes—and, for heaven's sake!—continuing these qualities into the second generation. I'm babbling, surrounded by words but unable to tell the way it has affected us. Simply:

God damnit

THANK YOU

Miriam
and
Kenneth

To Kenneth Patchen from James Laughlin (NDA)

November 15, 1965

Dear Kenneth:

It was good to hear from you the other night on the phone and I'm glad that there is prospect of something good for you from Texas. I'll be glad to cooperate along the lines we discussed.

Ann was kind enough to count the letter in the files here at Norfolk, and she found some 236 letters from you, 18 postcards, and 25 letters and cards from Miriam. There may also be some letters at the New York office, I'll have a look. Letters to Bob MacGregor are his, though I could approach him, if you want me to. He plans to leave the ND letters that came to him to Harvard.

As to the material which is "on deposit" (I have never given it to them outright) at Harvard, I'll try to get a list from them of what is there. The position on this stuff is that original typescripts or manuscripts belong to the author, proofs etc to ND. Harvard does not like to give this stuff up, as they hope to get it when I die, but they have to release the original scripts when the author requests them, and have done so in other cases. One rub, for them, is that they slipcased the material on certain books all together, a practice which I discouraged to the late curator, but he kept on doing it. I would just as soon keep the proofs there, to keep that phase of the overall ND collection complete.

I'm glad that Texas is willing to keep the material (your letters to me, my letters to you) restricted for a good period, thirty years certainly as a minimum. I don't think either of us want just any graduate student poring over our private lives and then gossiping about it to his friends. Perhaps it could be set up, if you wish, so that a reliable, mature scholar or biographer, one approved by both of us, of the heirs on both sides, could have access. But all of this should be carefully written up by the Texas lawyers, and approved by both of us, before we "deliver." I would plan to Xerox our letters before the originals left, but the same restrictions, with respect to the copies, can be imposed on Harvard. I'd also like to get from Texas copies of my letters on which I did not keep carbons in the early days.

I assume that you will be going over the tax angles carefully with Roberts. Their lawyers must know the ins and outs of this complicated side of it by now, and have stratagems for spreading payment over several years if that will reduce your tax liability for capital gains tax. We also want to make certain that I do not become liable for gift tax on the gift to you. $3000 can be given to any individual in any one year, tax free. That ought to cover it, spread over two years, unless they appraise the letters very highly.

[End of letter excerpt]

Western Union telegram to James Laughlin, New Directions from Kenneth Patchen (NDA)

Palo Alto, California
March 21, 1966

WESTERN UNION
TELEGRAM
W. P. MARSHALL, PRESIDENT

1966 MAR 21 PM 3 04

JTA149 (00)(00)SPE126 OA240
O PKA152 PD PALO ALTO CALIF 21 1043A PST
JAMES LAUGHLIN, NEW DIRECTIONS
3336 AVE NYK
VERY NECESSARY YOU KEEP YOUR WORD TO PUT NEW TITLE ON PRE CHRISTMAS LIST GIFTED HARD BOUND TWO COLOURS-PERHAPS SIMULTANEOUSLY PAPER SOOKS ALSO PARTIAL ECONOMY VIEW POINT BUT THESE CONSIDERATIONS MINOR ABOVE POINTS ARE NOT IMPORTANT TO ME YOU KNOW REPEAT IF FOR ANY REASON YOU DO NOT KEEP YOUR WORD I SHALL IRREVOCABLY END MY NEW DIRECTIONS ASSOCIATION IN ALL PHASES
KENNETH
(03).

To Kenneth Patchen from James Laughlin (NDA)

March 23, 1966
2340 Sierra Court
Palo Alto, Cal, 94303

Dear Kenneth:

Many thanks for your several recent communications and sendings, but I am afraid I must confess my head is spinning with all the complications of your intricate reasoning. I am glad, however, that you sent the follow up letter of clarification to your telegram, because I was rather negatively impressed by the tone of the telegram, but now that I see how your mind has been working I am quite ready not to take offence.

More than a business matter, it is, after all, given our long association, a question of whether I have faith in you whether I happen to like a particular book, and whether I really want to make a personal effort to help you, great a burden as it may be on my diminished time and strength. In both cases, the answer is very much an affirmative, so I will try to bear with you and do the best I can for you. But please, for your part, try to avoid all complications, and keep things just as simple as you can for me.

At first, I could not understand why you thought I had promised something about the picture-book, when I had not, but now I see that you have transferred the interest I expressed in "Alice" at the time of our discussion to this other book, since "Alice" was not ready on time. Very well, I will accept that, even though I don't think it is exactly logical.

The Lippincott sales manager was up here yesterday, and, while he is not exactly enthusiastic about the picture-book project, he seemed entirely willing to give it a good try. He feels, as I do, that such a book would have much greater success as a paperback, but if you absolutely desperately feel that you must have a book this year, and since we cannot release any more paperback until March of 1967, I guess there is no alternative but to experiment with it as a hardbound.

Our discussion yesterday ran along the lines that we would do a rather simple hardbound, and run some paperback sheets at the same time, which would then be released next March. But if you want to get into two colors, then we will have to reshape our plans entirely. From the preliminary conversations I have had with an offset printer who thinks he might be able to handle the job it appears to go that into two colors would enormously increase the cost of printing, and mean that we should think in the direction of a high priced limited edition. Probably something like 500 copies at a retail price of $10...and then remaindered those we get stuck with. And no paperback on it.

On the other hand, if you are willing to sacrifice the second color I believe we could run both a trade hardbound and a

[end of letter fragment]

To James Laughlin from Kenneth Patchen (NDA)

2340 Sierra Ct Palo Alto 94303
August 31, 1966

Dear Laughlin

Sorry to take so long thanking you for AIR-ing me a copy of the Hallelujah Anyway's jacket. I was supposed to enter hospital the day it came—last minute call off because of a strike of nurses. The call-off scrambled things more than ever: involved headache getting medicines since doctors thought I'd be rescheduled any minute. And I still have that uncertainty hanging over me, making it very difficult to do anything. The examinations, tests, x-rays, etc always make hospitalization an ordeal, but this off-again, on-again business complicates it almost beyond endurance. I don't (literally) know whether I'm coming or going and the doctors are in the same boat. And my back is giving me one of the worst times in years. I'll have a devil of a job getting into the flow of my work again—probably have to redo most of it. Such a setback at this time of general worry has my spirits in the dust—to put it mildly.

By this time I had hoped that something would happen to get us out of here. You remember I told you more than a year ago that I must somehow manage to get us to another place. Six years I've been imprisoned in this room! Miriam with two serious illnesses—nursing me, worrying how we'll get by much longer with no regular income. There are times when I wonder what's the point in it—and this is one of the times in capitals. I'm very pessimistic now about selling collection to library—and my bitterness is growing that in our situation no fund committee or foundation has given us a penny of help! (See by today's paper that the Rockefeller Fund has awarded Rexroth seven thousand dollars) It's clear that no one in the so-called literary community gives a damn whether I live or die. I take that back. Obviously they do care—verdict: die in a gutter, will not lift a hand.

It's something to think about. As the years pass, I see less and less point in any of it. My work—most of it done in pain added on pain—30 some years of it—and for what? What's the sense? Nobody gives a damn.

Sincerely yours,
Kenneth

To Miriam Patchen from William Packard (KPA)

October 12, 1966

Dear Miriam—

People (meaning me, or anyone) shouldn't take so long to answer a kind letter that meant so much to receive; thanks so much for writing, you know how much I love you both, and how I only wish the news of how you and Kenneth were getting on were somehow better, so damned much better, than it obviously is:—not even in terms of how much you both do truly deserve some peace and comfort and concern on the part of the community, but simply perhaps a "break", some happy accident that might begin to repay partially for all the years and years and years…

I am working, and hard, although I know the situation in New York theatre is terribly difficult and getting harder all the time, the commercial aspects are absolutely incredible and not worth going into, but most truly creative people here are discouraged, to say the least…That plus the Vietnam score plus the recent market slide has everyone a wee bit apprehensive, in a sort of silent way, that we may indeed be living in a kennel…

One dear friend here, Virginia Admiral, who knew you many years ago, says she is impressed by how many young students out at Queens College and elsewhere are "discovering" things like Albion Moonlight and Sleepers Awake; to which I said I wasn't surprised, I only hoped the message does more good to this generation than it apparently did to mine…

Sorry that Jonathan Williams hasn't followed through on publication plans for But Even So, can only hope he'll do so…And wonder if there's been any more thought to a "COLLECTED POEMS", and why New Directions hasn't initiated something like that…

Samuel French hasn't yet brought out the Phedre, it should be ready in a few weeks…And tho there was talk of more translation, I chose to go back to my own work over the next few years, and not do any more work in other languages…I don't know as I'm especially impressed by the vast number of competent (not a praise word for me) poets who spend their lives trying to get inside the minds and souls of other poets…So I'm hopeful I can do more, say more, get more down than I have so far, which isn't much…

One young poet, Steve Levine, recently published his first volume entitled SYNAPSE, and I wrote him to send you on a copy, as I thought you'd like it…He's somewhere out in California now, living on the Monterey Peninsula, I think…

Thanks so much for mentioning Harvey Breit, I will drop him a note to say I have been in touch with you and that you send greetings…

Now all good wishes and do write even if it is ghastly, and I know in my bones that things can't go on this way much longer…

My best,
B

To John Simon Guggenheim Foundation from Kenneth Patchen (GUG)

October 15, 1966
2340 Sierra Court Palo Alto, Calif 94303

Dear Secretary

I was awarded a Guggenheim Fellowship in 1936.

During the thirty years since then I have applied many times for a renewal of that Fellowship—I believe that the exact number of my applications is twenty-five (counting this one).

Now, in 1966, I again apply—and feel that the best argument of my case is to be found in the work I've done in these thirty years. I ask that your committee of selection examine the record of my creative activity—Who's Who, or any standard reference work of authors, will supply the information in cold outline form; any good bookstore will provide a more concrete and living basis for appraisal of my position in the literary community.

I know that Fellowships are not awarded on the basis of an applicant's need, but I think it fair to comment that during these many years of active production I have been a semi-invalid—and completely bed-ridden after a fourth spinal surgery in 1961. My medical expenses—larger now than ever—quite swamp my income from royalties, etc.

I would use the Fellowship renewal for creative work in poetry.

Sincerely yours,
Kenneth Patchen

Note: *Enclosed with this letter, on several sheets of paper listing his book publications.*

Chapter Eighteen: On the Side of Life (1967-1971)

To Kenneth Patchen from Alex Comfort (KPA)
University College, London

January 13, 1967
2340 Sierra Court Palo Alto

Dear Kenneth and Miriam,

Do forgive me. Not only did I not know about your troubles, but I was told K. had been over here and had been asking for me, but I wasn't in time to catch him. You must think me stupid or worse, but really the fault wasn't mine. I've been able to follow your fortunes only through your writing. Sometimes one loses touch with the man and what he is enduring, under the size and solidity of the structure he makes. I know I ought to have written before. My own problem has been the compulsion to live half a dozen lives, person, literary, everything—this makes me an ungrateful and unrewarding friend, because I lose all count of time between contacts. Forgive me.

I don't know what exactly happened, or why my colleagues haven't been able to help. You speak of a therapeutic misadventure—I suppose this means a bad mistake. Probably by now you've exhausted all advice, but tell me about it at least. If I'd known how ill things had gone, I'd certainly have come to talk face to face last time I was within reach, and I'll do so next time, whenever that is. Last time we corresponded I was trying to get you published here and did not succeed. Yet your influence is visible—possibly in disciples, like the folkniks, whom you wouldn't immediately recognise—from this side of the Atlantic. Whether this helps when one is sick I don't know. It may be a little bit like being under the skyscraper one has erected—still, you <u>have</u> erected it, and probably more than anyone you are the voice of decent anger on the side of life. In not being widely published here, you are only sharing the general and rather surprising neglect of the best American verse, and we may be readier for a Patchen invasion than now appears. I could imagine both your verse and your prose married to images in many media—film, television.

My sincerest sympathy in your troubles, but also my warm and continuing admiration for what you have done in spite of them. Send me your news.

Alex C.

To Miriam Patchen from Alex Comfort (KPA)

University College, London

January 23, 1967
2340 Sierra Court Palo Alto

My dear Miriam,

I think from your very clear account that it's obvious what happened. They probably did a gastrioscopic or esophagoscopic removal, which proved difficult: under anesthesia the spine must have been extended in order to pass the instrument, and damage must have been done.

What the outcome is I can't say myself. I feel sure the best thing will be this: I will try to find an orthopedic surgeon of top standing who is likely to take a personal interest in K. I tell him the story myself. I don't at the moment know whom to approach, but I'll make enquiries as soon as I get a chance. I won't suggest any more surgery or other intervention until I've had a good many words with colleagues—at least we mustn't make matters worse.

If you don't hear at once it won't mean I've forgotten. I have many medical contacts and travel a lot. Sadly, Lord Brain, the first man I'd have gone to, died last week. But there are others. You can rest assured that I'll try to help if I can see any hope of doing so. It shouldn't be necessary for things to be left like this.

Every good wish to you both. Good news about Cape. You will hear from me as soon as I can look around.

Yours ever
Alex C.

To the Patchens from Wayne Patchen (KPA)

February 8, 1967

Dear Children

Miriam I want to thank you for that nice letter you sent me. We haven't had much snow here so far this winter about 6 inches and that was only for a couple of days. Mostly 2 or 3 inches. I am anxious for spring to come so I can plant my garden. I have already got it plowed. I live here by myself and it gets lonesome some times as I haven't drove a car for 5 or 6 years since I was 80. May comes down and stays with me when Tommy is working night turn.. I have a bird feeder outside my kitchen window and you ought to see all the birds that come there. Haven't much to write about

Love Pop

***Note:** This is from Kenneth's father Wayne.*

To Miriam Patchen from Alex Comfort (KPA)
Department of Zoology, University College London

February 10, 1967

My dear Miriam,

This is about the most eminent opinion we have—from the head of the Medical Research Council's Unit. It does seem to offer some lines of action for Kenneth, so I've sent it straight to you.

Yours ever,

Alex

***Note:** The enclosed letter follows:*

To Alex Comfort from E.G.L Bywaters
Canadian Red Cross Memorial Hospital, Berkshire

February 9, 1967

Dear Dr. Comfort,

Thank you for your letter about Kenneth Patchen. The problem of natural disease are difficult enough, but iatrogenic disease is always a great deal worse since (perhaps fortunately) there are not enough 'cases' in each category to define a syndrome.

It is difficult to understand quite what is wrong with him, and the only possibility would be to have a definitive report on his illness from one of the doctors most recently concerned, together with the X-rays. His wife says he has a ruptured disc, presumably in the lumbar region. This is, I imagine, therefore probably a surgical problem, and I do not think our surgeons are any better really or any worse than the American ones.

I do know that there is a good physician, Boston trained, in San Francisco, Ephraim Englemann, and my feeling would be that if he has not already seen Englemann he should make an appointment to do so. It is seldom satisfactory to go by what involved relatives say, and I have had a number of pain problems from Americans referred to me in despair only to find that they were drug addicts primarily rather than pain problems, so I am somewhat wary of accepting cases except through people I know. It is obviously an extreme step to take to refer a patient from America, where there are very good centres and excellent physicians and surgeons, to some other place 6000 miles away.

In summary, I would be glad to review the X-rays if you thought this would be worthwhile, provided they were accompanied by a summary from an orthodox and recently visited physician or surgeon. I do not think that in the absence of this it would be worth going further unless he could see either Englemann at the San Francisco Medical Center or someone of equally good caliber. Alternatively, i.e. half way between San Francisco and London, Dick Freyberg at the New York Orthopedic Center (Hospital for Joint Diseases) is a very able and sympathetic physician. If this is a primarily mechanical problem of protruding disc, there seems to be no real reason why it should not be dealt with surgically <u>after</u> a physician's opinion.

Yours sincerely,
E.G.L Bywaters.

To James Laughlin from Kenneth Patchen (NDA)

February 28, 1967
2340 Sierra Ct. PA 94303

Dear Laughlin

Carolyn Kiser spent Saturday afternoon with us. Scherill, who drove her down from SF, phoned later to say that "she liked both of you very much, and was quite moved by the visit."
She said that I was first on the list to receive help from their fund for artists in need—that I definitely would receive help. We gave her a detailed account of medical costs and our need—on advice of doctors—to move to another area. She seemed embarrassed when we got down to these unadorned facts and figures, and it wasn't long before she led the conversation back into a consideration of literary and related matters—after once again assuring us that we would be helped, that we were not to worry.
She did stress the difficulty of cutting through the red tape in which all congressional committees are wrapped. So—I guess all we can do now is let her do her own work in her own way.
Immediately on the heels of that visit, which had required several days preparation, we ran into another interruption, this one lasting through yesterday. At work on the Collected again—and as I return to it, it strikes me that to leave out all the poems with drawings will give an unfair and distorted view of my work—particularly to someone encountering it for the first time. (And of course the things with drawings will never get into libraries at all.) Perhaps an alphabetical arrangement would overcome two difficulties: 1) a too apparent duplication of material already in paperbacks (Because It Is & Doubleheader); the possibility that Vol 1 & Vol 2 (in paperback eds) would not have an equal appeal. You might find that one of the books would prove much more saleable than the other—your guess is as good as mine which this would be, but it might be well (and safer) to make them halves rather than two separate entities.

[End of letter]

To Wayne Patchen from Miriam Patchen (KPA)
at 1200 Patchen Avenue, SE, Warren, Ohio 44481

April 25, 1967
2340 Sierra Court Palo Alto

Dear Pop,

It has been such a long time, more than a month, since your good letter came. Someone should have put a fire under me to get me started!

The weather here is—has been—something to discuss. This is really a desert—though people have managed at great expense to make it look otherwise. That is, the climate generally is consistent—warm daytime sun, cool nights and a rainy season from Nov11-Feb11. Hardly ever is there rain, except for a couple drops at any other time. This year the rainfall is the greatest in 100 years. It has been raining, hailing, thunder storming for 49 days—and cold. Kids are building arks; people are talking about webbed feet...And the heavy winter snows haven't melted yet so they expect trouble when a warm rain comes. Nature can still cause quite a bit of upset even if man is so smart to be able to go to the moon!

The other day we received (books) copies of a translation into Italian of Kenneth's Selected Poetry. I've probably not told you that he has translations of his books into French, German, Dutch, Swedish, Japanese, Spanish—and several have been published in England, of course.

What birds come to your feeder? We have one, too. However no very unusual ones come to ours. The highway construction removed many of the big trees and drove away the shyer birds and little animals. But when we first came here, some magnificent pheasants walked around as if they owned the place. Now we get warblers of varying kinds, phoebes, towhees, blue jays (they eat from my hand), starlings and sparrows, of course, a couple varieties of hummingbirds, robins, sometimes a blue bird, the meadowlark—and once an owl! Squirrels come for handouts and almost come into the house. Here we saw—and have—for the first time, black squirrels. Both the black and grey come every day. All this although we have two enormous cats. Our cats wouldn't dream of bothering "their" birds and animals, including a gopher which became very tame. The neighbors weren't thrilled about my friendship with a gopher. They (the gophers, not the neighbors!) are considered to be quite a pest.

Kenneth's medical picture is what it was. But someday—and soon, I believe—someone will come up with something which will help him.

I'm in good condition. My only problem is trying not to eat—close to starvation is considered the best level—and I like to eat!

And good news: a government grant has been granted to Kenneth. Just how much it is going to be, we don't yet know—but we know it will be at least $500 a month for 6-9 months until the big sum comes!

A Collected Poems of Kenneth's is to be published either late this fall or in the early spring. Much had to be dropped in order to try to cover the many books in 589 closely printed pages.

Kenneth will write you one of these days—honest! He's gotten so bad about letters. I write most of his—Affectionately

Miriam

To Kenneth Patchen from the National Foundation on the Arts and Humanities (KPA)

June 6, 1967
2340 Sierra Court Palo Alto

Dear Mr. Patchen:

I take great pleasure in informing you that you have been awarded $10,000 by the National Endowment for the Arts for your lifelong contributions to American letters.

This award will be paid in two installments: the first half will be sent to you as soon as you acknowledge receipt of this letter; the second $5,000 will be sent to you on or about December 15, 1967. We ask you to send us a brief report at the end of the first six month period, indicating what you feel you have been able to accomplish as a result of this award. And another brief, final report is required in June of 1968.

Please indicate your acceptance of this award and the conditions attaching to it by signing the carbon of this letter, and returning it in the enclosed envelope. Please indicate if payments should be sent to an address other than the present one. The reference number for this award is A67-I-185.

Heartiest congratulations to you, on being one of the first writers to be given an award based on a host of recommendations from fellow writers, editors and publishers throughout the United States. Their loyalty to you and your work must be a source of great gratification to you.

Yours sincerely,
Roger L. Stevens
Chairman

To James Laughlin from Kenneth Patchen (NDA)
30 October 1967
2340 Sierra Court Palo Alto 94303

Dear Laughlin

Infection beginning to subside—cost me two more teeth, in addition to the ten or so days lost—trouble complicated by allergic reaction to several of the sulfa compounds used (this allergy to medicines started with the violent penicillin flare up I suffered during surgery in 1956: great problem ever since.)

Thanks for copies of that letter from health insurance, and for your comments about it. Yes, I got in touch with doctor right off—he protested their ruling to State Medical Board, under which Blue Cross and the other health insurance companies function. Now it's a question of waiting for their decision. I'll bring matter to Roth's attention only if that decision goes against doctor's and my claim. He certainly is much too busy to take on just any old thing because of his position as Regent; but if it does come to point where our family medical attention is cut off—as it would be in event S.M.B's decision is thumbs down—I can only hope he will come to the rescue. We have a joint policy with Blue Cross, and Miriam is supposed to enter hospital for check up on the surgery she had about a year ago. As I said, we'll be hard put to find solution if health coverage is withdrawn, after something like a period of fifteen years of unquestioned service.

The contract for the "Collected," drawn up and signed on March 1st, does contain a clause stipulating that the cost of resetting pages taken from "Selected Poems" is to come out of my royalties. In a letter at time you estimated this cost at $6.50 per page. There are about 100 such pages, as near as we can figure.

[End of available letter]

To Kenneth Patchen from James Laughlin (NDA)

November 22, 1967
2340 Sierra Court Palo Alto

Dear Kenneth:

How does the enclosed look for the beginning draft for the biography to go on the back of the "CP"? I hope you can go to work on this to correct it and improve it right away.

Should there be something in the lead about your earliest writings, how you got started writing, the first things published perhaps in magazines before the first book?

Do I have the business about the football scholarship right, or am I just imagining that? Please note the two "injury"s that are circled. Were they related? Can you help me with an alternative phrase in the second paragraph so that we don't repeat "injury"?

This is the first time, I think, that we have officially dealt with your illness in a biographical sketch used on a book. Is this all right to do, and what do you want? Sad as it is, it seems to me it is one of the main facts of your life, and should not be concealed. But is this the right approach on it?

Are "Don't Look Now" and "Now You See It" one and the same play, or were there two different ones?

Cut the part about working for ND, if you want to, but I like it. I mean, I am always grateful for the marvelous work you and Miriam did there, and how you put up with me, I was so cranky then, as I guess I still am, I'll never know.
[End of letter]

To Jonathan Williams from Kenneth Patchen

December 4, 1967

"When is that J. Williams going to send me my copy of Kenneth's book ordered and paid for ($12) several years ago? Is he still wandering about abroad—I seem to remember you mentioned getting another card from him postmarked Austria. Outrageous, I say—no one has the right to be self indulgent and irresponsible with other people's property—and creative work at that! I know I wouldn't stand for it!"

That's signed by a very ill old woman, a friend of ours: Miss Winifred Bonnell.

Today Miriam returned Miss Bonnell's $12, and told her that I had decided to get my MS. back.

That is my decision.

We have returned what money has come to us: you do the same. No idea what I will do with But Even So—I have been patient with you to the point of utter foolishness—Now I want the MS. back.

Sincerely yours
Kenneth

To Kenneth and Miriam Patchen from Jonathan Williams (KPA)

[Letter fragment begins]

the printer (Low's, Chicago—which holds the mss in the safe) estimated would cost $12,500 to do properly, to your wants and mine. If I didn't send you a newsletter declaring these dreary facts it was because I didn't want to discourage you. I have every faith in the manuscript and intend to do it. But, just what do you expect me to do, until I have an economic base to work from. Go out and beg the money from the stones? So I went to England. I write more letters than any ten literary people you know and it isn't to feather my own nest. I'm not published by Laughlin, or anyone else to speak of and I happen to have a certain interest in my own work. It now develops that the University of North Carolina Press may issue a selected poems of mine—which, wow, will really cut a lot of ice with the perceptive American critics and poetry lovers. Anyway, I'm in England, by dint of borrowing a lot of money, not But Even So's. And I'm even in Austria visiting the tomb of Bruckner and earning my way reading Mahler poems to the bloody, stupid Austrians, courtesy the US Information Agency. No volley-ball. While I was doing this, I was also acquiring more lawyers in North Carolina, writing letters to Carolyn Kizer and Philip Hanes about one Kenneth Patchen, and waiting for something official to happen, so I could start publishing new books.

All of this ought to be fairly obvious and familiar to you by now, since you've seen me in action since 1948—for better or worse?

Kenneth, I have you on my mind and I certainly don't think it is my secret desire to keep you poor and ignored and your literary property in limbo. But, besides Kenneth Patchen, let us not forget there is an ideal community of writers I espouse. Their persons are difficult, to say the least: Dahlberg, Merle Hoyleman, Lorine Niedecker, Bucky Fuller, Ian Hamilton Finlay (who has just had a coronary thrombosis because of the tension he is under to get his work accomplished), Olson, Edson, Bob Brown, Mina Loy, Alfred Starr, Hamilton, Stevie Smith, Bunting, Grigson, Mervyn Peake, etc., etc., etc. And me. All I can do is try to push the whole thing along, jabber all over the country, write letters to Aspen Institute executives, and hope that the thing gets a firm economic solution. It seems to me you have to believe that I am engaged at all this with a proper spirit. If you think you are being exploited or dismissed or whatever it is you do think, then we'd better not deal with each other, for it makes me very angry indeed. Don't quote Winifred Harper Bonnell at me, who hasn't seen me since I devoted a month to your benefit in 1951; or someone named Steve Osterlund, who is in <u>no</u> position to know anything. Hire the CIA if you want to check up on my crimes against Kenneth Patchen. Jim Lowell knows how much <u>But Even So</u> costs and he knows how impossible it is to depend on the people who 'love' poetry. Recall, you once called them a pack of cheap sons of bitches. They still are. When I get money in hand I'll issue a new prospectus and get your book and many others out. You'll be the first to know. Until then, trust me or tell me once again to return the manuscript on a postcard. If you do the latter, I trust you won't expect anything else from me, except as an abiding reader. I'm sorry to go on at length but the air, again, must be cleared. I don't like being called self-indulgent. I wish I had a mountain boy to publish me. Huh?

Love to you both,
J. Williams

To James Laughlin from Kenneth Patchen (KPA)

May 9, 1968
[Letter excerpt]

I think if you had ten new men on staff you'd still overwork yourself. It was that way when you started, and has never been any different in all the years I've known you. Rough on you, but were it otherwise New Directions would be just another publisher. I trust that you will appreciate that there is nothing personal in my "strong words." What I do is so often done under conditions of nagging pain that when things go amiss for no accountable reason, exasperation can follow pretty swiftly—sort of an automatic protection device, the "ouch!" when one's toe is stepped on. The good is not to the toe but to the soul—

Tomorrow I'll send you a sketch of what I want for the tint block—and also a drawing to go with the dedication. That's fine about the hardbound! I'll try to draft something for the blurb. Royalties very handsome, very welcome, and very impressive—if I do say so. Thanks again. All good wishes! Kenneth

Excerpted first page of letter to James Laughlin:

14 May 68 2340 Sierra Court Palo Alto 94303

Dear Laughlin
As I said on my card of yesterday, your
splendid letter of the 10th arrived
just in time to prevent me from send-
ing a too hurried statement about
<u>But Even So</u> for the catalog. Your idea
of reproducing the covers pleases me
very much, as does your right on
target copy. Now I'll have time
to draft something better keyed
for appearance on the book than the
<u>splash-</u>rush thing I did.

For the copyright page:
None of these pages has appear-
ed before.
(Don't remember whether I sent
you this line or not.)

Perhaps you don't have the strength
you had at twenty, but for
heaven's sake you're in the prime
of your life! It's no wonder
you get tired and feel down

To James Laughlin from Kenneth Patchen (NDA)

May 14, 1968
2340 Sierra Court Palo Alto 94303

Dear Laughlin
As I said on my card of yesterday, your splendid letter of the 10th arrived just in time to prevent me from sending a too hurried statement about But Even So for the catalog. Your idea of reproducing the cover pleases me very much, as does your right on target copy. Now I'll have time to draft something better keyed for appearance on the book than the splash-rush thing I did.
For the copyright page:
None of these pages has appeared before.
(Don't remember whether I sent you this line or not.)
Perhaps you don't have the strength you had at twenty, but for heaven's sake you're in the prime of your life! It's no wonder you get tired and feel down when you have forty-eleven times too many dreary little nuisancy type tasks to perform day in and day out—nobody could keep up, you're bound to fall behind, and it's not in your make-up to every so often say, oh, to hell with it! and go off fishing or something. The point is, if you could work a hundred times more than you do, things would be just that much further behind-schedule and last-minute—for the simple reason that you are pushing into a rubber wall, and the harder you push…From time to time, back off, brush the mosquitoes away from your nerves, stop spitting into the wind—Thirty years without drawing a really free, relaxed breath—and you're surprised that you get tired and down!
[end of letter excerpt]

To Miriam Patchen from Barry Miles of Apple Records (KPA)
15 Lord North Street, London

December 13, 1968
2340 Sierra Court Palo Alto

Dear Miriam,

Sorry to have neglected you for so long but Apple have been very busy with the new Beatle album and albums from John & Yoko, James Taylor, George Harrison etc—their first batch of LPs and the first are always the worst to get out. This letter is to confirm that we would very much like to make an album with Kenneth and to tell you that there is a possibility I will be in California in late January, in which case maybe we could do something then or certainly get together and plan things. If all works well and I get to California I will certainly go to San Francisco and I see from my National Geographic map that you are very near there. If you have any ideas as to what you'd like to do please let me know as the series is completely wide open for straight poetry, poetry with pop, jazz, electronics, novels in music and words, interviews, statements of fact, fantasy and policy and whatever. So please don't necessarily restrict yourselves to the usual record format as it's not at all necessary. Soon I'll send you a printed form from Apple regarding their financial conclusions to do with this series, this will be the same for everyone. You may be interested to know that we are definitely doing albums with Allen Ginsberg, Richard Brautigan, Larry Ferlinghetti, Michael McClure and Charles Olson. Other people who have said yes but which we haven't made any arrangements with include Nathaniel Tarn with Pablo Neruda, Eldridge Cleaver and Norman Mailer and odd young English poets and Dutch ones.

Secondly you may or may not remember Long Hair magazine which I put out in London in '65 featuring the same sort of people that were in Jon Webb's Outsider magazine. If you have any new drawings, poems, prose you would like published I would be more than pleased to print them as there is nowhere near enough Patchen material seen in these isles.

Hope to see you soon,
Love,
Miles.

To James Laughlin from Kenneth Patchen (NDA)
July 24, 1969

24 July 69 2340 Sierra Court Palo Alto, Cal. 94303

Dear Laughlin
Your letter of the 14th must have via'd the moon since it took six days to reach me.
Roger, I read you loud and clear.
Ready-to-roll MS of new book for Spring '70 will be in your hands next month - probably toward its end.
Title:
PATCHENOPEDIA - FROM THE HAND OF
KENNETH PATCHEN
Particulars:
96 pages, including front matter.
The only type setting will be on copyright pg
since work is indeed "from my hand."
It carries forward fusion-of-media
character of Hallelujah Anyway & But Even So
to a logical new stage -
i.e., PATCHENOPEDIA
employs calligraphy and drawings
into (I believe) an exciting never-before dimension

And there is my news of that -
Several other matters (among them good word from the Corcoran Gallery of firm and official scheduling of Patchen show for November - main display section for a month, followed by national tour) I'll take up with you within a couple days.
All good wishes.
Sincerely yours,
Kenneth

To James Laughlin from Kenneth Patchen (NDA)
July 27, 1969
[Handwritten excerpt, see p. 317]

Sunday · July 27, 69 - 2340 Sierra Ct Palo Alto 2340

Dear Laughlin

Months ago you said you would send me the blurbs and considered quotes for Sleepers Awake and the paperback Collected Poems — as well as projected layouts for their covers. Of course without this material I am not only in the dark about things which concern me greatly, but I am unfairly cut off and handicapped in the supplying of texts and statements useful to our common purpose of making the most attention-arresting and market-orientated presentation of these so important titles.

In my opinion while our target should be youth before, during and after college, we must take into account the overt and covert miseducation of youth in literary (as in most other) things by the self-seeking cliques of poet?-professors which infest the halls of academe. We must hit hard — without falling into the easy and comfortable stance of understatement — The walls of silence and condescension about my work might seem to be impregnable after 30-odd years a-building — but they are not!

To James Laughlin from Kenneth Patchen (NDA)

July 27, 1969
2340 Sierra Ct Palo Alto

Dear Laughlin
Months ago you said you would send me the blurbs and considered quotes for Sleepers Awake and the paperback Collected Poems—as well as projected layouts for their covers. Of course without this material I am not only in the dark about things which concern me greatly, but I am unfairly cut off and handicapped in the supplying of texts and statements useful to our common purpose of making the most attention-arresting and market-oriented presentation of these so important titles. In my opinion while our target should be youth before, during and after college, we must take into account the overt and covert miseducation of youth in literary (as in most other) things by the self-seeking cliques of poet?-professors which infest the halls of academe. We must hit hard—without falling into the easy and comfortable stance of understatement—The walls of silence and condescension about my work might seem to be impregnable after 30-odd years a-building—but they are not! Things are a-stir whenever and wherever my work gets over or through those walls into the eagerly receptive hands of youth. The trouble is, and has been, that this has come about, not through any determined and concentrated effort, but through hit-or-miss happenstance.
I am asked over and over why no critical articles—even of a casual kind—have been published about my work. "Who the hell is keeping us away from what we want and need to know about so badly!" As I said, those walls are thick—a lot of people have been at the busy on them for a long, long time. Sure they'll come down, but must we wait another thirty years? I for one don't have them.

All good wishes.
Sincerely yours,
Kenneth

To James Laughlin from Kenneth Patchen (NDA)

October 13, 1969
[letter excerpt]
for a work done so long ago. I discovered that I had to recapture the experience— or at least a sense of it—that went into the making of

the fables before I could get the drawings to "work." A bit unnerving—particularly at first when more than a few ghosts rose from the pages. Odd how each work has its own special life which one sort of leaves behind—but not really.

Pleased that Jonathan came through in the way he did. When I was phone-tracking him down the east coast I did have some moments of big doubt. Well it worked out—and that's all to the good. Fred Martin is one in a million. He can grasp an idea about as fast as anyone I've ever encountered. And he's what I would call a good-hearted young man. Not many of those about, I sometimes fear.

Times like right now—I'm tired, and have fifty-eleven things to do.

All good wishes.
Sincerely yours,
Kenneth

Note:** This letter refers to Patchen's **Aflame and Afun of Walking Faces.

To The John Simon Guggenheim Memorial Foundation (GUG)

December 28, 1970
2340 Sierra Court Palo Alto, Calif. 94303

Dear Secretary

I wish to make application for the renewal of Fellowship for the year 1971. (Illness—including a stay in hospital—prevented me from doing so earlier.)

Have you a form for me to fill?

Do you wish me to send you copies of my recently published books?

I look forward to your instructions.

Sincerely yours,
Kenneth Patchen

***Note:** This was the last letter Kenneth Patchen ever wrote to The John Simon Guggenheim Memorial Foundation after 35 years of applying.*

To Kenneth Patchen from Frederick Martin (KPA)

December 23, 1971
2340 Sierra Court Palo Alto

Dear Kenneth,

I'm afraid that this will arrive too late for Christmas greetings but not too late to wish you and Miriam the best of all good things for 1972!

Gertrude has done her usual good job, I think, on the enclosed cover/ jacket design for IN QUEST OF CANDLELIGHTERS. The only slight suggestion I might have is to make the title a little bolder. And I understand that there is a "medium" face in the same font and Gertrude has agreed to see if this might work. We have also picked out two nice colors—an orangy-red and a nice warm brown. I think that either one would work but the choice is yours.

Please mull the design and let me have your decision with the return of the "comp" enclosed, by January 3. I'll be out in Chicago all of next week for the Modern Language Association meeting talking to some of the 10,000 professors. (I was impressed by the number of courses using your books last year as I think I told you. And I'll be interested to see if the trend is still growing.) So I won't be able to move ahead until early January. At that point I know the production people will want to pull out all the stops.

Can you think of any more publication dates I ought to include on the copyright page? I'll be sure to have the usual dedication "For Miriam" as you requested. And have you had a chance to look over the proposed catalog blurb I sent with my January 10 letter? I'd like to get started on this at the same time we start on the cover/jacket design.

Trust all goes well with you both. And many thanks for your dear/ deer Christmas greeting. Everyone enjoyed it—even the children!

With best wishes,
Frederick R. Martin

A Brief Chronology of Kenneth Patchen's Life

1911
Born in Niles, OH on December 13

1926-1929
Attends Warren G. Harding School, Warren, OH

1928
Publishes in school newspaper, works in steel mill that summer, courts Isabel Smith-Stein

1929
Attends Alexander Meikeljohn's Experimental College, University of Wisconsin; Poem "Permanence" published in *The New York Times*

1930
Attends Commonwealth Labor College one semester in Mena, AR; on the road in America labor orgainizing and writing

1932
Moves between New York and Boston; publishes "Lenin"poem in *Rebel Poet;* befriends Amos Wilder

1933
Meets Miriam Oikemus at a Christmas party in Boston

1934-1935
Works in rubber plant; marries Miriam while back in Ohio, June 28; moves together to Greenwich Village, New York; writes reviews for *New Republic;* living briefly in Rhinebeck, NY

1936
Publishes first book of verse, *Before the Brave* with Random House; wins a Guggenheim Fellowship and moves to Santa Fe, NM, then Phoenix, AZ

1938
Moves to Los Angeles and Hollywood, writes for films and WPA Writing Project; Kenneth sustains back injury

1939
Moves to Acton, MA, then on to Norfolk, CT; works for James Laughlin at New Directions home offices; publishes *First Will and Testament* with New Directions

1940
Moves back to Greenwich Village, New York City

1941
After dispute with James Laughlin, self-publishes *The Journal of Albion Moonlight,* anti-war novel

1942
Publishes *The Dark Kingdom* and *The Teeth of the Lion;* broadcasts radio play, *The City Wears a Slouch Hat,* with music by John Cage

1943
Publishes *Cloth of the Tempest*

1944
Wins Ohioana Award for *Cloth of the Tempest*

1945
Begins spending summers at Mt. Pleasant, NY; publishes *The Memoirs of a Shy Pornographer*

1946
Publishes *An Astonished Eye Looks Out of the Air, Outlaw of the Lowest Planet, Sleepers Awake, Pictures of Life and Death, Panels for the Walls of Heaven, They Keep Riding Down All the Time, Selected Poems*

1947
Moves to cottage at Old Lyme, CT, dispute with local library

1948
Publishes poetry, *To Say if You Love Someone*, and novel *See You in the Morning;* Befriends Kenneth Rexroth in from California

1949
Publishes *Red Wine and Yellow Hair*

1950
First major spine operation with help from Writers' fund

1951
Moves to San Francisc, Green Street apartment

1952
Publishes *Orchards, Thrones and Caravans*

1953
Publishes *Fables and Other Little Tales* with Jonathan Williams

1954
Receives Shelley Memorial Award; publishes *The Famous Boating Party* and *Poems of Humor and Protest* (Pocket Poems #3 with City Lights)

1955
Publishes *Glory Never Guesses*, silkscreen portfolio with Frank Bacher

1956
Undergoes spinal fusion operation; publishes *A Surprise for the Bagpipe Player*, silkscreen portfolio with Frank Bacher

1957
Moves to 2340 Sierra Court, Palo Alto; records *Kenneth Patchen Reads with the Chamber Jazz Sextet;* publishes *Hurrah for Anything* and *When We Were Here Together*

1958
Publishes *Poemscapes*

1959
Performance of his play *Don't Look Now;* records *Kenneth Patchen Reads with Jazz in Canada* with Alan Neil Quartet in Vancouver, sustains further back injury during surgery

1960
Publishes *Because It Is* and *The Love Poems of Kenneth Patchen*

1962
Befriends Joel and Zoe Climenhaga, works with him on his plays

1966
Publishes *Hallelujah Anyway* and *Doubleheader*

1967
Receives $10,000 award from the National Foundation on the Arts and Humanities for his "life-long contribution to American letters"

1968
Publishes *But Even So, Collected Poems*, and *Love and War Poems*

1970
Publishes *Wonderings* and *There's Love All Day*

1972
Kenneth dies at home in Palo Alto of heart failure on January 8; Tribute held at City Lights Poets Theater, February 2; *In Quest of Candlelighters* is published in May

* * * *

1984
What Shall We Do Without Us: The Voice and Vision of Kenneth Patchen published by The Sierra Club

1989
Kenneth Patchen Festival held in Warren, OH

1991
Awash with Roses: The Collected Love Poems of Kenneth Patchen published by Bottom Dog Press

2000
Miriam Patchen dies in Palo Alto March 6; biography *Kenneth Patchen: Rebel Poet in America* is published

2008
The Walking Away World and *We Meet* reissue of previous books are published by New Directions

2011
Kenneth Patchen: A Centenial Selection, edited by Jonathan Clark is published

Kenneth & Miriam Patchen

High School
Yearbook
Photos
Kenneth 1929
& Miriam 1931

Kenneth in Hollywood 1937

Kenneth in Norfolk, CT 1938
Working for New Directions

81 Bleecker Street Kenneth, Anais Nin,
unknown man, & Virginia Admiral 1940

Kenneth & Miriam in NYC 1945

Kenneth & Miriam Old Lyme 1947

Kenneth in the Village 1948

Kenneth & Chamber Jazz Sextet 1957

Kenneth at work on painted books, Green Street SF 1954

Philip Whalen, Michael & Joanne McClure with Kenneth, Palo Alto, c. 1959

KennethPatchen, Palo Alto 1967

Miriam Patchen, 1990

The Correspondents

Compiled by Larry Smith [with page references]

Amy Bonner (1891-1955) was a journalist and poet. From 1937-1947 she served as *Poetry's* eastern business representative.[92-93]

Harvey Breit (1909-1968) was an American poet, editor, and playwright. He was married to poet and playwright Patricia Rinehart. He co-wrote the play *The Disenchanted* with Budd Schulberg, about the life of F. Scott Fitzgerald. Breit began his writing career at *TIME*, where he worked from 1933 to 1934. He befriended the Patchens while living in the Village and plotted with Patchen to launch the radical literary publication PULSE in 1939. He wrote an early critical appreciation of Patchen's work in "Kenneth Patchen and the Critical Blind Alley," *Fantasy*, 6 (1940). He became a columnist and editor for the *New York Times Book Review* from 1948 to 1957. Breit also edited *The Selected Letters of Malcolm Lowry* (1964). [54-55, 270]

Bennett Cerf (1898-1971) with friend Donald Klopfer was a co-founder and publisher of Random House Publishing. In 1925 the two men bought the rights to the Modern Library series from Boni & Liveright and went into business. In 1927 they began publishing general trade books which they had selected "at random." He and senior editor **Saxe Cummins** negotiated the contract for Patchen's *Before the Brave* in 1935.Random House posthumously published Cerf's autobiography, entitled *At Random: The Reminiscences of Bennett Cerf.* [45]

Alex Comfort, (1920-2000) was a British medical professional, anarchist, pacifist, conscientious objector and writer, best known for *The Joy of Sex* (1972) which played a part in what is often called the sexual revolution. He wrote the preface to Patchen's *Outlaw of the Lowest Planet: Selected Poems* (1946) and consulted with Miriam Patchen later about Kenneth's health issues. [195, 301-303]

E.E. Cummings (wife Marion) (1894–1962) was an American poet, painter, essayist, autobiographer, and playwright. During W.W.I he enlisted in the ambulance corps and was stationed in France where he was imprisoned for suspicion of espionage (*The Enormous Room*, 1922). For a time he lived in New York and Paris. He and Marion Morehouse, a fashion model and photographer, had a long common-law marriage while residing at 4 Patchin Place in Greenwich Village. Here they befriended Kenneth and Miriam Patchen. [110, 113, 118, 123, 188. 190, 194-195, 198-201, 204-205, 211, 212, 214, 218-219, 225, 227, 229, 230, 244, 248, 254]

Robert Duncan (1919–1988) was an American poet. He taught for a time with Charles Olson at Black Mountain College in North Carolina and has been associated with the 1950's Beat West Coast Renaissance.During the 1940's in Greenwich Village he and Russell Sanders were intimate friends with both Kenneth Patchen and Patchen's nemesis, Anais Nin.

Lawrence Ferlinghetti (1919-   ) is a poet, novelist, playwright, painter, liberal activist, and the co-founder of City Lights Booksellers (1953) & City Lights Publishers (1955). Moving from Greenwich Village to San Francisco, he became a main figure in the San Francisco Renaissance and publisher of the Beat Movement writing. An intimate friend of Kenneth and Miriam Patchen, he often transported him to the hospital and published two of his books in the Pocket Poets Series. In 1998 Ferlinghetti was made Poet Laureate of San Francisco. [207, 208]

James Thomas Farrell (1904-1979) was an American journalist, short story writer, and novelist whose most famous work is the *Studs Lonigan* trilogy which focusing on the working-class life of Chicago's South Side Irish. Farrell was also active in Trotskyist politics and joined the Socialist Workers Party. [59, 70]

C. Wrey Gardiner (1901–1981) was a British writer and poet, editor of *Poetry Quarterly* (1939-1953) and publisher of Grey Walls Press of London in 1940 which published Patchen's *Outlaw of the Lowest Planet: Selected Poems* (1946). [159]

James Laughlin (1914–1997) was an American poet and the editor and publisher of New Directions Publishers, which he began with the 1936 annual publication of *New Directions in Prose & Poetry* an anthology including authors such as William Carlos Williams, Ezra Pound, Elizabeth Bishop, Henry Miller, Marianne Moore, Wallace Stevens, and E. E. Cummings. He became friends with the Patchens in 1939, hiring them to work briefly in the early Norfolk, CT offices and eventually publishing many of Patchen's works. In 1992 Laughlin won the Distinguished Contribution to American Letters Award from the National Book Awards. [57,65, 67-68, 71-75, 78-81, 90, 96-99, 103, 119-120, 122, 169, 172-173, 176, 179, 202, 208, 232, 235, 257, 261-265, 274, 288, 293-294, 296-297, 305, 308-309, 311-313, 315-316]

George Leite (1920-1985) was a California author, poet, publisher and bookstore owner active in the San Francisco Bay Area in the 1940s and 50s. He was the founder of Daliel's Bookstore on Telegraph Avenue in Berkeley, California, where he published *Circle Magazine* which featured writers such as Kenneth Rexroth. He lived for a while in Henry Miller's cabin on the Big Sur. [136-138]

James Boyer May (wife Geraldine) (1904 - 1981) was a poet, essayist and a publisher. He ran the small but influential literary magazine *Trace* from 1952 through 1970 in Los Angeles. *Trace* printed listings of small press activities and jazz. He and his wife befriended the Patchens in the late 1950s and 1960s and would host them when they traveled to Los Angeles.[241]

Alexander Meiklejohn (1872-1964) was born in England, of Scottish parents. He became an American education pioneer, philosopher, university administrator, and free-speech advocate. He founded the Meiklejohn Experimental College at the University of Wisconsin, which Patchen attended in 1929-1930. He later served as dean of Brown University and president of Amherst College. In 1945 he was a U.S. delegate to the founding meeting of UNESCO in London. He was selected by John F. Kennedy to receive the Presidential Medal of Freedom. [26, 27, 28, 29, 30, 31, 33, 38]

Henry Miller (1891-1980) He dropped out of City College, rejecting formal education, and began working various labor jobs. In 1929 he and wife June opened a speak-easy in the Village, then travelled Europe in the 1930s settling in Paris where he met Anais Nin, and later Lawrence Durrell. His *Tropic of Capricorn* was published in Europe in1939. He returned to U.S. in 1940 where he befriended Kenneth Patchen. In 1946 he wrote a critical tribute, *Patchen: Man of Anger and Light* (Padell). With some driving coaching by Patchen, he did a road tour of the U.S. (*The Air-Conditioned Nightmare*). He did watercolor paintings and married Janina Lepska, then moved to Big Sur, CA. Many books were written in the 1950s, then Grove Press published the first U.S. edition of *Tropic of Cancer* followed by famed censorship trial. [94-95-99-1-2, 135, 143-145, 146-148, 152, 156-158, 165, 177, 179-181, 186-189, 192, 220, 224, 226-227, 279, 280, 289]

Henry Allen Moe (1894-1975) was the first director and eventually president of the John Simon Guggenheim Foundation from 1925-1963. He was also first director of the National Endowment for the Humanities, and was a president of the American Philosophical Society from 1959 to 1970. [49, 51-52, 60, 63, 68-69, 82, 115-117, 139-142, 174, 181, 185, 196, 204]

Harriet Monroe (1860 –1936) was an American editor, scholar, literary critic, poet, and a patron of the arts. She was the founding publisher and long-time editor of *Poetry* magazine, which debuted in 1912. Monroe supported such poets as Ezra Pound, T. S. Eliot, William Carlos Williams, Carl Sandburg and others, among them Kenneth Patchen. [35-37, 39]

Lewis Mumford (1895–1990) was a native New Yorker who became an American historian, sociologist, philosopher of technology, and an influential literary critic. He is noted for his study and writings of cities and urban architecture. In 1919 he became associate editor of *The Dial*, an influential modernist literary journal and later worked for *The New Yorker* where he wrote architectural criticism and commentary on urban issues. [42, 46]

Alan (Al) Neil (1924-) is a Canadian pianist, composer, visual artist, and author. Neil was a central figure in the 1950s and early 1960s at the Cellar, a musician-operated Vancouver club, where he accompanied such US jazzmen as Carl Fontana, Art Pepper, and Sonny Red. The Alan Neil quartet from this period (Dale Hillary, alto sax; Lionel Chambers, bass; Bill Boyle, drums) recorded in Vancouver, British Columbia, with Kenneth Patchen on the LP *Kenneth Patchen Reads with Jazz* (1959, Folkways) (photo 1989 by Chris Cameron) [246-248]

Miriam Patchen (1914-2000) born Miriam Oikemus of Finnish parents who emigrated to the Boston area. She and her parents were members of the Communist Party of America. She attended Massachusetts State College in 1933 where she became known for her radical ideas, then met Kenneth at a Christmas Eve party in Boston. He persuaded her to come an live with him in Greenwich Village. They were married in Ohio in 1934. [44, 221, 249-250, 281-288, 290, 298, 302, 303, 306, 313]

Wayne Patchen (1883-1967) father of Kenneth Patchen, worked in the steel mills around Warren and Youngstown, also did remodeling of homes in the area. After wife Eva's death he traveled the U.S. and visited the Kenneth and Miriam in California. Photo is of Wayne and Kenneth, Rhinebeck, NY 1935.[44, 221, 303, 306]

Henry Rago (1915-1969) was a poet and editor of *Poetry* magazine from 1955-1969. He was also a Professor of Theology and Literature at the University of Chicago, jointly in the Divinity School and the New Collegiate Division. His book of poems is *A Sky of Late Summer* (Macmillan 1963). He became Patchcn's chief correspondent for *Poetry*. [211-212, 216, 223, 228-231, 233, 238, 240, 242, 259, 278]

Kenneth Rexroth (1905-1982) was an American poet, translator, and critic. He is regarded as a central figure in the Berkeley and San Francisco Renaissance and a major influence on writers of the Beat Movement, focusing on Nature, labor, and Eastern writing. He is the author of more than 50 books, including *An Autobiographical Novel* (1964; expanded 1991), most with New Directions Publishing. In 1948 he travelled east to Old Lyme, CT to meet Kenneth Patchen, and later encouraged the Patchens to move to San Francisco. [163-168, 171, 175, 182-184, 190, 220, 222, 236, 238]

Harry Roskolenko (1907-1980) poet, novelist, autobiographer, journalist (pseudonyms of Jean de Ballard, Elizabeth Goode, H.R. Rose, Harry Roskolenkier, Allen V. Ross, Harry Ross, etc.) was born in New York and was self-educated, working various labor jobs before joining the US Army in 1942. In the 1940s he befrinded Australian poets of the *Angry Penguins* group. He edited an Australian issue of the American poetry magazine *Voices* (1944). His memoir of his childhood is *When I Was Last on Cherry Street* (1965).[64, 66, 70]

Karl Shapiro (1913-2000) an American poet appointed the fifth Poet Laureate in 1946. His *V-Letter and Other Poems* won the Pulitzer Prize for Poetry in 1945; he served as editor of *Poetry* magazine for a number of years in the 1950s.[190. 193]

Isabel Smith-Stein was a classmate and early love of Kenneth Patchen. She was the daughter of two of Warren, Ohio's leading doctors from the wealthier North Side of town. She met Kenneth on a science club field trip to the steel mill, and they were members of "The Literary Club" at Warren G. Harding High School, along with Walter Potashnik (Benton), Cecil Gordon, Catherine Yoxheimer, Doris Lamb, and William Congalton. Kenneth sought an alliance and romance with her and after high school wrote to her at Ward-Belmont girl's school in Nashville, TN. In later life she married a writer and college professor and lived in Arlington, MA. [17-25]

Wallace Stevens (1879-1955) was an American Modernist poet who spent most of his life as vice president for the Hartford Insurance Company in Connecticut. His poetry won both a Pulitzer and National Book Award, and in 1955 his *Collected Poems* won the Pulitzer Prize for Poetry. Patchen wrote to him repeatedly for financial backing.[107, 109-110, 112, 114, 115, 121]

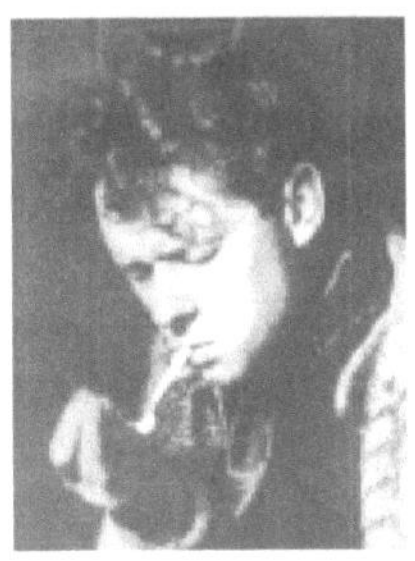

Dylan Thomas (1914-1953) (wife Caitlin) was a Welsh poet, playwright, and fiction writer. His public readings and hard drinking, particularly in America, won him great acclaim, though he died in New York November 1953. He wrote a long letter to his American peer Kenneth Patchen in 1939, and he and wife Caitlin visited the Patchens briefly in San Francisco in 1952. He is perhaps best known for his poetry play, *Under Milk Wood.* [83-89]

Leon Trotsky (1879–1940) was a Bolshevik and Russian Marxist revolutionary and theorist and the founder and first leader of the Red Army. After leading a failed struggle of the Left Opposition against the policies and rise of Joseph Stalin in the 1920s, Trotsky was expelled from the Communist Party, deported, then assassinated in Mexico on Stalin's orders. An ally of radical artists and wrote *Literature and Revolution* (1924). In 1939 Kenneth Patchen wrote to him asking for contribution to his planned PULSE magazine. [54-55]

Louis Untermeyer (1885-1977) was an American poet, critic, and editor. He was appointed the fourteenth Poet Laureate Consultant in Poetry to the Library of Congress in 1961. Known for his Leftist views as a critic, Untermeyer was among the first to include Patchen in a broad anthology, his *Modern American Poetry* anthology (6th edition, 1942).[111-112, 159-160, 178]

Amos Niven Wilder (1895-1993) was an American poet, critic, and theology professor and an intimate friend of Kenneth Patchen from 1930's on. His *The Spiritual Aspects of the New Poetry* (1940) was one of the first treatments of Patchen's poetry. He also wrote *Theology and Modern Literature* (1967), and *Thornton Wilder and his Public* (1980). His brother was the playwright Thorton Wilder. [41-43, 46, 50-51, 56-57, 60-62, 69, 90-92, 93, 108]

Jonathan Williams (1929-2008) was an American poet, publisher, essayist, and photographer.As the founder of The Jargon Society, he published poetry, experimental fiction, and photography, including Patchen's book of *Fables* (1953). He was a close friend of the Patchens from their days at Old Lyme, CT, in 1949 on. [309-310]

Thomas Wolfe (1900-1938) child of a stonecutter and a hill country school teacher, grew up in his mother's boarding house. He abandoned playwriting, and after three years of writing and revision published *Look Homeward, Angel: A Story of the Buried Life* (1929) one of the great coming-of-age novels. In 1935 Wolfe published *Of Time and the River*. He died of tuberculosis of the brain. From the manuscript he left, Harper & Brothers produced two novels and a book of short fiction including *The Web and the Rock* (1939) and *You Can't Go Home Again* (1940). Patchen admired his writing and sought his patronage. [53]

Jasper Wood (1921—2002) (wife Nancy) was a Cleveland, Ohio ad writer, photographer, filmmaker, and advocate of the arts and free speech. He admired and befriended Kenneth Patchen in 1946 when he hoped to publish "On the Side of the Angels" a magazine of the arts under Patchen's guidance, then attempted to publish a book of Patchen's to be entitled *Panels for the Walls of Heaven*, which was ultimately published by Bern Porter Books. He did publish one book by Ernest Hemingway, *The Spanish Earth*(1938). He became an advocate for Cleveland renegade poet d.a.levy and others. He and his wife Nancy remained lifelong friends of the Patchens.[123, 126-133, 135, 138, 142, 145-149, 152-155, 157, 293]

Kenneth Patchen (1911-1972) was a poet, playwright, fiction and fable writer, artist, and performer of poetry-jazz, working in the tradition of engaged writing which he helped to forge in America. Producing almost a book a year for 36 years, his work stands as an exposed girder in the structure of American character and art. His friendships with such writers as Amos Wilder, Lewis Mumford, James Laughlin, Henry Miller, Kenneth Rexroth, Dylan Thomas, Lawrence Ferlinghetti and others place him at the center of dissident writing in America. Rising from his native grounds in working-class Ohio, he became a leading figure among Leftist thinkers and artists in Greenwich Village's 1930s and 40s. In the 1950s he moved to the West Coast where he created artistic blends of poetry and art, and poetry and jazz. Finally crippled with back pain during the last decade of his life, he created the wonderful picture-poems. For four decades, on East and West Coast, by the force of his own will and his native genius, Patchen molded a life and art as one. With the loving support of his wife Miriam he endured the pain and travail of years of struggle to recast an art based on truth and striking beauty. His is one of the great stories of American literature.

The Editor

Allen Frost lives in Bellingham, Washington, with wife Laura, daughter Rosa and son Rustle. He was born in La Jolla, California, and graduated from Bowdoin College in Maine. He has lived and worked in Seattle, Washington; Portland, Oregon; and Huron, Ohio. He works in the library at Western Washington University. His *Ohio Trio: Fictions* appeared in 2001 from Bottom Dog Press, followed by *Bowl of Water* written between 1989-2002. *Another Life* is drawn from limited edition poetry chapbooks written 2002-2007. *Home Recordings* appeared from Bird Dog Publishing in 2010. He contributed an article to the collection *d.a.levy and the mimeograph revolution* (2008). He is an associate editor of Bottom Dog Press.

Larry Smith is the author of *Kenneth Patchen: Rebel Poet in America* (2000) from Bottom Dog Press and professor ermeritus of English and humanities at Bowling Green State University's Firelands College. He and daughter Laura Smith edited *Awash with Roses: The Collected Love Poems of Kenneth Patchen* (1991; reissued 2010). He is a poet, fiction writer, editor and literary critic. He directs Bottom Dog Press in Huron, Ohio where he lives with his wife Ann.

www.ingramcontent.com/pod-product-compliance
Lightning Source LLC
Chambersburg PA
CBHW030422310726
48979CB00009B/1573/J

* 9 7 8 1 9 3 3 9 6 4 5 5 3 *